ACCLAIM FOR ERIN HEALY

Afloat

"The writing is vivid and smart."

—*Publishers Weekly*

"Healy's story is original and engrossing, with a unique plot and relatable characters."

—*Romantic Times*, 3-star review

"[*Afloat*] is full of danger, intrigue, and compelling characters. Readers will enjoy the way [Healy] intersperses supernatural elements into this action-packed novel."

—*CBA Retailers + Resources*

House of Mercy

"Supernatural and spiritual elements abound in Healy's novels, and this one is no exception. Unusual storytelling helps to make the message stronger and more thought-provoking."

—*Romantic Times*, 4-star review

"The complex plot of *House of Mercy* will appeal to those who crave supernatural suspense. Once again, Healy leads readers to a place where they can see the physical and spiritual meet, where they can glimpse the mercy of God in an unexpected form."

—*CBA Retailers + Resources*

"*House of Mercy* is a story of a family who must all learn to trust and to forgive in order to heal. A story of suspense with a bit of the supernatural. A story full of symbolism depicting the love of God. A great read that kept me turning the pages."

—LYNETTE EASON, BEST-SELLING, AWARD-WINNING AUTHOR
OF THE WOMEN OF JUSTICE SERIES

"Healy's dramatic story will find an audience with those who enjoy Cindy Martinusen Coloma."

—*LIBRARY JOURNAL*

The Baker's Wife

"Healy's fascinating plot is fast-paced and difficult to put down once started."

—*ROMANTIC TIMES*, $4^{1/2}$-STAR REVIEW, TOP PICK!

"A tightly woven, character-driven suspense story . . . should appeal to Dekker fans as well."

—*LIBRARY JOURNAL*

"A combination of suspense, mystery, religion, and even romance weaves this tale into a cohesive, compelling read."

—*NEW YORK JOURNAL OF BOOKS*

The Promises She Keeps

"Complex characters, a plot steeped in imagery and eloquence . . . a beautiful tale of eternal love . . . Healy thrives when telling tales of spirituality and mystery."

—LIFEISSTORY.COM

"... A smartly written story ... *The Promises She Keeps* will undoubtedly be enjoyed by established fans of Healy's writing, and those unfamiliar with her work, or even the genre, should give this captivating novel a read."

—5MinutesForBooks.com

"An intricate book . . . Healy is highly skilled. . . . *The Promises She Keeps* is beautifully written."

—The Gazette (Colorado Springs, CO)

Never Let You Go

"Heart-pounding suspense and unrelenting hope that will steal your breath."

—Ted Dekker, *New York Times* best-selling author

"Fans of Ted Dekker will appreciate Healy's chilling story of the dangers on the road back to hope and faith."

—Booklist

"Keeps you glued to the pages until the very last."

—Tosca Lee, *New York Times* best-selling author of *Iscariot* and The Books of Mortals series with *New York Times* best-selling author Ted Dekker

Never Let You Go

"... Will appeal to readers who like to be on the edge of their seats."

—Library Journal

STRANGER THINGS

OTHER BOOKS BY ERIN HEALY

Motherless (Coming Winter 2014)

Afloat

House of Mercy

The Baker's Wife

The Promises She Keeps

Never Let You Go

With Ted Dekker

Kiss

Burn

STRANGER
THINGS

ERIN HEALY

®

THOMAS NELSON
Since 1798

NASHVILLE DALLAS MEXICO CITY RIO DE JANEIRO

Published in Nashville, Tennessee, by Thomas Nelson. Thomas Nelson is a registered trademark of Thomas Nelson, Inc.

Thomas Nelson, Inc., titles may be purchased in bulk for educational, business, fund-raising, or sales promotional use. For information, please e-mail SpecialMarkets@ ThomasNelson.com.

Published in association with Creative Trust Literary Group, 5141 Virginia Way, Suite 320, Brentwood, TN, 37027.

Publisher's Note: This novel is a work of fiction. Names, characters, places, and incidents are either products of the author's imagination or used fictitiously. All characters are fictional, and any similarity to people living or dead is purely coincidental.

Library of Congress Cataloging-in-Publication Data

Healy, Erin M.
  Stranger Things / Erin Healy.
    pages cm
  ISBN 978-1-4016-8958-2 (Trade Paper)
  I. Title.
  PS3608.E245S77 2013
  813'.6--dc23

                          2013023736

Printed in the United States of America

13 14 15 16 17 18 RRD 6 5 4 3 2 1

For my BLS,
who keeps blooming in astonishing color
fire after fire after fire.

THE HOUSE APPEARS TO BE A TRAGEDY.

It's an abandoned structure that sits far off the road, a ruined place gutted by fire and battered by weather. Stone walls hold up a metal roof. Where the two meet, fat spiders lie in wait for their next meal. The trees that surround the place are indifferent, and someday the weeds will swallow it completely.

That's one way of seeing it.

Close your eyes. Spin around. Drink the air. Then look again: The house appears to be a triumph.

It's a peaceful home nestled under sheltering trees, its stone walls a fortress against harsh weather and unwelcome visitors. The metal roof catches sunshine and sends water sliding into a rain barrel at the bottom of a gutter, where white birds have come to bathe. On the shady porch, strong with new boards and fresh paint, a graceful swing waits for its occupant to return. A glass topped off with lemonade and ice sweats on the rail.

Darkness sweeps in. A cloud passing over the sun brings the tragedy back to life. A chill creeps up the path leading from the grove. The glass of lemonade falls to the rocks and shatters.

Then wind shoves darkness out of the way. Sunshine raises the triumphant house from the dead. Orange poppies spring out of the ground. A woman in an ocean-blue dress emerges from the house to pluck some for her table.

A black scorpion lies in wait among the flowers.

Here, light and darkness jostle for attention. Both visions are real, but which one is more true?

Listen: there are footsteps on the path. People are coming. People who will give an answer to this question. There will be an argument. Expect worse than a civil dispute.

But keep an eye on the woman picking poppies.

ONE

THE CLOSET WHERE BECCA WAS TRAPPED HELD every nightmare she'd ever had, plus one that had never violated the borders of her imagination until now.

Outside of the closet, a gas lamp burned in an empty room. The lamp's unnatural white light and dizzying stink came into the tight space through a crack in the locked door. Sawdust from the unfinished floor stuck to Becca's sweaty palms and formed a gritty paste. Her breath was noisy and her heart was a frightened cat trying to claw its way out of her throat. If she wanted to avoid a split lip, she should follow orders: shut up, sit down, stay put.

Becca got to her feet and pressed her cheek against the wood, looking through the gap for her opportunity to disobey. To survive. Better to live with a split lip than die without one.

Outside the closet, only fresh floorboards made the burnt-out carcass of a room suitable for humans. It seemed there was no electricity here. There was definitely no heat. For the most part there was fear, and something else that Becca couldn't name: a sensation that the place was unstable, that the floor might open up and swallow her.

She wrapped herself up in her arms. If she could keep her head, she might be able to see her way out.

Jett, the boyfriend who turned out to be a liar, was gone now.

He'd promised her a candlelight picnic and privacy, when what really awaited was a crumbling house and a man who looked her over as if she were something to eat.

That man, who had an unfortunate resemblance to her step-dad, had forced her into the closet. She raked at his grip with her free hand; she kicked at his knees, at his groin, and screamed. But he hefted her in as if she weighed no more than a pair of shoes and he was just tidying up the house. She beat on the door with her fists, and though it rattled, it held firm.

At first she had feared for Jett. Would the man kill him if he didn't get away? Her eye found the crack for the first time and she looked out—shouting, questioning, pleading—and saw something more terrifying than a murder. Cash exchanging hands. The man gave Jett a thick bundle of bills. Jett caressed those bills, kissed the stack, and left the house without her.

His betrayal silenced her. She pressed her hands to the door, which was now a shield separating her from worse horrors, and wondered if there was a handle she could grip from the inside. Something to prevent the man from opening it. No. The panel was smooth and flat.

But he seemed uninterested. He stood in the shadows of the opposite corner of the room, where the glare couldn't reach, and studied the illuminated panel of his phone. He tapped, he scrolled.

He said, "You're not as strong as you think. Accept that as quick as you can."

She wasn't sure he was talking to her. The crack in the door put him in a tight frame. He had Hollywood looks equally fit for an unwitting hero or suave bad boy.

He continued, "Things'll go better for you when you do."

Slowly she lowered herself to her knees and moved her finger-tips over the surface of the ground, searching for something besides sawdust and spiders, something useful for self-defense or escape. A nail, for example, that she might slip between the door and the wall to dislodge the latch.

"What's your name?"

She didn't answer. Dust clung to her hands.

"Jett said your name is Becca."

"Then you don't need me to tell you," she snapped. She remembered the fake ID—Jett's idea, so she could get into his favorite club. The card was still in her jeans pocket. She fished it out, thinking new thoughts about the things he had often talked her into doing there after just a couple of beers.

Today the manager had asked her if she wanted a job.

In the closet, Becca rose from the floor and leveled her eye with the crack.

The man's eyeball was there, staring into her black hole. She flinched and knocked her head against the underside of a stair. The ID card dropped from her fingers and lightly slapped the floor.

"You're right," he said. "I don't need you to tell me anything." His words were thick against the wood, for her ears only, though as far as she knew they were alone. "In fact, don't speak at all. Or I'll shut you up myself."

She believed he would.

"What are you doing here?" he demanded of someone else. An unexpected visitor? He moved and the crack filled with light.

"Hey, Uncle Phil." The voice was thin with undertones of whine, like Becca's little brother's. But a kid her age stepped into the skinny view, an athletic boy, all-American clean. She recognized him at once. Brock Anderson. They'd gone to high school together before she dropped out, but she knew him by reputation: star pupil, king of the wrestling mats, and when the adults weren't looking, the Tom Sawyer of troublemaking.

Uncle Phil? Brock would be no ally of hers. Would he?

Brock took in the run-down room. "When I told you about this place I didn't think you'd actually be interested. It's a dump."

"I'm waiting for someone, and you don't want to be here when he comes."

"Was that Jett I saw leaving?"

"As you should be."

"I need to talk to you," Brock said.

"We both have phones."

"I wanted to see you."

The pair stood on the other side of the gas lamp and faced off like bright halves of the moon. Behind them, the ceiling bent their dark shadows at an aggressive angle.

"You here to ask for money?"

Brock sniffed and looked embarrassed.

"Get out. And don't ever follow me again."

"Look, I'm freaking out. I lost my scholarship!"

"Not my fault," Phil said.

"It wasn't my fault either. And you know Mom can't pay for Cornell."

"No, after her latest incompetence she probably can't afford a Happy Meal."

"But you're rolling in cash. Mom says—"

"Do you think she can say anything that would matter to me?"

"Why do you think I'm the one talking?" Brock spread his hands wide. "Help me out here!"

Taking advantage of their argument, Becca lowered herself to her knees and patted the floor for the ID card. Now was the time to tinker with the latch if it could be done at all.

"I don't give handouts," Phil growled.

"Then make it a loan."

"I'm not a bank either."

"Then . . . then . . ." Shadows shifted across the crack in the closet door. Becca found the card, slipped it under the latch, looked out through the crack at the two men who faced off, one desperate, one indifferent. The plastic met resistance.

Brock was saying, "Let me work for you, just one year. Now through next summer. Give me something to do. Anything."

At this Phil's expression changed from irritated to amused. His eyes darted to Becca's closet. She snatched the card back to her racing heart.

"You think you can earn enough for Cornell that fast? Just what is it that you think I do?"

"Mom says something criminal." Brock's laugh was a snort. "Not that you care what Mom thinks."

"Anything successful must be criminal. It's how she excuses her résumé of failures."

"That's what I said."

"I doubt it."

Brock gestured to the ruins. "I think you flip houses. You've got enough of them."

Phil watched him, tapping his phone against his chin.

"I can work, Uncle Phil. I'm good with a hammer and paintbrush." Brock crossed his arms.

"Tell me how you lost your scholarship."

"Wasn't my fault."

"Do you have a story or not?"

Brock rolled his eyes. "Teacher gave me a D at the end of the term, a totally subjective grade. She was completely unfair."

"Old hag with an ax to grind? Teacher for fifty years, angry about today's slacker youths?"

"Not exactly. She's the one who brought us up here on a biology field trip that one time."

"So I have her to thank for the house."

"I guess. It's when I first saw it."

Phil looked at his watch. "Contest the grade."

"Tried. But Ms. Diaz is some kind of darling, won a bunch of teaching awards. Everyone's all gaga over her. Hot too. Probably sleeping with the principal."

"Oh, that type," Phil said.

Type. Becca knew Ms. Diaz, and it took no special brains to guess that Brock had finally met a teacher who wouldn't be charmed by his flashy intelligence into letting a few assignments slide.

"You mean *your* type," Brock challenged, and his uncle laughed agreeably.

"Unattainable," Phil said. "Until she learns she's not." He put away his phone, his thin tolerance of Brock replaced by some kind of fresh interest.

In her closet, Becca believed she had glimpsed her imminent future with Phil and felt sick. It would take more than silence to save her skin; she knew it the way she knew when her stepdad was about to throw a plate at her head. She worked the card back into the door, and it went in far enough to tap the latch before snagging in some unseen joint of the hardware and refusing to dislodge.

Brock was saying, "So, about a job?" when the gas lantern popped and Becca jumped, bumping the door. The latch jangled and the card remained pinched. She held her breath. Brock's head turned toward the closet.

"What was that?"

"I think I could come up with something for you to do," Phil said as if he hadn't heard Brock's question. But he was moving toward Becca. She pressed herself against the back wall, then thought there might be a better way. She had just enough room in the short storage space to throw herself at the door if he opened it.

"So you're offering me a job?"

"I'm offering you an opportunity."

"Why? I mean, to do what?"

"Now you sound like you're not sure. Get your head square, Brock. Once you tell me yes, I won't take no for an answer."

Phil was so close now that the crack in the door turned opaque.

"No, no. Just tell me what you want me to do."

"Take your revenge," Phil said.

"Reve—? What? Against who?"

"The teacher."

"Diaz? What do you care about her?"

"I care about you, Brock."

Becca couldn't see anything beyond her prison now, but Brock spoke with a frown in his voice. "I'm really not interested in her. I mean, I'm mad, yeah, but she can't give me money for Cornell any more than Mom can. I only want some money."

"You'll get plenty of that too."

"How?"

"A little harmless fun. You like a good laugh, so what's the problem?"

"Uh, you said revenge."

Phil's voice spun away from Becca as he said, "Okay, forget it."

"No, no! Okay. Sorry. Doesn't matter what. I'll do it. Just say when."

Phil cursed.

"I mean it," Brock whined. "I'm sorry."

Phil made his nephew wait an agonizing time before saying, "Then we'll start now."

He released the door latch, and as soon as the panel began to swing outward, Becca punched it with the full force of her weight. The door should have caught him in the face. The shoulder at least. It might have broken a few of his fingers.

Instead it flew free. She saw the shadowy form of him standing aside as she burst out. She heard the door strain its hinges before snapping back. But she was in the clear.

The problem was she couldn't see which way to go. The white light of the lamp stunned her eyes and made duplicates of everything in the room—floating black silhouettes that wouldn't hold their position.

But the biggest black hole seemed to be the front door, so she leaped toward it on feet that were far more certain than her eyes.

An unseen obstacle cut off her escape at her ankle and she sprawled. Splinters entered her hands when they took the fall. The crown of her head met a sharp corner and the black spots in her vision came apart like dandelions in the wind. She was shrieking and hugging her leg to her chest. She rolled to her side. The pain in her shin had teeth.

"Hold this," Phil said to Brock, handing something over as he knelt beside Becca. She kicked at him and the pain stole her breath. She clutched her knee and feared she might pass out.

Then what would they do to her?

Sawdust bit into Becca's cheeks and lined her lips. She forced her eyes open, willing them to stay alert. If she couldn't see, if she didn't pay attention, their advantage over her would only grow.

In front of her eyes, the wide plane of the fresh wood subfloor reflected the bright glare of the gas lamp. Gradually it came into focus, and as her sight adjusted, the light seemed to change. The white light behind her gave way to gold rays that seemed to surround her. Liquid sun poured over the floor like paint, drowning woodchips in a creamy yellow puddle as it spread.

Then the paint turned into a carpet of softness, silky as chick feathers, rich as melted butter, warm as a window in the sun. She smelled fresh lemon cake and felt safe, even hopeful.

The promise came and went in the space of a breath.

A needle stabbed Becca's arm and everything golden turned ashy. The carpet vanished. Becca lifted her eyes to Brock. A baseball bat hung from his fingertips as if he'd never seen one in his life and didn't know what to do with it.

"Help me," she gasped.

He took a step back, looking as if he'd just walked into a pit of venomous snakes. Because he had, of course. They both had.

"What are you doing?" Brock whispered.

"Starting your training," Phil said. "We're going to put her in your car."

The words had no effect on her. The pain eased and she could hear herself breathing. Brock swayed. Or that might have been a trick of her mind. She closed her eyes even though she knew she shouldn't.

"Brock! You're working for me now, whether you sprout a conscience or not."

Brock cleared his throat.

"You said yes, Brock." Phil swore again. "It's too late now to say no. You can have money or you can have trouble. Are we clear?"

They both sounded so far away.

"Yeah. Yeah, we're clear."

Then the unstable floor beneath her back did open up and swallow her. And Becca fell out of this world and into a realm where nothing bad ever happened, so long as she wasn't looking.

THREE MONTHS LATER

MONDAY

TWO

SERENA DIAZ'S HIGH SCHOOL TEACHING CAREER ended while it was still technically beginning, before she had finished paying off her college debts and while tenure was still a distant goal. It ended at the beginning of the week, near the beginning of the school year, on a fair Southern California morning.

The principal of Mission Acres High School in North Hills intercepted her that morning before she reached the teachers' lounge. He invited her to his office without looking at her. The half pout, half squint balanced atop his teepeed fingers was directed at his desk, as if Serena had caused such deep personal offense that he couldn't bear to lift his eyes.

Serena held a paper cup of coffee and a six-inch stack of graded papers, which she held on to as she lowered herself onto the chrome-and-vinyl seat. She slipped her tote off her shoulder and let it rest against her ankle. The window beside Mr. Walter's desk had a soft-focus dampness in the lower corners that the morning sun hadn't yet erased. The first wave of students had begun to arrive, and they collected themselves in small groups on the grass outside and around the lockers in the exterior halls. The daylight wasn't warm yet. Some clutched sweatshirts across their narrow bodies, others held on tightly to summertime, refusing to give up their flip-flops and tank tops until the fashion became physically unbearable. For some it never did.

"Ms. Diaz," her boss began, and she wondered why he didn't call her Serena as he usually did. "Brock Anderson is in your science class."

Serena's defenses went up. "Fifth period, yes. AP environmental science." She took a sip of her coffee.

Brock was a sharp student but a bit of a troublemaker—not the reckless kind but the smart kind, the type who knew how to do the barest of minimums to achieve his desired results, though on occasion this practice failed him.

"He got a bad grade on his first big test of the year last week. You can imagine his reaction. Is it about that?"

Mr. Walter all but impaled the fleshy pouch under his chin on those steepled fingers of his. Still he would not look at her. "Yesterday evening I received a phone call from CPS."

"Child Protective Services?"

"Yes."

Serena tried to imagine what kind of harm might have come to the trophy-winning athlete. Brock had seemed fine when she last saw him—which, come to think of it, was the previous Thursday.

"He was absent Friday," she said. "Is he all right?"

"He's made some disturbing allegations."

"About whom?"

"About you, Ms. Diaz. About you."

She set her coffee on the lip of Mr. Walter's desk, then leaned back in the seat and straightened the papers on her lap, wondering what kind of crooked lines connected the dots that were CPS, Brock, and her.

Mr. Walter finally lifted his eyes to the window. A bit of rising sunlight that caught his glasses caused his piercing blue eyes to seem faded and watery.

"Thursday evening Brock told a friend he was planning to take his own life."

Serena caught her breath. Surely not because of one test? The news brought her forward again in the chair.

Mr. Walter continued, "The friend told his parents, the parents contacted the Andersons, the Andersons took their son to their family doctor to be evaluated. He was admitted to a behavioral health center for the weekend."

"That's terrible!"

Serena reached out to touch Mr. Walter's desk, as if she might find the right thing to say among the pen cup and stapler and glass apple paperweight. This was a new experience for her, a heartbreaking one. But she couldn't see Brock's thinking and wondered if she should feel guilty about the effects of that grade.

"I knew he was angry about the grade, but I had no idea. Brock's entirely capable of getting an A before the semester's end, if he would just—"

"Brock told the social worker assigned to his case that he wanted to die because you had . . . you had engaged him in an inappropriate sexual relationship in exchange for the promise of an A on his transcript."

It took Serena several seconds to personalize the entire meaning of what he had said, identifying each phrase and part of speech as being spoken about *her*. She couldn't speak.

At some point she'd received training in what to do should the unthinkable happen, should an angry student concoct a potentially devastating lie and drag it out into the public. There were precedents in the district. A history of teachers accused, both truthfully and falsely. But at that moment Serena couldn't remember a bit of what she had been taught. All that came to mind were the latest guidelines for how to do CPR.

"That's ridiculous," she said. "Mr. Walter."

And in the formality of her boss's name, Serena got a fresh picture of her unfortunate position. It wasn't Serena Diaz and Mac Walter having a conversation here, colleagues Serena and Mac having a tête-à-tête regarding a difficult student. It was supervisor Mr. Walter and relative newcomer Ms. Diaz, still so new that the principal, who tough-loved all students as if they were his biological children, probably knew more about Brock Anderson than he did about her. She was in her second year of teaching at Mission Acres. Brock was in his fourth year of ingratiating himself to authority figures with his fingers crossed behind his back. He was a talented graffiti artist, a low-key rebel who didn't lack any intelligence, only self-discipline.

"He also alleges that when he finally got the courage to oppose you, you retaliated by giving him an unfair low grade that sabotaged his Cornell scholarship."

"I did not do any such thing," Serena insisted.

She gathered up her papers again, this time like a shield over her heart.

"I'll talk to him." Serena stooped to grab the straps of her tote bag. "We'll work out whatever it is that has made him so angry."

"You'll do nothing of the sort."

"Why not?" She stood. Her heart was already trying to flee the scene. Apprehension stiffened her joints and turned her bones into heavy lead rods. "There's no reason for him to make up that kind of story. I'll just find out why he—"

"Stop. Please, I need to finish." Mr. Walter's A-frame fingers parted and he placed his hands on the desk. He stood, leaning forward slightly, braced on his fingertips as if his legs might give way at any second. She sensed what was coming before he said it.

"You know I have to suspend you immediately, pending an investigation. You'll still be paid of course."

"Students can do that? Just say the word and send their teachers home?"

Her tone was all wrong. Embarrassment shut her mouth. She *did* know suspensions were routine in these situations, if the suspicions were at all credible. And sometimes even if they weren't.

"It's for everyone's safety. After what happened at Miramonte . . ."

He didn't say more; he didn't need to. Mr. Walter referenced the case that had recently devastated a Los Angeles elementary school, in which a delayed investigation into one teacher's lewd acts resulted in the entire school staff being replaced and relocated.

"I'm sorry. Yes, of course. I know."

"You understand that it's my highest priority to protect the school and all the students here."

"I feel the same way."

"There will be an investigation."

Serena's shock morphed into fear then. What exactly did Brock have that made his story credible? She pressed her lips together and nodded, then found the courage to meet his eyes, which had finally turned to her when she least wanted them to.

Mr. Walter straightened and sighed, and she saw in the deep lines of his brow something she had never noticed before, a hint that the distaste in his frown wasn't for her after all. Maybe it was distress, like a chronic pain that undergirded every day of his existence, that things like this even happened at all. Really, which was worse: Brock's story as a horrific reality or as a perverse fantasy aimed to take down a promising teacher?

Somewhere beneath the suffocating shock, she found her professionalism. "You can expect my full cooperation. I don't have anything to hide."

Mr. Walter removed his glasses. "Serena."

The lead in her bones softened. A quiver had overtaken her, a low vibration like a predictable California earthquake. She didn't notice it until he spoke her given name, and then she thought she might crumble. She managed not to.

"Don't speak to anyone," he advised. "Most of all Brock. Take his accusations very seriously, even if they're false. Call the teachers' union. Please tell me your dues are current."

She nodded weakly and recognized these instructions as the ones given to her in the training session that she couldn't retrieve from her memory.

"They'll refer you to an attorney," Mr. Walter continued. "They'll even pay for it, if you are in fact not guilty and you file a not-guilty plea, should this go as far as court."

That one word, *court*, took Serena's breath away. Lance. She had to call Lance.

"Is there somewhere you can stay besides your home?" He asked the question with the gentleness of a worried father—someone like her own father, who had asked this question of hundreds of women over the years before offering them the safety they so desperately needed. "Because the press is going to hound you."

The press. A reality far, far worse than court. She couldn't think. She didn't know where she should go. Not to her family. The press would make their lives miserable too. So many women counted on her family for safety, for shelter, for a place to heal quietly.

"I'm never going to get to teach again, am I?" Serena murmured. "Public opinion will see to that, no matter what the truth is."

Mac Walter averted his eyes again, powerless to disarm the bomb Brock Anderson had just dropped in her lap.

"Please let me know how I can help."

THREE

FIRE FOLLOWERS DIDN'T GET TOO MANY ANONY-
mous tips. In fact, Christopher Larsen couldn't remember the small
nonprofit ever receiving one. The call rang in as he was doing his
last morning lap in the backyard pool, and it went to voice mail
before he had time to haul himself onto the deteriorating patio and
fetch his towel.

He dried his hands and face and listened to the message while
the rest of him dripped. That morning between eight and ten,
said a level-toned man, members of Phil Lancet's notorious sex-
trafficking network would pass through the Angeles National
Forest via the Big Tujunga Road, transporting new girls out
of Los Angeles. Two Caucasian men in an unmarked blue van,
heading north from Sunland, would be carrying four, maybe five
girls.

If not for the mention of Lancet, Christopher would have
thought he was dealing with a hoax. Fire Followers, which aimed
to prevent girls from being lured into sex trades in the first place,
didn't conduct anything like sting operations after the fact. There
was no reason to alert the Larsens' tiny, localized aid organization
before the FBI or LAPD—which is exactly what his contact at the
FBI said when Christopher called him to relay the information.

"It smells sour," Special Agent Dale Montague said to Christopher after listening. "Be there in a sec," he said to someone off the line.

"Other than it being anonymous and vague and possibly misdirected, what's to keep you from throwing your entire department at this one?" Christopher asked lightly.

"Finite resources, my friend. No idea who the caller was?"

"An adult male, or a very hairy woman."

"That narrows the field."

"Could be someone who hates Phil Lancet. Someone who knows we've picked up his trail again recently."

"Or just someone who hates you." To someone else Dale said, "Not Randall, Randolph."

The tip could have been concocted by someone inside Lancet's network to cause Christopher some grief. What better way to stir up a cause like Fire Followers than to pelt it with cherry bombs? Call them to arms, then laugh at the bewildered expressions when they realized the opponent was fabricated. Of course, Christopher didn't say this. Dale would already be thinking it.

"But what if the information is good? Maybe the guy who called is just someone who doesn't want to be investigated." He could hear Dale speaking over a hand-muzzled mouthpiece, requesting a file that pertained to some other case.

"Someone who doesn't want what?" he asked Christopher.

"To answer your many questions about how they know about a trafficking scheme. Maybe it's someone with a score to settle—someone with John Roman's group. It's not a secret that he took my sister—"

"Did they name Roman?"

"No, but Lancet and Roman go together like peanut butter and jelly."

"It's a squishy theory," said Dale. "Very soft. The Jell-O hasn't had time to set."

"What can it hurt to send someone to check it out? Just one person?"

"You're one person, aren't you? You've got my direct number. Call me if something gels."

"Dale—"

"What's the appropriate sentiment here? That I hope you find something or that I hope you don't?"

Dale was a good man, a dedicated agent, an attentive husband, an involved father of three boys. Maybe because he was all those things, an overabundance of legitimate needs—not to mention bureaucratic red tape—competed for his attention every day. There just wasn't enough Dale to address everything with equal thoughtfulness.

Christopher wanted a cigarette to take the edge off his frustration. He might have one in the car.

It was already seven thirty and Sunland was a solid half hour away from Christopher's Santa Monica bungalow in decent traffic, which Southern California's never was. So he hopped into his old blue Kia while his swim trunks were still damp. He pulled a T-shirt from several random articles of clothing that he kept in the back, not because it was strategic, but because he never had time to organize unimportant things like his wardrobe. This particular shirt had been in his car since it was given to him almost a year ago by a friend who never passed up a gag: *Don't shoot!* the front pleaded. *I'm not Christopher Dorner.* The shirts had sold by the thousands during an infamous LAPD manhunt for the former police officer, in which angry authorities misidentified—and then shot—several innocent civilians, including a woman. Christopher's friend thought too much of the outlaw sharing his name.

When the single layer of cotton didn't ward off the chill, he layered this with an oversized button-down that had been wadded in the passenger footwell.

A cellophane-wrapped package of cigarettes tumbled out from under the shirt. Empty.

He would have to settle for loud music. Christopher turned up the radio.

The day promised sun after a weekend of light rain. Southern California had three seasons: sunny, rainy, and Santa Ana windy. The worst of the hot summer winds were behind them now, and for the rest of the winter the rain would try to overpower the sun. With the occasional exception, it would lose. The morning fog was lifting, rising above the concrete freeway as if it had given up its ghost.

He pushed his sunglasses onto his nose and headed east, thinking about the possibility of John Roman being so close at hand. Christopher had thought about the elusive Roman every day for the last twelve years, starting even before he knew the man's name, on the day he learned that his little sister had disappeared. Christopher and his closest friends had pulled Amber out of Roman's underworld two years later, when she was sixteen. But Roman's evil industry had continued to expand and prosper. These days he was invisible and protected behind his armies of well-paid pimps and traffickers and groomers, Phil Lancet chief among them.

At the stacked interchange between the 10 and the 405, Christopher honked at a driver with out-of-state plates who had dropped well below the speed of traffic and seemed confused by which lane she should be in. He made a swift pass to get ahead and narrowly caught the northbound exit. No time to lose. He might already be too late.

Six weeks ago Lancet had made a daring appearance at a fundraiser aimed to end violence against women. It was there that Fire Followers had managed to pick up his trail.

They did it through the woman who attended the fund-raiser with him. Even though she was easier to track than Lancet, it took them a week to confirm that she was a high school science teacher from North Hills named Serena Diaz. The 405 passed straight through North Hills. Christopher could see Mission Acres High School from the freeway and hoped something had kept her away from those kids today. The school parking lot was filling up. Unhurried students loitered on the grass and shot baskets on the asphalt courts.

A young high school teacher cozy with Phil Lancet. Few ideas turned Christopher's stomach the way that one did. When adults in positions of trust started victimizing young people for a life of prostitution, the world would implode.

But for six weeks, the FBI's investigation had been bogged down by the red-tape requirement of confirming Lancet's identity. A positive ID seemed neither urgent nor likely, Special Agent Montague argued, since Serena Diaz was, from a legal point of view anyway, as pure as the ocean breeze. Did Christopher know her parents ran a shelter for abused women in Pasadena called the Safe Place? Maybe Lancet—if that was the man with her at the fund-raiser—had become a convert.

Christopher didn't believe it. He knew of the Safe Place, had even sent a woman their way once, but children didn't always follow in their parents' footsteps. Sometimes they tried to erase the tracks entirely.

It took him forty minutes to reach the Big Tujunga Road. At eight ten, he turned his salt-rusted little SUV around and parked on the other side of the road where he would best be able to spot a blue van carrying two Caucasian men. If the vehicle existed at all. He hoped they weren't already on their way up through the forest.

He leaned across the passenger seat and retrieved a few photographs from the glove box.

Phil Lancet. Tall like a palm tree, angular and lean. His ability to intimidate came from his measured self-control—precise, almost graceful—rather than from brutish muscle. He was fair, with a mess of blond locks that nearly reached his shoulders. The hairstyle in this picture taken five years ago was far longer than he wore it now in the company of Ms. Diaz.

Serena Diaz. Olive-skinned, brown-eyed, young. She could pass for eighteen, Christopher thought, though a reluctance to smile made her look older and the résumé he'd unearthed put her at about twenty-four. Thick black hair fell to her collarbones in tight ringlet curls. Playful down, seductive up. The light in her eyes might be kindness or mischief. Easy for a woman like that to play whatever role she was thrown into.

Jett Anderson. A sun-bronzed college dropout who'd had a lucky swim in the gene pool. Fire Followers believed he was grooming girls for one of the local underground networks—maybe Roman's, maybe not. Today Christopher's friends were tailing Jett, who liked to talk his girls out of school on different days of the week, reducing his chances of being discovered as a man of many women.

Jett was new on their radar. So were the other four young men in the stack of pictures. Maybe Christopher would see one of them in the van today.

No photo of John Roman. Amber had seen him, known him more intimately than anyone twelve years ago, back when he groomed and then abducted her. After her escape she'd tried to work with police artists to develop a sketch but was never happy with the results. Always close, never accurate. Since then, her memory of Roman's appearance had become fuzzy, while her recall of his monstrousness kept its high-definition clarity.

There was hardly any traffic on the Big Tujunga Road on this weekday morning in October, so Christopher got a good look at each car as it sped past. And although Serena Diaz was at the front of his mind, and although less than fifteen minutes earlier he'd wished for something to separate her from her students, he was not prepared to see her here, driving north into the Angeles National Forest.

She was not driving a blue van, but a sensible gray Volvo, and as far as Christopher could see, there were no men riding with her.

Even so, he pulled out onto the two-lane road, turned around for the second time, and followed her.

Serena didn't call Lance right away. He had a court appearance that morning, and the sound of his recorded voice mail message would only confirm just how alone she was. After her meeting with Mr. Walter she fled Mission Acres High School, escaped North Hills, and drove east to her favorite place, into the not-very-majestic mountains that formed the Angeles National Forest.

In all the world there were only five chaparral plant communities, and in North America the only one was here on the coast of Southern California, stretching down to Baja. As a biologist, Serena loved the privilege of living in such a rare place. The humility of these chaparral hills' south-facing slopes stood in sharp contrast to the boastful glamour of the state's popular culture. These were simple hills covered in shrubby bushes and dense grasses, not the American ideal of beauty. The toyon, the chamise, the ceanothus were all so common and unassuming that they'd formed almost invisible backdrops in hundreds of Hollywood films and TV shows.

The Angeles National Forest held the Los Angeles basin firmly between itself and the Pacific Ocean as if to prevent its smog, real and figurative, from spreading to other parts of the country. It was rugged and scrappy. It was prone to drought and wildfires.

It was also resilient and optimistic, and Serena needed an inspirational dose of both.

Observing nothing of her concrete-jungle surroundings, she drove to Sunland, then to the Big Tujunga Road, then onto the unpaved roads of the Station Fire burn scar, where more than a hundred and sixty thousand acres had been leveled by a blaze in October 2009.

She drove for some time over the uneven, narrow road, about three-quarters of a mile, at a slow pace. Then, at a spot where two toyon trees formed something like a low-hanging arch, she parked. The toyon were evergreens that bore white flowers in the spring and heavy clusters of small red berries in the winter. The hardy plants were also known as California holly and, many believed, had given Hollywood its name.

Serena's Volvo balanced half on and half off the road in a margin that couldn't really be called a shoulder, her car crowding the recovering shrubs.

In the trunk were sturdy hiking boots, field notebooks, extra water, and a camera, items she kept close at hand for her frequent treks into this familiar territory. But today she left them behind. She kept her sensible Clarks on her feet and didn't worry about protecting her best slacks and tailored jacket. What use would she have for this outfit now? She left the graded papers strewn across the passenger seat, along with her tote and her phone. Let someone find them. They were part of a life that didn't belong to her anymore, though she would have to defend it.

Serena hiked to the place she had visited repeatedly, a place so familiar that she didn't have to do any thinking to get there.

The region had made a good recovery since the terrible burn. Green life danced larger than the black skeletons on a ground scattered with riotous wildflowers, purple and yellow and orange, life that stayed trapped in seeds until a fiery heat created the tragic circumstances that would make it possible for them to bloom. Fire followers, they were called.

When she had first come upon the site just a year after the Station Fire, back when she was completing her student teaching requirements, the compacted mess of organic life reduced to its carbon essence still covered the ground. Its ashy remains swirled around her hiking boots like tiny mourning ghosts. Over the seasons they gathered weight.

At first Serena came to document nature's recovery for her students. Burn areas were great training ground for fledgling botanists. Sometimes a few of them came with her for extra credit or just for bona fide passion. Some would jump at any field trip that took them out of school. The California lilacs and coffeeberrys, smooth manzanitas, and tangled masses of greasewood would take years to return to their former state, and Serena intended to observe their every step.

She photographed and notated and researched and took her discoveries back to the classroom. Restoration was evident almost immediately in the green shoots that sprang from sheltered crown roots at the base of plants like toyon and yucca. She saw it in the new seeds prepped for germination by the smoke and heat and nitrogen compounds that only a fire could create. It sprang up in the form of wildflowers that bloomed like crazy the first spring after destruction.

The magnet of optimism had drawn her to this forlorn site again and again. Where others saw wreckage, she saw the promise of hope.

Today, however, something about the area was foreign and frightening. She walked slowly, both glad for the distraction and unnerved by it. What was the cause? The smells from the weekend rains? The shadows cast by a sun that hadn't quite broken through? No—it was the hour, she finally decided. She'd never come so early in the morning on a weekday, not so late in the year. The light made everything look different. But also the same.

Her mind was loud with overlapping thoughts, like the senseless rumble of people raising their voices over each other in a crowded place. She walked for half an hour before the true reason for her unease finally rose above her mental chaos.

The wildfire was years past. The crisis was over. So was the summer. At that very moment, there should be no wildflowers here at all.

FOUR

HOW COULD SERENA NOT HAVE NOTICED HIM, Christopher wondered as he brought his SUV alongside her parked Volvo. Was it an act? He felt oddly undecided.

She had left her car at a gap between two shrubs. The recovery in this spot had been swifter than in other parts of the Station Fire area, maybe because the hillside here seemed to form a sort of football-stadium bowl that could capture more water during the rainy season. In any case, the scrubby bushes were taller here, small trees.

As he pulled around to park behind her, he decided to have a closer look at the contents of her car while he waited for her to return.

But when he swung his legs out of the Kia, put both feet on the ground, then stood in the joint where his car and door formed a V, dread came over him like a rogue wave at the beach. It was the kind that came when your back was turned, the kind that drove your face down into the sand and then handed you over to the strong fingers of an undertow, dragging you out to sea before you could catch a mouthful of air. It almost knocked him right back down into the seat of his car. He had felt this dread on two other occasions in his life: once after being knocked off his surfboard by a wave lurking behind the one he caught, and once when he got the news that Amber had been abducted.

This time he didn't know the why or what of the sickening feeling, only that it required a response. Do something or a life will be lost. Maybe Serena's, maybe some young girl whom she'd victimized. He paused only long enough to bend into his backseat for something to protect his feet. Flip-flops. And he grabbed his yellow knit cap, the one with ridiculous tasseled ear flaps. He rarely wore it, though Amber had given it to him. It wasn't the best item for a man who usually needed to keep a low profile. He had the unsettling thought that it would stand out in a place like this, should someone need to search for his body drowned on dry land. It might even be visible from the air. And his sister would know he really did like the hat after all.

He plunged into the growth after the dark-haired mystery, quickly spotting her light shoe prints in the rain-dampened ground. Ground thick with wildflowers.

The blooms made no sense to him at all. All this new growth— what was it doing here now? He reached down and plucked a flower the size of his big toe, a bright orange fire poppy with four petals, the California version of a four-leaf clover. He didn't know a lot about flowers, but these fire followers held special significance for him, and he did know they shouldn't be in bloom right now.

Christopher moved on, perplexed, pinching the slim stem between his fingers.

The farther he walked into the bowl-shaped territory, the thicker the toyon grew. He was headed slightly downhill now, forced to keep to the right as the growth became taller and more hedge-like. The shrubs took the shape of trees and twined arms with manzanita and coffeeberry bushes. The lushness of the growth was as mystifying as the flowers scattered across every inch of bare ground; he couldn't walk without stepping on something colorful, and the silky flower petals tickled his ankles and were caught under his heels by the snapping-jaws motion of his flip-flops.

The sounds of human movement reached his ears from the other side of the thick bushy screen. Christopher couldn't see an end to the hedge. So he decided to go through it.

The process brought the ocean back to mind. That memory of trying to get out of the strong arms of an undertow and to the surface for air. Of being dragged back under, abraded by seashells and sand on the shallow floor, before it fell away to frightening depths. Only this time his arms and legs were scraped up by branches.

He finally reached the clearing, his yellow cap askew.

And all the mysteries of the past half hour seemed elementary compared to the sight that greeted him then: Serena Diaz, slowly approaching a grand stone house fit for a center spread in *Sunset* magazine. A massive place, quiet and safe, that would have brought Amber to her knees in gratitude. *This is it*, he could imagine her saying. *This is the house for all the Fire Followers. I want it.*

And he wanted nothing more than to make the house Amber's, so she could transform it into a home for other women who had very particular needs. Simple needs that were not simply filled. But Amber would be the one to do it. He was so convinced of this that he believed he saw her, right there on the wide front porch, held up by wide white posts and framed by a pretty white slatted rail, swinging on a porch swing and laughing with several other women.

Fire Follower women.

She was beautiful. She was whole. She was dressed in blue.

Serena Diaz was approaching the women, and Amber rose to meet her.

The fire poppies were following Serena. Christopher looked twice at the sight that finally tore his gaze away from the image of his sister. No, the flowers weren't following her in the sense that they were walking on feet; they were springing up out of the ground in each place where she took a step. They were shooting straight up, then falling out like a fountain to the sides, growing into each other, forming a lush carpet of blazing sunlight. Knobby orange buds emerged at the end of each stem and then popped open like popcorn. More toyon sprang out of the ground. White petals dropped like snow. Red berries took their place. Whole life cycles of fire-hardy shrubs began and ended and began again right there in this bizarre place where nothing made sense.

It couldn't possibly be real.

And then suddenly, it wasn't.

The abandoned house stood before Serena like something made more noble by suffering. It stood, barely, in a blackened clearing where no wildflowers bloomed. She hadn't noticed when she'd left them behind.

As she approached, she felt small. Beneath her shoes, damp leaves shifted and released mildew scents. All around the gutted private dwelling, thick scrub oaks were thinned to skinny charred sticks fifteen feet tall. Yucca stubs like black pineapples crowded the stone walls. A bird launched itself off the rotting sill of a window and flew away, kicking up flecks of blistered gray paint. These floated briefly in front of the glass warped by fire.

The house was an accidental discovery Serena had made one day when she wandered from the hiking trail. It was easy to imagine that any road to the solitary home had long since been covered by neglect. Once upon a time, a driveway might have swooped by the front porch, before the chaparral reclaimed the space and absence cluttered the house with shrunken spider skeletons and hollow insects.

In the upstairs windows, gray curtains that once had been white caught the breeze let in by the breached front door. Everything was gray: the sky, the ground, the stone walls, the dull roof, and even her own disbelief in Brock's accusations.

The old place was topped by a sloping metal roof. Its porch was brittle cinder too weak to support a person's weight, and only the wide brick steps were suitable for walking on. The window glass sagged, but the building was erect. Sooty. Stubborn.

Serena admired this kind of stubbornness, the kind that resisted devastation. It was why she had needed to come here on this particular morning.

And yet the very act of running toward solace might look like an attempt to evade the law.

Behind one of the blistered windowpanes, one corner of the dingy curtain rose and a girl's face appeared, startling Serena. She halted in the ground cover. Never before had she encountered anyone here.

The rippled window distorted the young woman's features, making her look old and angry. But Serena had the unshakable impression that she was catching a glimpse of her younger self, though all the girl's features seemed exaggerated by the melted glass. The two shared curly hair, wide-set eyes, and narrow chins.

Serena lifted her hand in greeting but her twin did not. The two stared at each other until a creaking board jerked Serena's attention to the first floor.

A physically unimpressive man stood in the gap where the door should have been, separated from her by the charred porch and wide steps leading down into the tangled growth. Lacking any fat to ward off the dampness, he seemed folded in on himself for warmth: elbows tucked into his ribs, back stooped, chin drawn down to his chest. The cigarette in the corner of his mouth glowed.

Serena glanced back up at the window. The girl was gone. The fabric curtain was still.

The man removed the cigarette and exhaled smoke.

"'S private property here," he said. His tone was more factual than hostile. He had a mild accent that she couldn't place.

The information was no news to Serena. The forest contained several inholdings, though she'd never looked into the details of this particular house. But for the occupant to return today of all days seemed unfair.

"Sorry." Serena retreated a few steps. "Never seen anyone around before."

His thumb fiddled with the cool end of his tobacco. His friendly smile surprised her and took years off his age.

"You come often?" he asked.

"Time to time. Since the burn."

"What for?"

She gestured to the land. "Recovery." Her passion to explain the work was gone today. "I'm a teacher."

He nodded in that polite way people offered when their care was superficial.

"You rebuilding?" Serena's question was dumb in light of the scene: there were no vehicles, no contractors, no signs of productivity.

"Yes." The word was sudden, a reaction to an idea he'd never considered before. "Yes, we are. Do you teach landscaping? We could use someone eventually."

She smirked. A biology teacher landscaping in the national forest? She glanced around at the stark space, and when she looked back at him his smiling eyes were fondling her. The heat left her skin and the air felt strangely chilly on her cheeks. He took another draw from his cigarette and stood aside as if to give her space to enter. She saw then that some temporary boards had been laid across the unstable ruins between the brick steps and the front door.

Serena withdrew. She wouldn't find what she needed today anywhere near this man.

"Offer you some coffee?" he said when he saw her turning. "No electricity yet, but I've got a thermos."

She tilted her face up toward the window where she'd seen the girl. "No. I need to get back. And I see you've got company."

"Hm? There a mouse in the house?" The man jumped off the porch over the steps and came out far enough to see for himself. The behavior was so full of boyish curiosity that she thought she might have imagined his ogling. Serena joined the man in looking up.

His hand closed around her arm and shocked her like an electric jolt. It charged her heart and cut her down at the knees. She dropped all her body weight into an effort to break free, but his sinewy fingers were steel strong. She shouted. He struck her in the temple with the bony heel of his hand. Tiny stings of cigarette ash showered her forehead. She stumbled. He hit her again, this time on her ear. She fell to one knee.

The whole world smoldered right in front of Christopher's eyes, then vanished like smoke. The women on the porch, gone. The spectacular stone house, reduced to charred ruins. The wildflowers, ash. The person who was coming toward Serena from the house was not Amber at all. Was not even a woman.

But Serena remained.

Serena, and a woman cowering behind the glass of an upstairs window.

Two women plus someone accustomed to treating women as less than human.

There was no time to sort out what fantasy was happening in this place; the reality was clear enough. The grip on Serena's arm was malicious. Christopher could see the man's harmful intentions in the glassy surface of his eyes. He heard the ill will in the smooth lies. It was a language Christopher knew and hated. No matter what Serena's association with Phil Lancet might be, she didn't deserve what this man would do to her. No one did.

Glowing ash from the man's cigarette rained onto Serena's skin. He struck her on the side of the head. She fell.

Christopher saw the craven man's gun.

Like a dream, like magical fire poppies rising up from burnt ground, a plan to get her out of this mess formed in his mind.

"Serena!" He stepped forward and shouted her name without thinking, but the moment required no thought. There was only one right behavior in such a situation: to save a life. "Serena!"

She turned and saw him. Her attacker stopped striking, one hand still raised over her head. She twisted free, or he released her, and she bolted. Christopher caught her against her will, but she yielded.

He wiped ash off her forehead with the tail of his shirt, an intimate gesture that should have been awkward. It felt to him as natural as touching a friend, and the gesture was accompanied by a strange and stabbing sadness that he had not met her sooner.

"I mean it, Serena, one of these days you're going to go walk off a cliff and I'm not going to be able to find you."

The confusion in her eyes said she didn't recognize him and might not choose to trust him, but she didn't pull away. He'd seen this kind of fear before. She wasn't the first woman who'd put her hand in his, knowing intuitively that rejecting help would mean almost certain death.

The stranger calling her by name had tumbled out of the twiggy scrub behind her, slapping the branches away from his face, dressed all wrong for this terrain in flip-flops, swim trunks, and a short-sleeved button-down open and flapping over one of those horrible Christopher Dorner T-shirts. He wore a knit winter cap in bold African colors—yellow, red, green—with a slim plastic visor and earflaps and tassels that dangled to his armpits.

He might have been right at home down on the Venice Beach boardwalk, but these mountains were a long way from there.

His smile was oafish and apologetic. And kind. She had no idea who he was, how he knew her name. Or if he would join this other guy in harming her.

Had he followed her from the school?

He must be a journalist. A parent. An ambulance chaser. A PI hired by Brock's family.

"I mean it, Serena, one of these days you're going to go walk off a cliff and I'm not going to be able to find you."

The words were gentle but didn't explain a thing. He smelled of chlorine and cigarette smoke. He rubbed something off her forehead with the tail of his shirt. His touch urged her to trust him, though she knew she couldn't. His wide hands were firm on her waist, confident, the way a ballroom-dance instructor had once taught her partner to lead. Lance, Lance. She should have called her boyfriend, left a message, told him where she was going. She focused on the ground and saw the man's left foot was bleeding where a twig had scratched his skin.

"My sister wanders away," Venice Beach said to the other man, turning her head to see the ear that had been struck. "Thinks she's Darwin making new discoveries in the wilderness. And she's brilliant, really amazing. But she has special needs."

Serena thought the man examining her head might be the one who wasn't typical. But she kept her eyes pointed at the ground. She'd read once that a victim had a greater chance of surviving an attack if she didn't study her attacker too closely.

He continued saying to the brute, "Thanks for finding her."

"It was nothing," the other one said. The words were flat.

"Can I give you anything?" Venice pulled a wallet out of a pocket in his trunks and opened it, then fished out a couple of bills. Serena considered running off again, decided against it. "Buy yourself a nice dinner. You and a friend."

The man accepted whatever amount was handed to him. He seemed to remember his cigarette and lifted it to his lips while counting the cash as if he'd just sold a car or a piece of furniture.

"You need a ride anywhere?" Venice pressed. "Looks like you're alone? I've got a car down the road."

"No."

"Well, thank you, then. Thanks from the whole family. We'll get outta your hair." He encircled Serena's shoulder and steered her away from the house, straight back into the skeleton thicket. She turned reluctantly, not knowing whether she had just dodged a bullet or was allowing herself to be led from one slaughter to another.

"Amber's worried sick," he said for the benefit of the other man. "Only Kaleo believed I'd get you back home for dinner."

She didn't know any Ambers or . . . or . . . She hadn't caught the other name. Home for dinner sounded like an ominous event.

He lowered his voice. "Why did you come here?"

She pretended not to hear.

"These people will kill you."

"What people?"

"Unless you're working for them. Even then, no guarantees. How did you know about this place?"

Serena decided to make a break for freedom within the scrub. She should be able to outrun any man in flip-flops, and she was confident of the way back to her parked car. The stranger pushed aside some new growth that stood in their way and let her step through first.

"Can I trust you?" he asked her. It struck her as a ridiculous question coming from a man dressed as he was.

"I don't know," she muttered. "You seem to have mistaken me for someone else."

"Serena Diaz," he said. He was behind her when a gunshot whipped the air.

Serena whirled to see the gun that had let the round loose. Her ears were ringing. Her lungs were frozen.

Venice Beach was not holding a weapon, but she couldn't make sense of what he did have in his hands: a baby doll with silky black hair and a frilly pink dress. Where had that come from? Under his hat? Nothing else she saw was logical either: a green clearing so wet with dew that it wouldn't burn were a torch put to it; a pristine stone house worthy of a billionaire; a group of young women sitting on the porch in wicker furniture, heads bowed together over books.

Was this death?

The last scrap of morning dew dropped off a branch above her head and dribbled through her eyebrows into her eyes. The lovely view vanished.

When she blinked, she saw blood oozing through Venice Beach's T-shirt. The man on the charred porch was aiming for a second shot with just one confident hand, cigarette lazy at the corner of his mouth. He closed one eye and leveled the barrel.

She was quite alive. For another second at least.

Christopher put himself between her and the gun, calculating the risk.

The plan almost worked.

He heard the shot but didn't feel it. She turned around. She saw him. She knew.

Oh, if only she could *really* know, and see what he had seen: his strong sister, made stronger by this place, where she'd never been. And Serena coming to meet her like a precious friend, walking wildflowers into being as she arrived. Amber would be okay, even if she didn't know it yet. But Serena . . .

He pushed her toward safety.

"Run," he said as he fell.

Serena ran.

FIVE

SERENA COULDN'T INSERT HER KEY INTO THE CAR'S door lock. Her hands shook so badly that she dropped it twice into the loose dirt. The key buried itself in a blink.

Her vehicle was still in the narrow road, two wheels in the shallow ditch and two on the packed earth. On her knees, breathless, she ransacked the dirt for that key. It was unfortunate that the old car's electrical system was so shoddy that her key fob no longer worked. It was unfortunate that she'd decided to come here on this unfortunate day.

An SUV, one as inexpensive and road weary as her Volvo, had squeezed in behind her on the shoulder. She glanced at it while her fingers searched for the keys. Did that car belong to Venice Beach? It was a Kia, its blue paint along the roof already giving way to rust from the salty ocean air. If not for the possibility that a man with a gun was about to burst through the ground cover at any minute and start firing at her, she might have taken the time to poke around.

Venice Beach's fading eyes rattled her. They were all she could see as she searched the soil: his chocolate brown eyes waning to the dry beige of desert. She'd never seen such a thing, a man's eyes aging to the end of life in an instant.

The bullet had struck him, hadn't it?

He was dying back there by the house, wasn't he?

While she made a frantic effort to save herself.

Her hair, ratty with leaves she had snagged on her escape, brushed the dirt as she searched. Then the key's jagged teeth bit into her hand and she closed her fist around it. Dirt packed into her fingernails. She stood, raised her trembling fingers to the lock one more time, and realized that she never locked her car up here, not the way she did down in the city. She jumped in, slammed the door, and put the key in the ignition.

Her return to the paved road was a hasty, jarring ride. She left the dirt lane behind her without checking for traffic and might have been struck by an oncoming blue van if it hadn't been turning onto the very route she fled. The driver craned his neck for a look at her. She stepped on the gas.

Halfway down the hillside a mild burnt odor crept in through the vents and she realized she'd forgotten to release the emergency brake.

If these things had happened yesterday, Serena would have called the police. But yesterday was so long ago, and the police were the last people in the world she wanted to talk to. She traveled at such speed over the road that on one curve she drifted into the oncoming lane and startled an old Volkswagen. The driver laid on his horn. She slowed and dug her phone out of the console next to the driver's seat. It took her multiple attempts to get the number she wanted. But when Lance answered on the first ring, her body dialed back the adrenaline.

Lance would put sense into her head. Lance would sort out how to right everything that had gone wrong.

"Serena? Where are you?"

She took a relieved breath. "Big Tujunga Road."

"Running off right now without telling anyone where you're going is not the brightest idea you've ever had."

"Someone shot at me."

"Shot at—you mean like an angry parent?"

"No, no. Someone was at the house."

"What house?"

She'd only known Lance for a couple of months, and she had mentioned the old house before, but with the beginning of the new school year she hadn't had time to take him there.

"The Station Fire house." She registered his odd choice of words late. "What do you mean, an angry parent?"

He spoke more softly into her silence. "It's all over the news feeds. I saw it the second I stepped out of court. I've been trying to call you. Are you okay?"

"No, no. I'm not okay. There's a man. Lance, I just left him there. I think he's hurt. I don't know what to do."

"Are we talking about the person who shot at you?"

"A different man. He helped me."

Already, the sloping hillsides were making way for the faded asphalt roads to straighten out. At the next bend, chaparral yielded to land cleared by humans. Lance's silence prompted her to apologize.

"I know, I know, I should have called you first. But I needed time to think. It's a lie, Lance. Every last word out of Brock's mouth."

"Brock Anderson, the one who gave you so much trouble this summer."

Of course—the media wouldn't have released his name. He was still seventeen, a senior coming around the curve to adulthood. She was surprised the school hadn't suppressed the story for a while longer.

"Yes, that's him."

"Serena, listen to me. I can tell you're upset. We need to talk about everything that happened today. Then I can help you sort out this shooting. Do not go home, do not go to the police. I want you to come straight to my house."

"I should call the teachers' union first, go through all the right channels."

"I'll take care of it. We can do that here. Lucky you, to be dating a defense attorney before any of this even started. Brock picked the wrong woman."

A few stones on the heap of her mind tumbled away. "They're not going to tell me I have to use someone else? There's not a conflict of interest or anything?"

"Where's the conflict?"

She couldn't think of any, really. Who could more passionately represent her than a man who cared about her personally, who would believe she couldn't possibly be involved with a student because she was so completely involved with him?

It was the best thing for a woman in her position to do. It was also the easiest thing to do. She drove another quarter mile believing this.

But the brown-eyed man with the free curls was asking if he could trust her as she sped down the road away from him.

"Would you call an ambulance?" she asked. "The police? I can't believe I left him."

"As soon as you hang up. Tell me again exactly where this place is." She heard the rustling sounds of him rifling his desk for a pen. She told him, as best as she was able, how someone might be able to reach the house without having to hike in. Maybe the shooter had cleared an access that she failed to see. It had never occurred to her to look.

Lance asked, "How bad is he hurt?"

"I don't know. I couldn't see." She searched her memory for clues and couldn't come up with anything but those fading brown eyes. "What if he's dead?"

"Was he shot? Was there blood?"

"I think so. I don't know. He just . . ."

He just what? Had he fallen down? Had he followed her out? She couldn't remember. Her foot came off the accelerator and the car slowed. Behind her, someone honked and then passed. Why couldn't she remember anything about the man except those eyes? He was dressed oddly, she recalled, but already those details were eluding her. What color was his hair? How tall was he? Had he spoken with an accent?

The sensation of his confident hand on the small of her back, turning her around, caused her to pull off the road. She drifted into weeds lining the barbed-wire fence of someone's property on the edge of Sunland.

"Serena." Lance's voice was firm, calling her thoughts back to the conversation.

"I should go back. I'll wait for them, show them where he is."

"Imagine that one of your students came to you with this story. Would you advise her to go back, alone?"

"Lance."

"It's a reasonable question, just one of a million I can think of. Are you prepared to explain why you were present at a shooting instead of being in a police interview room?"

Of course not. The question made her angry.

"Leaving a man to die might be the first wrong thing I've done today," she said.

"You shouldn't have left LA, Serena. Even the appearance of trying to run away will harm you right now. You must be the perfect angel that the rest of us know you to be. Your story is everywhere, your face—"

"There is no story! Lance! I didn't do anything. What they're saying . . . Oh my gosh, Lance, I never . . . I would never . . ."

"Honey, I know. I know."

Lance's voice soothed. She hadn't realized until that moment just how much she had feared his reaction to the news—that he might believe it.

"What are they saying?" she dared to ask.

He hesitated, then: "More than you want them to."

"Why would Brock do this? Why would he pick a lie that is just as bad for him as it is for me?"

"Don't worry about it now. Get off the phone, drive straight here. I already have so many of your things. You'll stay as long as you need. No prying eyes. No difficulties for your family."

The car continued to idle at the side of the road. Outside, the sun pushed aside the very last of the low clouds and hung in a pale blue sky.

"You're a good man, Lance. Thank you."

"It's the least I can do."

She let the silence sit between them until he said, "Okay, I'll see you in a half hour or so?"

But a troubling detail was festering in Serena's brain.

"If you call the ambulance, they'll figure out I was the one there eventually."

"Serena, really, focus on what only you can do. I already have a plan to avoid that. I can take care of you. I *will* take care of you."

"Can we make an anonymous tip?"

"Something like that. Stop worrying."

"Thank you, Lance, for everything."

"Just get here as quick as you can."

He ended the call first.

Serena sat in her car for an immeasurable amount of time. From this position of safety, it was impossible for her to stop worrying about what had happened to the brown-eyed man who had saved her life. He knew her name.

What was his?

Why had he intervened, for a woman who would be shunned by the rest of the world for the rest of her life?

As she turned her cell phone over and over in her fingers, a bird landed on the hood of her car, noticed her, then jumped away, wings rattling the air. The creature left bits of dirt behind on the hood. To Serena, they looked like flakes of old gray paint. Like ash.

Behind her: a great mystery. Ahead of her: the slow and torturous death of her career, her reputation, her lifelong dreams, which had begun when she was a child who gathered her dolls onto her lap and taught them how to read.

The raven-haired doll in Venice Beach's hand was the exact replica of one taken from her when she was a child. She'd surrendered it to another little girl who'd come to the Safe Place with her mother, years and years ago. The child stole it, and the mother shamed Serena into letting her keep it.

What was that man doing with her long-lost doll? It didn't matter that he wasn't doing anything with it, that the scenario was just a fleeting illusion.

He was real enough. If she didn't try to help him, she'd be guilty of worse than Brock's claims.

Serena put her phone back in the console and pulled the steering wheel of her car into a U-turn.

SIX

SERENA DIDN'T THINK SHE WAS BEING FOOLHARDY until she reached the unpaved turnoff that she had peeled out of so recently, her tire tracks mingling with others in the rain-softened earth. She slowed and thought of the blue van that had arrived as she was leaving. The thought prevented her from turning off the road and returning to her previous parking spot. The van might still be at the house. More men to outnumber her.

This was probably the only road that could take a vehicle to that abandoned house. Over the next half mile, any car coming would not be able to avoid any car going. The drivers would have to make a cooperative effort to pass each other without incident. Serena had no way of knowing if the shooter had departed, resumed his business inside the gutted house, or was on his way down the curving hillside with reinforcements at that exact moment.

The other sets of tire tracks near hers were wider, deeper. Did they belong to the shooter, or to Venice Beach, or to someone else? Her untrained eye found it impossible to determine exactly how many tracks there were and which way they'd carried their vehicles.

So Serena passed the turnoff and stayed on the main road for another mile. Once last spring her ambling field studies had taken her all the way through the burn area from her parked car to the main road, and now she tried to recall exactly where she'd come out. It was a difficult thing to make landmarks out of chaparral shrubs.

The runoff of winter rains had created natural gullies in the mountainside, and at one point the road had been built up over a wide pipe drain. She remembered walking over this small rise on the long route back to her parked car. Taking a wild guess, she parked on the first shoulder wide enough to hold her car, then prepared to return to the house.

She changed into her hiking boots this time and retrieved a lightweight day pack from the trunk of her car. It contained a compass, a trail map, a small first-aid kit, a bottle of water, and a protein bar. She trekked south by southeast, wondering how she would get Venice Beach out if he was too hurt to walk.

She didn't like thinking of him as Venice Beach. She didn't like the place. Obviously he wasn't Christopher Dorner, but she would call him Chris until she could find out the truth.

She hiked for an hour and a half before her surroundings became truly familiar and her jitters came back.

The sweat from her brisk trek mingled with new perspiration as she approached the back of the house. She stooped, though the spiny yucca here were just tall enough to hide her. From this angle she could see the faint lines of a driveway long overgrown behind the house, then burned clear. Struggling green shoots poked through black tangles of shrubs along the umbilical cord that connected the forgotten structure to a world that had moved on.

Twin mats of broken branches that followed the old path suggested that a large vehicle had been here recently. Someone had brought the shooter and the woman she'd seen upstairs, then left them here. Or was a car here the whole time, hidden by the house? Chris had said something about offering the man a ride. It might have meant anything.

Serena trod carefully in a wide circle around the structure, going the long way to avoid having to cross the drive, where she might be exposed.

As she came to the front, her attention flitted between the gaping doorway and the stand of scrub oak where she'd last seen Chris. She knew before she reached the spot that she had taken too long to return.

He was gone.

He'd left his sandals behind.

One flip-flop was half buried in a mildewing pile of oak leaves so close to her that she almost stepped on it. The other stood upright, impaled on a twig, as if it had been snatched off a reluctant foot.

The twig had also caught a scrap of shirt, which Serena thought might have been his. The piece was too tiny and blood-soaked to know for sure. No sign of the knitted yellow cap.

On the other side of the thieving twig were two divots that cut through dirt and leaves like ski tracks. Heel tracks. She wished they had been footprints instead.

Serena would have to enter the small clearing to follow those tracks, but her courage failed her here, now that Chris's death seemed certain. This was the very spot where she'd turned around at the sound of the gunshot and watched his hands reach out to her, push her away. Those brown eyes were still so lifelike in her memory, telling her to go.

She thought she could hear his voice. *Run*.

Serena felt the physical sensation of being pushed and took a staggering step backward. But this time she didn't flee. She couldn't run away because her legs wouldn't hold her up. They buckled and she went down, and the damp earth quickly cut through the thin weave of her slacks. There, in front of her, was the body of Chris, facedown as if he'd thrown himself on her mercy.

He had been shot in the back.

Her intellect told her that she was just seeing things, the way she saw the doll, the way the old stone house had suddenly appeared to her restored and hospitable in a fresh world where everything was new. *This isn't really him*, she told herself. *This is some kind of post-traumatic stress response. A subconscious mechanism the brain uses to make sense of the unbelievable.*

Still, she reached out to touch his head, to test her brain, to deny the man's death.

She made note of his hair this time, wavy like the meat of a walnut, with a cowlick right on the crown.

Her hand was outstretched, quaking. She could see every creamy brown strand and the shadow her palm cast over them. How could this not be real?

The body was yanked right out from under her, jerked away with such violent speed that she screamed and then covered her mouth. The one who'd shot at them was pulling Chris out of the brush, that cigarette still limp in the tobacco-stained corner of his lips. He didn't look at Serena; in fact, he behaved as if she weren't even there, sitting squarely in front of him.

His arrival changed the quality of what Serena was seeing, muting the true-to-life colors and high-definition textures. A sepia-toned pall that matched the stains on the man's lips and fingers fell over the scene. This didn't change the fact that she expected to be shot.

The strange view brought to mind time-faded home movies, but with a macabre twist. It was as if someone had strung up a translucent sheet by the corners, lashed it to the trees, and projected their old-tech video onto the fragile surface. She watched, motionless with fascination and fright and something like motion sickness thumping between her ears.

The parallel marks in the ground weren't made by Chris's

heels, she soon saw, but by his arms, his elbows and hands leaving tracks in the dirt on each side of his head as the shooter dragged him away. The hem of his T-shirt crept up to his armpits, bunching around his thick chest. If he wasn't dead, the soil invading his nose and mouth would soon see to it.

Serena's head filled with tears, backing up into her throat.

In spite of the unnatural speed that initially snatched Chris out from under Serena's outstretched hand, she could see now that the dragging took considerable effort. The shooter was shorter, lighter, and far less muscular than Chris, and judging by his breathless grunting, the very definition of unfit. No one emerged from the house to help him.

When he got Chris as far as the side of the house, then prepared to turn the corner and drag him to the back, Serena rose to follow. It was foolishness following a mirage, but she had to know why Chris had helped her. Once the men were out of sight, she might never see him again.

She heard Chris groan and thought perhaps he wasn't dead. But she was witness only to a vision from the past, not to the reality of the present.

Four or five steps into her decision she passed through a gauzy, sticky thing that caught her lips and eyelashes like a spider's web hiding in dim light. The sensation of a spider on her cheek came in an instant. She swiped wildly at her face, blinking, sputtering, and spinning. It seemed eight-legged heebie-jeebies had overtaken her and no amount of shimmying inspections of her clothing or her skin could get rid of the feeling.

She peeled off her blazer and shook it out, and the snap of the fabric was like a summons from a trance. What was she doing, announcing her presence to the ill will in this isolated world?

In the ensuing stillness, she watched the gap at the front door and waited for someone to emerge. No one did. She had unintentionally trampled Chris's tracks while trying to shake off imaginary spiders. They were as real as the web she found in the ends of her hair, and they continued to trail up to the house and around to the back.

Hiding now was pointless and would only waste more time. Serena slipped back into her jacket and jogged to the corner of the house. Here, where the ground was comparatively flat, she could see a reddish brown smudge between the elbow tracks. Blood.

All the marks—the smooth soles of the skinny man's leather shoes, the dragged body, the terrible blood—ended abruptly at the structure's rear entrance, as if the acting had ended and all the players simply got up and walked off the set.

Serena reached out a hand and touched the stone wall. It was as real as she was, as sturdy as her racing heart. She let the wall hold her up through a beat of indecision. Her ears detected only the high-pitched tone of silence. The only human she could hear was herself. Even the birds had stilled.

The tickle of a spider grazed the back of her neck. She flicked it off.

Then she stepped into the blackened house.

SEVEN

THE THICK WHITE OLEANDER BUSH SPILLED OVER A
low wall that was covered with chipped plaster and ancient pink
paint. Both were probably seventy-five years old. The dark green
leaves and woody stems were effective on the freeways as a median
between opposing lanes of traffic. They also did a decent job of
concealing Will Brenner and Kaleo Iona from the couple across the
beach-access alley.

The narrow asphalt lane was really a shared driveway to the
dozens of single-car beach-house garages that had been lined
up here since the forties. The houses themselves, built atop the
garages with tiny rooms and big sun decks that competed for the
ocean view half a block away, stood so close together that Kaleo
liked to claim he'd once passed a neighbor toilet paper through the
bathroom windows.

Will's ginger ponytail was snagged behind him on a long-
dead oleander blossom, and the petals came apart when he leaned
forward to look through the viewfinder of his telephoto lens. The
couple loitered at the bottom of a painted metal staircase that ran
up the outside of one of the beach houses. Kaleo doubted the girl
was yet fifteen. Her makeup, her hair dye, her flirty clothes made
her look older, but her true age was evident in her smile—when
she showed it. Shy, hopeful, naive. Not yet hard. She possessed the

kind of innocence-in-denial that was an irresistible temptation to sick men.

She sat on the bottom step looking up at the man, who was slim and clean-shaven and apparently all of sixteen. Kaleo knew he was actually twenty-three, and that his name was Jett Anderson, and that he had served Phil Lancet coffee on more than one occasion at the coffee shop where he worked. Of course, this was not proof that Jett was a criminal—on the contrary, he was a sponsored surfer required to stay on the up-and-up—but the nature of Phil Lancet's business practices caused the Fire Followers to keep Jett close in their sights. And what they'd seen made Kaleo restless.

Today Jett wore a wetsuit unzipped and unpeeled to the waist. His dark hair looked like a sea urchin, spiky and stiff with sea salt. A fall storm had churned up some good Malibu surf earlier. Jett's board stood against the closed garage door. He crossed his arms and leaned forward slightly, attentive, while the girl spoke to him with all the animation of a ventriloquist. They were out of earshot.

"Turn around already, would you?" Kaleo muttered.

"Patience," Will muttered for the billionth time.

"We don't have forever," Kaleo said. They both had paying jobs, Kaleo as a 911 dispatcher and Will as a frame builder down at Aaron Brothers, and Mondays were the only day off they had in common. Will also moonlighted as a private investigator, though most of his gigs were ones such as these—pro bono work for the Fire Followers, which consumed every free hour they could afford.

"The Roman Empire wasn't destroyed in a day," Will said. His curly red beard tickled the wide leaves as he spoke.

"We've been at it ten years already," Kaleo complained.

It was an old routine: Will, meticulous and painstakingly attentive to detail; Kaleo, pawing the dirt. They were a pair, Kaleo thought, a regular Hollywood odd couple: the fair-skinned Will and the Pacific Islander Kaleo, the burnt and the bronzed, the brains and the brawn. Kaleo hated to imagine what people thought of them crawling around in hedges.

Fire Followers was a fledgling, globally-minded nonprofit, the result of Amber Larsen's near death in a Las Vegas brothel. Christopher had found her, rescued her, and then held her hand during a physical, psychological, and spiritual recovery that had taken almost a decade and still needed tending now and then. But as she grew healthier, together the siblings dedicated themselves to protecting women and children from the sordid domestic sex trade—the luring, the transporting, the imprisoning, the prostituting. It hadn't been hard to convince Christopher's best friends Kaleo and Will to join him in the cause.

Even now, Kaleo couldn't get the statistics out of his head. Human trafficking was the world's fastest-growing criminal enterprise behind drugs and weapons. Seven years was the life expectancy of a young woman lured into that hell that trended toward younger and younger girls and more violent, more perverted activities. Most couldn't get out before it killed them.

That particular abyss was far deeper than Christopher and Amber could manage alone, and so they started at home, with the trafficking of girls in the Los Angeles basin. The best way to save these young women, in the Larsens' opinion, was to prevent them from being taken in the first place. Abroad, girls were lured away from home and out of poverty with the promise of well-paying jobs. Here in the United States, where fewer people lived on the brink of starvation, targeted girls were often those living in emotional poverty. They weren't promised a paycheck, but the comfort, security, and kindness of a man who seemed to understand their pain and know the way around it.

Not until it was too late would they learn that the man who listened to their stories with so much compassion and comfort would drive a knife into their trust and then become their pimp. Or sell them to one.

The Fire Followers crew attempted to alert parents. They raised community awareness. They raised money for free community clubs where young women could find the resources, support, and understanding they lacked at home. And they left the traffickers and pimps to authorities—except when it came to John Roman, the man who had abducted Amber before he became successful enough to get others to do that work for him. And though Fire Followers had seen plenty of victories across the years—a few brothels closed, a few women rescued, a few girls saved before they ever left home—the man they all sought seemed to have disappeared.

"Ten years overall," Will said. "But only six weeks where this dude Jett is concerned."

"All right, all right, six weeks," Kaleo said. "Six weeks, and we still can't prove Jett's working for Phil. We can't even definitively prove yet that Phil works for Roman."

All they had were really good educated guesses, nothing that would hold up in court. Roman was both savvy and invisible. Christopher liked to call him Bin Laden, comparing his sex trade to an Al Qaeda network in which no individual possessed any significant knowledge about the overall operation.

"Jett's been grooming three different girls at the same time," Will observed.

"So he's an immoral pig."

Will straightened in the close quarters and held a branch out of his face as he turned to look at Kaleo. His red-framed glasses were slightly askew on his nose. "If a groomer's going to work three girls at a time, it's going to take longer than usual. And maybe he can afford the time, if Phil's not in a hurry because he's got other business at present."

"Or maybe he's not very good at his job," Kaleo said. "He's a rookie with three irons in the fire and desperate hopes that he'll be able to use just one of them. *Or*," Kaleo continued, "what if Phil's life is about to be turned around by a magnificent woman. One Serena Diaz. I might have paid attention in biology if she'd been my teacher. Maybe he's turning over a new leaf. Maybe he's about to break ties with Roman, and Jett is being prepped to take his place."

Will shook his head, not even trying to keep up with Kaleo's thinking.

Kaleo gave up. "Where's Christopher?" he asked.

"Texted earlier. Said he's chasing a tip up on the Big Tujunga Road."

"What kind of a tip?"

Will freed his long hair from an oleander branch. "Something about a transport. And Serena Diaz."

Kaleo sighed. "Okay, so she might be the Bonnie to Phil's Clyde, just as we thought."

He tipped his head toward Jett, who had finally taken a seat next to the girl on the narrow step. They sat shoulder to shoulder now, he still listening, she still talking, hardly moving her mouth. "There's your shot," Kaleo said.

Will put his eye back to the viewfinder and clicked away.

"No one on Roman's payroll gets off of it," Will said. "No one wants to, no one gets to. Especially not as lucrative an asset as Phil Lancet."

"And if Serena works for him, she works for Roman."

"Do you realize how much time we spend on theories we can't ever prove?" Will separated himself from the camera and looked at his watch. "Christopher should have checked in by now."

Kaleo braced his arms on the plastered pink wall and stretched out his back. "Reception up there is spotty. He'll call when he can."

At the foot of the metal steps, Jett had put his arm around the girl's shoulders and pulled her into a sideways hug. He kissed the top of her head, and Kaleo saw the wet trails of eye makeup coming down her cheeks. It might be nothing less than what it seemed, a kind soul comforting a heartbroken one. Or it might be something far more sinister, something the four cofounders of Fire Followers had seen over and over again.

Will swore. Apparently he thought it was the latter. "Don't do it, sweetheart," he mumbled.

The girl turned her face upward and let Jett kiss her. Will took pictures and Kaleo knew his redheaded friend took pleasure in none of it.

Jett took over the conversation now, capturing the girl's attention with words that earned him that sweet smile.

Will withdrew from the chipped wall and began to put his camera away. His brusque movements shook the oleander as if he were a bear.

Kaleo started collecting their things. "Time to pay Mom and Dad a visit."

Will stuffed his camera into the bag. "We don't have enough yet."

"What do you mean we don't have enough? We've seen this a bazillion times. It's not like we're prepping for a court appearance here."

"We've got nothing on Jett but a few pictures of him playing the field. They might make his other two girlfriends angry, but they won't put him in jail. He's got no record."

"I'd rather prevent a crime than wait for one to be committed."

"We all would. But you can't argue that Phil's stepping out of the business and at the same time risk blowing up our only current connection to Roman," Will argued.

"But now we've got the lovely Ms. Diaz," Kaleo quipped, trying to prevent an argument from breaking out.

He looked back, but now his view of the girl was completely obscured by the thick bush. This was the stage at which Kaleo could never walk away, never be satisfied with the easier work of raising awareness. Lots of people were sympathetic to the cause, but too few could devote their time or hard-earned money to it.

"Today we might stop *one* girl from stepping across the line into hell," Kaleo said. "*This* is when we save lives, Will. If Jett can't even close his first deal, Phil won't have him, and that's one more predator we keep out of the business."

"He'll just find someone else," Will insisted. "Another Jett. There are as many of them as there are girls who need saving. We have to bide our time. Be patient. Wait for the right moment to get to Roman. Isn't that the real goal? If we can get to Roman, we can get hundreds of girls out, keep thousands from ever going in."

Kaleo shook his head, hating the oversimplified arguments. "We're both right, you know. I just can't. I just can't walk away from her."

Kaleo squared his shoulders to block Will from heading too quickly to their little sedan. "That girl over there needs us to hurry, not to wait. She's someone's daughter. Maybe someday she'll be someone's wife. What if she were yours? I mean, I know you have your eyes on Amber, but—"

Will cut him off with a warning glare. "What would Christopher say?"

"You know: 'Don't be late!'"

"Being on time, at the *right* time, isn't being late."

"Sometimes it is."

He saw the first sign of a cave-in: Will squinted behind his glasses and wrinkled his nose. "What's her address?" Will finally asked.

Kaleo patted his pants pockets. "You've got that information, not me." A slip of paper crinkled under his hands. He pulled it out.

"But I've got the teacher's address handy." He grinned and waved it under Will's nose.

"Good." Will pulled the strap of his camera bag over his head so that it crossed his chest. "If anything's happened to Christopher, I can track her down and sell her to the enemy," he said.

"Funny," said Kaleo as the men headed to the car parked in front of a stranger's garage. "Very funny. You're a regular comedian."

EIGHT

SERENA STEPPED THROUGH THE REAR DOOR INTO what must have been a kitchen. A chipped sink, released from its burned counter, tottered on old plumbing. Some of the pipes protruded from the wall, dry and corroded. A pudgy refrigerator, smoke-stained and droopy, had fallen through the floorboards and left its door open. Beneath the odors of decay, Serena smelled droppings left behind by animal invaders. Probably opossum. Squirrel. Raccoon.

Wide plywood boards had been laid down over the destroyed floor like a ramp, leading out of the kitchen.

She had entered the house the first time she'd come to the area but not since. The structure had been dangerously unstable then, so although this decrepit kitchen came as no surprise, she was caught off guard by the sight behind the useless refrigerator. A new wall had been erected. It was a frame, really, sturdy two-by-fours assembled to take the load of the upper floor. Whoever had built this either didn't care about finishing work or hadn't gotten to it yet. There was no electrical, no drywall, just a remodeled view of the living room space beyond.

Four years after the Station Fire tore through the old house, evidence of smoke still tainted everything. The scent of fresh-cut wood was stronger than anything else. Similar restorative framework braced every interior wall that she could see.

The open living area also had a new subfloor, which was covered by plastic. There were new stairs too—unfinished boards without a rail—ascending to the second floor. A partially open door under the stairs revealed a shadowy cove and a rumpled sleeping bag, a camp stove, and a brown cardboard box that might have held canned goods. It was Serena's first clue that the man who'd dragged off Chris's body might return.

A light cross breeze moved through the house from the gaping front entry to the back door where Serena stood. She listened to the stillness and heard no human noise.

If the occupant had taken Chris to some other location, had the woman upstairs gone with him too? But the man had seemed surprised when Serena mentioned seeing her. What if she was hiding, an unknown houseguest? She might know something about the shooter. She might have seen the attack.

"Hello?" Serena called.

This house hid many secrets. That was all Serena knew for sure. She moved across the hazardous kitchen floor to the plastic and went upstairs, one hand on the smoke-stained wall for balance.

There was an exposed needle and syringe lying on one of the steps. She avoided it and continued to the top.

The woman Serena had seen lifting a curtain and peering out was not there.

The floor up here was also new but lacked the plastic sheeting. A fine layer of sawdust covered the entire area. Serena had expected bedrooms, maybe a bath. There were neither, just an open floor, like a loft, with three windows facing the front of the house, flanked by the cheap curtains, and a low-sloping roof at the back that gave the room the shape of a trapezoid. Each of the windows had nine French panes of melted vinyl dividers and bubbling glass.

In the far corner a five-gallon bucket appeared to serve as

a toilet and smelled like it too. Not even the smoke or sawdust masked that awful scent. Why hadn't the woman opened a window? Large nails driven at angles deep into the sashes answered that question.

Serena crossed to the far side of the room, to the third window, where she'd seen the woman's face peering out at her. From this height, on this side of the window, she was granted a unique perspective.

The damaged glass distorted everything. It caused the forest's burn scars to look more Halloweenish. Its emerging greenery seemed painted on by a child.

It wasn't the sort of place Chris would have just wandered by.

Three toyon bushes, with their feather-shaped leaves clustered like fluffy boas, marked the spot where Chris had put his arm around her shoulder and turned her away from the house. It was easy from here to see exactly how the scene might have ended without his intervention, and might end yet, if she didn't leave soon.

Serena was disappointed not to be able to meet the woman who might have seen it all.

A gray dot in the middle of the window caught her eye. It was balanced in the corner of the center pane, a disk larger than a dime and smaller than a quarter just sitting on the narrow frame. When Serena reached out to touch it, the graze of her fingers knocked it to the floor.

It made a crater in a bank of sawdust. She stooped to pick it up.

The silver-colored thing had a depression on one side that was the size of her thumb. She thought it might be a type of worry stone, the kind sold at stationery stores and tourist gift shops, for keeping in one's pocket along with loose change. When anxious, a person could fish it out and rub the smooth surface. It was a simple stress-relieving technique that Serena found comforting even then as she caressed the surface.

On the opposite side of the piece was an engraving of a four-petaled flower. A poppy, Serena guessed.

Serena slipped it into her pocket at the same moment that voices rose outside at the back of the house. They entered the room downstairs, heavy feet thumping the plywood, before she could make any decision about what to do.

Her palms broke out in a sweat and she became hyperaware of the room's stink and stale air. The shooter might have returned with an accomplice. She held her breath and hoped that these were the authorities Lance had promised to call. But if—when—investigators came up here, she would have nothing to do but admit her presence was awkward.

She looked out the window. There was no one there. She hated not being able to see the road, not being able to figure out exactly how many people were here.

Then she realized they weren't speaking English. Nor Spanish, which she also knew, though she caught a few words that might have been Latin American variations. So many languages swirled in the cultural soup of Los Angeles. There were two voices, and they argued. Even though she couldn't catch the meaning, the tones of berating and cowering were the same in any tongue.

Serena remained as still as the house. She feared what she might have to do if they stayed.

They moved around at the foot of the stairs, clumsy oafs who knocked into everything regardless of the fact that they were in a wide-open room. Or not clumsy, just free of all respect for anyone and anything outside their own skin. One of them kicked the box and the other objected with a shout. The camp stove groaned as it was picked up and dropped onto the muting layers of sleeping bag.

That bothersome sensation of a spider tickling her arm under her snug sleeve resurrected itself. She didn't think it could have done so at a worse time. Unless the men kept up the ruckus, getting the itch out would make attention-getting noise. Mind over matter, mind over matter. She closed her eyes. She breathed slowly. She focused on the men's argument, on the location of their voices in the house. Though the nerves in her skin insisted that the spider was real, her logic assured her otherwise.

The men left the house. She waited. It seemed like she waited forever, and that torturous spider was just as determined. And then finally, she heard the sound of heavy tires driving away over dusty earth, the sound she had missed when they arrived. Serena exhaled and rapidly peeled off her jacket, needing to swat that eight-legged imagination. She scratched her arm vigorously and shrieked when a large brown ball of legs fell from her skin to the dusty floor.

She shivered as it scurried away, scaling tiny sawdust mountain ranges and crossing wide sawdust fields. As it fled to the nearest crevice, Serena noticed the disturbances in the dust as recognizable imprints: down the middle of the room, a passage marked by shoes, most notably the distinctive ridged soles of her hiking boots. The others were foot-shaped but bore no pattern, like a ballet shoe.

And on each side of this aisle rectangular objects had flattened the dust before being snatched up again. They were as long and wide as a person. Serena thought of bedrolls. *Four*, she thought. Maybe five. They weren't perfectly preserved.

Had more than one person been hiding up here?

The dust would not say for sure.

Serena went back downstairs, noting that the stove, the bag, and the box had all gone with the men. She went back outside, this time through the front door. Everything looked so terribly normal. She asked herself what she was hoping for and why. Nothing that had happened to her here today was even about her.

Was it?

Chris's murder and the mystery woman continued to haunt her

imagination. As did all the other things she had seen and could not explain.

Serena didn't want to be here if or when Lance's anonymous call finally delivered a few willing investigators. She left quickly. The return trip would take longer than she wanted, as she would have to scale the surrounding hills rather than descend them this time.

As she hiked, she rubbed that stone bearing the poppy and wondered what the last woman to finger it had seen to make her leave it behind.

NINE

FAR FROM THE COAST, AT THE BASE OF THE FOOT-
hills that rose behind Pasadena, Serena pulled her car into the tiny
parking lot at the rear of the Safe Place, then sent a message to
Lance, who'd called five times and sent a dozen texts during her
return to the abandoned house.

All's well. One more stop then will come right to you.

The parking lot had room for six vehicles, and Serena saw her
parents' compact Hyundai in one of the four occupied slots. Its
front bumper touched a terra-cotta-colored stucco wall. The bar-
rier was an intruder-discouraging ten feet high and topped with an
invisible security system.

Enid and Esteban Diaz wouldn't turn on the evening news
until after they went home for the night, and Serena hoped to be
the first to tell them what others would be saying.

As she approached the rear entrance, a wrought-iron gate built
into the stuccoed wall, she withdrew her security pass from her
purse and waved it in front of the scanner. The gate clicked open,
and she pushed it inward onto a scene that was perpetually unexpected for this part of the city. A redbrick herringbone walkway
led the way to safety under a canopy of jacaranda trees that, in June

and July, were saturated with purple blooms. A handful of second-ary purple jacaranda blossoms might open up for Thanksgiving. For Enid, such an event would be like getting an extra holiday.

Beyond the trees, a garden her mother had designed and tended looked like it belonged at a French cottage rather than an urban shelter. It was always in lush condition, even through the wet winters. Cultivating it was Enid's gift to the residents who needed a quiet place to sit or a welcoming place to work. More than one abused woman had found a new purpose and skill in this small world of trees and flowers.

The gate swung shut behind Serena and locked. Even this far from the building's restaurant-sized kitchen, she could smell the garlic and chili of pozole, the pork stew that the Safe Place staff made every day, winter and summer, no matter what other foods were on the menu. For Serena, these were the scents of stability and fearlessness. As long as there was pozole, there was home.

If only she could stay on this side of the gate and block the rest out—Brock's lie, the imminent investigation, the assault of cruel men, and the death of a stranger—she would. But she knew she couldn't stay long.

Her phone vibrated. Lance.

No more stops. Come now. Investigators are impatient.

Investigators. She shivered though the temperature was fair. She would hurry.

Enid wasn't in the garden at the moment. The brick path led Serena through the tunnel of trees and then stepped up onto the red-tile porch that ran the width of the building. Multiple arched windows lined the walk. Serena sought the door all the way at the end. Here she passed her ID in front of another scanner and heard the lock release. She went in.

The old carpets in the cozy building, which Serena believed had been a small hotel in the 1940s, sat atop thick pads. These gave the flooring a domed look and caused her shoe to leave temporary depressions as she walked down a dim hall. Rope lights hidden by drop-down molding high on the wall gave the place a warm if not really updated look. The age of the place was comforting, as if it could boast of weathering lots of crises. Enid and Esteban had never been ones to put their money into cosmetic improvements. There was barely enough for the triage, her father was known to say: a hot meal, a warm bed, toiletries, a change of clothes, company, and the promise of professional help when the time was right.

In a distant room, an upbeat Latin rhythm created irresistible energy. Like pozole, music was always in the house.

A toddler gripping his mother's finger offered her a soggy cookie as she passed them. The mom was just a child, no older than some of the kids in Serena's classes. If the young mother stayed long enough, she'd be able to attend classes of her own here: parenting, cooking, self-care, job hunting, service skills, and maybe even some trade courses. Whenever possible, her parents tried to help those eligible to take the GED, to expand their limited options.

Serena smiled at the child and politely declined the cookie, but she avoided meeting the mother's eyes. When Serena was six, and a guest her same age had run off with her prized baby doll, Serena had tried to take it back. The incident happened in the TV room on the other side of the garden, and Serena hadn't thought she might need her parents' help. The six-year-old's mother, perhaps conditioned by hardship to be fierce, had run Serena over with her words: "What's a ratty doll to you, rich brat? Too spoiled to share your toys? Think my girl don't deserve half what you got?"

Serena, shamed by the sallow woman who had leaned over her, could think of nothing but what she'd heard her father say on more than one occasion: "We don't help people because we pity them, but because we might have something they need." And Serena felt very, very angry that the little girl had needed her favorite doll. But she let the girl have it and didn't breathe a word to her parents. Serena came very close to hating the other girl, whose name she never wanted to know, who played with the doll in careless ways that Serena couldn't bear to watch. When the mother-daughter pair left the Safe Place, Serena never saw the cherished baby in the perfect pink dress again.

Until that morning.

Over time her memory of the toy faded, but Serena grew into an uneasy wariness of the women her parents served. She never knew what to say or do, certain that every action was on some level flawed, a potential offense to the very women they were trying to help. Her parents' generous second natures, the part of them that gave so appropriately and naturally, eluded her. Teaching was a better fit, a helper's work marked by clearer boundaries of propriety, authority.

Or so Serena had thought.

At the end of the hall, where a sheer curtain hid a barred window but let in plenty of light, Serena knocked on an office door.

"Enter," her father's voice invited.

When Serena pushed the door open, she found him studying his computer screen. Her mother was there too, sitting on his desk. The rhythmic music that she'd heard upon entering came from the small CD player on the windowsill.

"Mija!" Enid slipped down and came around, arms outstretched. "What a nice surprise. But why aren't you in school?"

"Because I've been suspended."

Enid Diaz embraced her daughter, but not before her face registered surprise. "What is this?"

Her father turned around to silence the music.

"It's nothing. It's just procedure. An angry student filed a complaint. You remember the one from the inquiry this summer?"

"And just like that they send you away?" Enid protested. "That boy is trouble."

Serena's father took off his glasses and set them down as he stood up. He was a great bear of a man who might be fearsome if he ever got angry, an unlikely figure in this facility designed to set women's minds at ease. And yet he seemed to instill a sense of protection rather than threat.

Esteban Diaz kissed the top of his daughter's head, and in the secure hug that lasted a second longer than usual she sensed the other trait that had made this line of work absolutely perfect for him: he could see beneath the surface of a thing and know exactly what was going on without prejudice or invasion. He knew enough of "procedures" to grasp the seriousness of her suspension.

Serena said, "You'll hear a lot of unpleasant things said about me in the days to come. I just want you to know that none of it is true."

"Of course not," her mother said. "What has this student said?"

"If it's unpleasant, she doesn't need to repeat it," said her father.

"He claims I had sex with him."

Enid set her lips in a thin line. "You never were one to break news gently."

"I didn't want you to hear it from anyone else."

"They have not frozen your pay?" her father asked, leaning back against the desk and crossing his arms.

"No."

"And you have a good attorney? Your Lance, perhaps?"

"Yes. He's already at work on this for us."

Her mother sputtered. "It's that boy who'll need a good attorney before this is over, isn't it? I can't believe young people say such things about their teachers!"

Serena put a calming hand on her mother's arm. "The school must take it very seriously, *Mamá*. But you shouldn't worry."

Enid patted Serena's hand. "I know better than to worry about you, *mija*. You're my feisty one. But I can be angry for you, can't I?"

"So long as you take it out on the weeds."

"I have some roses to prune." Enid said it as if she planned to cut them off at the roots.

Her father was regarding Serena with a gaze that suggested he understood all she didn't want to say: that she didn't know how long an investigation would take; that she might not be able to save her reputation no matter the outcome; that child predators in positions of trust, whether truly guilty or merely accused, were regarded by the public as more despicable than murderers.

"What can we do to be of help?" he asked.

"I don't know yet," Serena said, fishing into her pocket for the second reason she had come.

"Do you want us to tell David and Natalie?" Her brother and sister.

"They might find out before I can reach them. So if you talk to them before I do, please tell them I'll call." She'd call David, at least. Natalie, who not only believed that people were capable of heinous things but was smugly satisfied when anyone did something that reinforced this view, might consider Serena guilty until proven innocent. Boys, Serena could imagine her saying, liked to boast of sexual conquests. They'd never lie about being sexually humiliated. Ergo, Serena would be the one with something to hide.

Intellectual logic, not the good and bad of human nature or even the bonds of family love, governed Natalie's worldview.

Serena found the worry stone imprinted with the poppy and held it out to her father. He twisted to retrieve his glasses off the desk and placed them on his nose before taking the piece from her hand.

"I wonder if you've ever seen this symbol before," she asked, indicating the flower.

"And what makes you think I have?" The question was genuinely curious, but Serena couldn't avoid feeling like he could, if he wanted to, expose all the events of her morning as if she held them in an ice block and his questions were a well-placed chisel.

She half hoped he wanted to.

Serena shrugged. She thought he might have seen it because the woman at the window where this stone appeared might be the type of woman who needed a shelter like the Safe Place.

"It's probably just some mass-produced thing," she said as he shook his head. "Something from a tourist trap."

"It looks like a poppy," her mother said.

"A fire poppy, I think," Serena added. "See the texture on the petals?"

"Like wrinkled tissue paper," Enid said to her husband, as if he were having difficulty seeing what his daughter meant.

She had no doubt that her father didn't need clarification, just as he had recognized the ice block she'd brought into the room. But he kept his chisel and hammer stored.

"May I keep it?" he asked. "I can look into it for you."

Serena nodded. Esteban put the stone on his desk next to the pencil cup.

After a moment's pause Serena said, "I'm sorry I can't stay."

Her father nodded once and smiled at her, but his kind eyes were pained today. One of the women he'd always succeeded in protecting was about to face trial as a modern sort of witch. "Let me walk you out," he said.

Her mother kissed her on the cheek and held on to her hands an extra moment. "You are an adult, of course, but you understand you are also my baby girl."

"I know, *Mamá*."

"Please consider staying here for a time."

"You know it would be bad for the other women if I did."

Enid conceded reluctantly. "Then find another way for us to help."

"I will. I will. I love you."

Esteban offered Serena his elbow and tugged her close. They walked down the hall's spongy carpet and back out to the gardens with the red-tile porch and the orange stucco and the infinite shades of green.

"I am listening to everything you don't say," her father said. "Your thoughts are very loud today."

Serena smiled. "I'm sorry."

"It's to be expected. But what is it that can't be said?"

So many things. "Nothing. Yet. Everything works out for people who tell the truth, right?" Serena said hopefully.

"The truth is the only thing that ever got anyone out of trouble. But as for everything working out . . ." Her father tilted his head to one side and shrugged. *Sometimes yes, sometimes no.*

"I think I saw a man die today," Serena said.

Her father's eyes widened. "You think?"

"He might still be alive, but when I went back to help, he was gone."

"The authorities have been notified?"

"Yes, Lance called for me." Her father's thoughts were loud in her ears too: *You left. Lance called on your behalf. What are you hiding?* Serena studied the garden. "He was hurt protecting me."

"You need that kind of protection? Was it connected to the boy at school?"

Serena shook her head. "Completely unrelated, though I do think this might go down as one of the worst days of my life. The man was a stranger. It was a coincidence."

"I'm glad God thought to arrange it for you."

"I doubt that man shares the same sentiment."

That shrug again. "But what if he does?"

"How could he?"

"You have pronounced this day one of the worst of your life. But he is a stranger, you say—what do you know of how he chooses to see the world?"

"Could anyone think that dying for a person you've never met is a good way to go?"

"And yet men and women do it often—our service people, our fire fighters, our law-enforcement officers. Good Samaritans."

Serena saw his point but feared he didn't see hers. "In reality, do you think they *want* to die?"

"Reality is both more and less than it seems. Well, from my perspective," he added with a dry humor.

"What do you mean?"

"I mean, you see death as tragedy. Some see it as destiny, especially if it's for the sake of another human being. Or take this: I see a broken woman come through these gates"—he gestured to the secure entrance—"and I see a jewel. Her abuser sees trash. Some people see a lost cause. Others see their life calling. It's all real, but it's not all equal. Perhaps this might help you when you become overwhelmed with all the different ways of seeing these present problems that face you. You must focus on what is *more*. Greater. Better. Truer."

It was possible—but chances were that stress was precipitating a mental breakdown. That's all there was to it. That was *her* reality.

"I'll try to remember that," she said.

Greater, better, truer. But she feared that Brock's lies might be more powerful than all that together.

TEN

LANCE LIEBOWITZ LIVED IN AN ELITE NEIGHBOR-
hood in Pacific Palisades called Castellammare. It was near the
beach, a short jog down the sand from Malibu.

Castellammare, Italian for "castle by the sea," was built into
the hillsides just above the Pacific Coast Highway. At first glance
the elite community appeared to belong to a gathering of aging
architects too competitive to let anyone have the final word. Homes
of every imaginable style were featured here, from modest bungalow to overstated Italian villa to angular modern monstrosity. And
in Serena's opinion none of it would win the ultimate competition
with Mother Nature: eventually, a landslide would wipe out the
sturdiest retaining wall, the hot pink bougainvillea would overtake
every column and archway, and the Seuss-like palm trees, wobbly
in the wind, would prove more powerful than the numerous webs
of electric and phone lines.

But this was a shallow outsider's view, and the first thing she
had to admit after Lance invited her to his home six weeks earlier was that she fell hard for his house, a Spanish-style adobe with
round-arched windows and a red-clay tile roof. The creamy walls
turned to gold at sunset. They surrounded a courtyard and a turret, which was the main entrance to the house. As spectacular as
the seven-bedroom mansion was, with its mission-style furniture

to go with the Mediterranean architecture, what Serena really adored was the view. Entering through the turret, Lance's guests were treated to a sixty-foot panoramic view of the ocean through a wall of sliding windows. And if these interfered too much, they could be pushed aside and left behind for the porch, suspended in ocean breezes.

From up here Serena could sit with her world quite literally behind her, facing vacation-worthy views of Santa Monica, Palos Verdes, Catalina Island, and the soothing Pacific.

She found herself there now, sitting on Lance's balcony, without a clear memory of all the turns or steps she had taken to arrive. Today the peaceful view failed to soothe. Serena thought of her students crowding the halls outside their lockers, passing on the gossip surrounding Brock's absence and her sudden disappearance. She reminded herself that something far worse than Brock's lies had happened today. A man had lost his life.

Keep it in perspective, Serena kept saying to herself. She would, by coming up with a plan. In the rare cases when her entire class failed a test, it was up to her to retool the lesson plan. This would be no different.

Lance was handing her a highball glass full of crushed ice and Diet Dr Pepper. He had poured himself a glass of wine, something red and expensive from his well-stocked racks. She looked to him, knowing he would be her calm, her logic, her law.

She tilted her head back on the upholstered patio lounge. He dragged a chair alongside her and leaned forward, bracing his elbows on his knees, waiting. The afternoon sun cut through her jacket at a comforting angle.

Lance forced nothing out of Serena. Never had. He waited like a man who could easily wait for the earth to revolve around the sun. He possessed a rare and unflappable patience, she'd always thought, and the trait had the dual effect of appealing to her and arousing her own *im*patience. Something about him reminded her of a hunter who sat still in a hide for hours on end in spite of unbearable heat and flies.

He was as handsomely outfitted as his house, in slacks from Canali on Rodeo Drive and a pale green shirt that was two different shades, depending on how it caught the light. It was open at the throat, and Lance's expensive cologne did more than the view to settle her down. She had never asked what it was, preferring the mystery. The only detail reminding her that he was first her boyfriend, and second her attorney, was his footwear. Instead of the usual Italian leather slip-ons, he wore dress socks with felt house slippers.

The carbonation that escaped her soda misted the back of her hand.

"I saw a man die today."

For a little while that was all she could say.

He took the soda out of her hand and set it on the short drink table by her chair so he could sandwich her fingers in both of his hands.

"You want to tell me what happened?" he asked.

"Should we just call the police and tell them everything at the same time? I suppose I'm going to have to tell it all more than once—all the things that didn't happen and the terrible things that did. I don't think I can do that too many times."

"You and I are meeting an LAPD detective at seven thirty. In public, on neutral ground, friendly as possible."

A new kind of fear breathed down Serena's neck. "You set an appointment?"

"It's an act of good faith. You're cooperative, a model citizen. You have nothing to hide." He stroked the back of her hand. "And you went missing. I had to give them something."

Serena sat up on the lounger and lifted her legs off the cushion so that she faced Lance, their knees touching.

"I'm so sorry. I should have done what you said."

He didn't scold her or say anything at all, and she loved him for it.

"I think they moved the body, Lance."

"The man who was with you? The one who was shot?"

"I went back and—"

Lance sat ramrod straight and let go of her hand. But his calm expression didn't flinch.

"I know, I know. I'm sorry. It was stupid, but I wanted to help him."

"And?"

"And he wasn't there. They moved him."

"Who's they?"

"They, he, I don't know. Whoever shot him, whoever was there at the house. There were two men."

"I thought you said there was only one."

Serena told Lance almost everything that had transpired since she left Mr. Walter's office that morning. She told him about Venice Beach, and she told him about the woman she saw at the window, the worry stone she'd found inside.

"You went inside the house? Serena."

Lance asked to see the stone. She told him she'd given it to her father.

"I had to tell them in person," she defended.

But Serena withheld details of the visions. They had no bearing on the facts of her predicament, and she had no idea how Lance would react to her seeing things. He might question her reliability.

"Is it possible that there were two men there from the beginning?" he asked. "The one who shot Venice plus one more?"

Serena supposed it was.

"Then it's possible that one shot him and the other talked sense into the shooter. And what I mean by that is, maybe someone took him to a hospital."

This possibility had never occurred to Serena. It would explain the hasty departure and the need for them to return afterward.

"I'll make some phone calls," he said. "He has a unique description. We should be able to find out pretty quickly if anyone matching it was treated in an ER for a gunshot wound today."

Serena placed her hand over her heart. "That would help me feel better." Even if the feeling was only temporary. Because he might be dead. Those brown eyes might be buried in the national forest in a shallow grave. "He saved my life. I don't even know his name. Tell me why that feels like a crime?"

Lance picked up a pen and a yellow legal pad that had been sitting under his chair, unnoticed by Serena until now. The top sheets of the pad were covered in scrawling notes.

"I understand why that man's situation is overshadowing everything else in your mind," he said. "But we really need to get a handle on the matter with Brock Anderson." He looked at the notepad.

The sun shifted and the ocean breeze picked up as if conspiring to give Serena a chill. She looked at her untouched soda.

"What am I being charged with, exactly?"

"Nothing yet."

"But when I am?"

"*If* you are, unlawful sexual intercourse with a minor."

Serena shuddered. "Like statutory rape."

"Essentially the same thing."

"I didn't force Brock to do *anything*."

"Force isn't part of either definition. Age is. He's under eighteen, you're more than three years his senior—seven, to be precise. You're in a position of trust. That's about as bad as it gets."

"You mean it's a felony." She wasn't asking as much as stating her shock.

"Yes."

"Lance." She looked him directly in the eye. "We never even did anything consensual."

"I believe you."

She exhaled. "I heard once from a former teacher who was accused that getting a not guilty verdict isn't the same as factual innocence. Is that true? It just means they can't prove guilt beyond a reasonable doubt. He was found not guilty but lost his job anyway."

Lance didn't say anything. He looked at his notes. She interpreted this as agreement.

"I'll lose my job no matter what happens."

He looked up at her quickly. "We're going to keep this out of court," he said. He leaned in. "You're not going to have to worry about guilty and not guilty and factual innocence, because this is never going to go to trial. I promise you that."

It seemed preposterous but Serena decided to believe this because the alternative was too overwhelming.

"And if it all goes south we can always go to Vegas," he said with a half smile. "Easy place to get lost."

He was joking, of course. She hated Vegas and he knew it—though right now that particular jungle held a little bit of appeal.

"I'd rather you be the amazing attorney you are."

Lance sipped his wine. "That would be a better strategy. I might have to make you a partner."

"Does that mean you'll waive my fee?"

He leaned over to offer her a light kiss. "You are my current pro bono case. How much do you want to tell me about Brock?"

Serena sighed. "You already know about our dispute over his term grade last year. He's smart, the type who can get As most of the time without working too hard. Student council, varsity wrestling team, community volunteer."

"He sounds perfect."

"Not perfect, but broadly liked. He has a rebel streak, he just doesn't want it taken out on his transcript. I bet that half the trouble blamed on other kids could be traced back to him if anyone looked hard enough."

"So he's a troublemaker?"

"Juvenile pranks. Nothing to be arrested for." She turned to Lance. "Why haven't I been arrested yet?"

"Investigations into these kinds of things can take a long time. Police could arrest you whenever they want. If public pressure gets hot enough, they might. But it's more likely they'll hold off until the DA says he's got enough evidence to get a conviction."

At the word *evidence* he let go of her hand and looked back at his notes, and Serena felt strangely abandoned.

"What kind of evidence do they need?" she asked.

Lance hesitated. "It depends. Some kind of convincing proof that Brock knows something he shouldn't." He smiled half-heartedly. "That butterfly tattoo on your hip, for example. What the inside of your house looks like. Other personal details. Have you ever texted him?"

"I don't text students."

"Called him?"

Serena closed her eyes to think. "He helped with the science fair last year. I think I called everyone a few times about that—some schedule changes, last-minute details. We had one unplanned meeting."

"We?"

"The administrators and judges—volunteers. Brock was helping judge the sophomore entries."

"Have you ever met with Brock privately?"

"No!"

"Even in the classroom?"

Serena groaned. "A couple of times. After the fiasco with his grade last spring, I tried to give him extra attention. Purely as a teacher."

"Facebook friend?"

"That page is private. As you know." She had a policy against friending romantic partners. In her experience it led to unnecessary complications.

"And why do you think Brock would make this kind of claim?"

"Because he thought he had something mastered that he didn't, and that's too hard for him to admit. Have you ever heard of anything so stupid?"

"It's happened." He tapped his pencil on the page.

"It shouldn't." She held her hands together in her lap as if that might help her bring the volume down. "Kids today think they're not responsible for anything but are still entitled to success."

The corner of Lance's mouth twitched.

"What? You think I'm wrong?"

"I think you're just mad at Brock and you really care about your students more than that."

She did. She loved her students and had a hard time understanding why a good kid like Brock would concoct this kind of lie. Everybody blew it sometimes. The high achievers were proud and strangely insecure about even the smallest failures, but something about Brock's lie just didn't suit him. She couldn't puzzle it out.

"I've wondered if his parents might be involved," she said.

Lance's eyebrows went up. "Why?"

She shrugged. "I don't know them except for the way his mother handled the inquiry over the summer. In some ways she seemed more upset about it than Brock did. Maybe all the pressure to perform comes from her."

"All the more reason they wouldn't want him involved in a scandal like this, don't you think?" The force of his voice stopped Serena's train of thought. She looked up at him. "If you start imagining he's strategy. Her impression of these scandals was that attorneys squirreled away their clients at every opportunity.

"What? Why?"

"If Brock had made this kind of accusation against his neighbor Joe, well, the media really wouldn't care about that kind of thing, would they?" Lance posited. "But when a child says a teacher has misbehaved, everyone wants a piece of her hide. We're going to have to be aggressive with this, Serena. We're going to have to be bold. We're going to have to be the ones who get both the first and the last word. It's the best way to keep the damage to a minimum. If we don't come out strong and fast, they'll eat you for dessert."

Serena hesitated.

"It's not like I'm proposing a press conference or anything."

Nothing about this was right. Nothing.

"You think they're going to convict me without due process?"

"The public does it all the time."

"Without being arrested? Without court? Without evidence?"

Lance sighed and straightened. She knew then that he'd been withholding something.

"Not completely without evidence," he said. "Brock claims he has pictures."

not to blame for his own actions, you're going to complicate y
case. It's a nightmare for everyone, no matter what's true and wl
a lie."

Serena nodded and stayed silent.

"So here's what we're going to do," Lance said. He put d
his pencil and took her hand again. "We're going to fight thi
two fronts, a public one and a private one."

She seized upon the idea of a fight. Of having something t

"Tonight we'll meet with the detective. You listen, I'll
It'll be our interview as much as theirs. We're going to fin
how much they think they have and what they're still fishing

She nodded.

"Tomorrow you are going to call Brock Anderson."

"Oh, I don't think that's a good idea. Mr. Walter—"

"We'll go through Brock's attorney. The conversatio
be recorded for your protection. The goal will be to get Br
admit he's made everything up. I don't expect that to actuall
pen, but I think we can make some headway in your defen
tell you what to say. And what not to say."

"Do you have the call set up?"

"Not yet."

The prospect was both invigorating and frightening.
the chance to clear this all up with a phone call, well, who w
want something so simple? But she dreaded something t
couldn't put her finger on. She thought maybe fishing for ir
tion from Brock was something the police should be doi
perhaps they were reluctant to do that kind of thing when
to victims.

"Later tonight we'll record a video for you to pos
We'll preempt the public opinion. I'll have a statement wr
you to read from."

Serena physically withdrew, so surprised was she

ELEVEN

ON DAYS LIKE THIS KALEO FOUND IT EASY TO DOUBT that good efforts counted for much.

He and Will had devoted seven hours to printing and distributing photographs. They began by printing the photos of Jett Anderson's three young targets. They took these to Kaleo's contact at the LAPD and got a promise that they'd be passed on to the appropriate task force, but that was all they could do. Until a crime was committed, the pictures of young couples behaving harmlessly would not trigger any police action.

Kaleo grumbled at this, having a love-hate relationship with the LAPD ever since a knee injury knocked him out of the academy and he became an outsider in a place that had started to feel like family. Even ten years later, the sting remained and often showed up in the form of criticism of their procedures.

"Told you it was too soon," Will said as he drove out of the station lot.

"Kick me when I'm down," Kaleo retorted. "At least the girls' families will care."

The first house contained a foster mother who was irritated about having been aroused from her nap before her five kids were due home from school. She seemed well intentioned but exhausted, trying to catch much-needed sleep before her next graveyard shift.

She and her husband split shifts, she explained, so that there was always an adult at home.

Kaleo apologized and handed her the paper photos of the girl in her care with Jett, sitting together at a neighborhood park.

"This man is believed to be connected with a prostitution ring," Kaleo explained. "We think he's working on recruiting your daughter, and these other girls." He showed her their images as well. "We're here to ask for your help in doing whatever it takes to protect her."

"Like what?" the woman said, and Kaleo was stunned to see that she was asking sincerely. "I mean, I can't control who she hangs out with. Why don't the police arrest him if he's as bad as you say?"

"We're working with the police," Will explained. "But he hasn't actually committed a crime yet. We don't want it to get that far. These men prey on girls who feel misunderstood or unloved by their families."

"Of course she feels unloved," the woman said. "She's fourteen and both her parents are incarcerated. Nothing I can do about either one of those things, no matter how many meals I cook for her or how often I wash her clothes."

"Maybe you could show her these pictures," Kaleo said, prepared with copies of Jett with the other girls. "Tell her what we think. Advise her not to go anywhere alone with him."

The woman snorted.

"Do you care?" Kaleo asked sharply.

"'Course I care," she said. "It's the kids who don't."

At the second house, a Beverly Hills gem with three Mercedes parked in the wide driveway, the girl's father threatened to report Kaleo and Will to the police for violating his daughter's civil liberties, taking photographs of her without her consent.

"That's the only crime I see here." He slapped the stack of

photographs with the back of his fingers. "I think *you're* the per-verts, stalking sweethearts with a telephoto lens. That boy's decent. Has a job, has surfing sponsors. If these pictures show up anywhere but right here in my own hands, I'll come after you and shoot you myself. But not with a camera." He slammed the door in their faces.

Kaleo stared at the closed door for a full ten seconds before Will pulled him away.

"Why do these people even have kids?" Kaleo asked as they walked back down the stamped concrete driveway to their clunker at the curb. "I guess it shouldn't come as a shock."

"The day I'm not shocked by this is the day I quit," Will said.

Kaleo yanked on his driver's side door handle so hard that the lever snapped off in his fingers. He glared at it. "You're right. You're always right, and it's starting to get a little annoying."

Will opened the door for him from the inside.

"Not every day's like this one." Will's encouraging words contradicted his frown. "Think of all the parents we've met who've done the right thing."

The third parent, not in Beverly Hills, had bloodshot eyes and track marks up her arm. "Someone wants her, he can have her," was all the woman said, shoving the photos back into Kaleo's chest. "One less smart-mouth asking for my money."

Whereas the failure of the day reduced Will to an introspective mass of disheveled red hair in the passenger seat, defeat had the opposite effect on Kaleo. He drove faster than legally allowed back to their office, hardly paying attention to the familiar route. His brain was hammering out new resolutions, invigorated plans so that they might have at least one success to sleep on when they finally hit the sack tonight.

Christopher still had not returned or called and was not answering his cell phone. He had either forgotten (again) to keep it charged or was bleeding in a ditch along the Big Tujunga Road. It was ten o'clock at night. It was time to find their friend.

Dividing his focus between the road and his phone, Kaleo dialed Christopher's sister and put her on speakerphone.

"Kaleo," she answered cheerfully. Next to him, Will straightened in the seat and squared up the glasses on his nose.

"Hey, Amber. I'm looking for your brother. He happen to be with you?"

"No, haven't talked with him today. We've been up to our eyeballs at the booth."

One of Fire Followers' many endeavors to raise funds involved selling handmade items at local festivals and street fairs. It was Amber's dream to have a home that sheltered prostitutes trying to get off the street. Somewhere other than prison, which was presently the only option for many of them. The fact that prostitutes were treated as criminals rather than victims troubled Kaleo, but putting the women in jail was all that the law could do to keep them off the streets and put a roof over their heads. It was a poor, temporary fix. Outside of prison, sheltered beds were scarce and resources were few. At present, Fire Followers didn't even have the means to employ their own people. Still, they held on to the goals.

"Did Christopher miss a meeting?" Amber asked.

Will opened his mouth and Kaleo cut him off, lying to her immediately. At age twenty-six, Amber had already experienced her lifetime allotment of suffering, and Kaleo shot Will a look that said they shouldn't add to her collection. Besides, he still half expected to find Christopher at their home, bleary-eyed from working so hard on an online campaign that he just hadn't heard his phone ringing.

"Yes, he's late," Kaleo said.

"He's never late." Worry came into her voice and Kaleo regretted his mistake.

"He's never late for you girls," Will said quickly. "But when it comes to Kaleo and me, well. If you hear from him, lay the guilt on thick, would you?"

"William, hey!" Worry: gone. Sunshine: everywhere. "Anything for you."

Kaleo rolled his eyes. *William.* Like he was royalty or something.

"I'll even throw in a guilt trip for forgetting Kaleo's birthday," Amber said.

"My birthday's not until next week."

"Trust me, he's forgotten," Amber said.

"In that case, I'm asking for lobster at Gladstone's."

"Does a Gladstone's bib with a picture of a lobster count?"

"If it's from you, little sister."

"Nice."

"And tell him to call me."

"Will do."

"Thanks, Amber."

"Bye, guys."

Fire Followers' "headquarters" was little more than a small Santa Monica bungalow purchased by the Larsen family grandparents back in the 1940s. The lawn was lush, but tall hibiscus blocked most of the windows and dead palm fronds brought down by the weekend rain littered the driveway and sidewalks. Orange sprays from a large bird of paradise plant gave the yard a splash of fall color.

The car bounced as Kaleo hit the overgrown driveway and shot all the way to the detached one-car garage in the back corner of the property. Christopher's car was not there. Kaleo jumped out of his Toyota the way one did at LAX when about to miss a flight and hurried past the backyard pool and into the house through the slider on the back porch.

The woven grass mat under Kaleo's shoes was layered with years of tracked-in sand that had taken all the shine off the old linoleum floor. Even blocks away from the beach, the granules seemed to wander inland of their own accord. The mat was frayed at the edges, like the tips of Will's wiry red hair, and its square panels were separating at spots where the hand-stitched seams had given out. Kaleo felt one more strained thread pop apart under the weight of his footsteps. He crossed the dining room and passed the living room, where the TV was blaring a local news channel.

"Christopher!" Kaleo hollered down the narrow hall toward the three bedrooms and miniscule bathroom. Christopher had the master bedroom. Kaleo and Will took the smaller ones. Amber lived with girlfriends in cleaner quarters.

No answer.

Christopher's parents had remodeled the house in the eighties, but their children had no aptitude for decorating. Christopher and Amber had never replaced the mauve sofa set and teal green bedding and brass-and-mirror home accents. They just couldn't bear to spend their money on aesthetic details when it was needed for so many more important things.

The Larsen bungalow was the Fire Followers' office because it was paid for, and because an office lease in Los Angeles was even less affordable than new paint and wallpaper. So they covered up the sickly eighties decor with what really mattered to them:

Promotional posters Amber had designed for Fire Followers, featuring brilliant landscapes of wildflowers poking up out of a charred hillside.

Printers' boxes full of event flyers, which they attached to windshields, palm trees, and café bulletin boards.

Maps of Los Angeles, of Mexico, of Central America, Eastern

Europe, and Asia. Amber had big dreams, though she knew they had to start small.

Computer terminals for Kaleo and Will and other volunteers to run their activism through social media and other outlets, especially the numerous college and university campuses of Southern California.

A dry-erase board mapping the status of their efforts to track the movements of known recruiters.

Photos of naive young women who thought they were worldly wise, and of predatory young men pretending to be innocent of everything but true love, tacked and taped over every wall of the living room.

Kaleo poked his head into Christopher's room and took a quick inventory. Morning bed usually straightened before lunchtime, still unmade. Backpack, gone. Running shoes for his daily evening run, still sticking out from under the bed, waiting for feet. By all appearances, Christopher had left after breakfast and not returned.

In his own bedroom Kaleo grabbed his trail maps, his hiking boots, his prepacked gear for day hikes, a jacket, and fresh batteries for his high-powered flashlight. He knew the Angeles Forest, but it wasn't his habit to spend time wandering around there after dark. The place wasn't exactly lit up like the Hollywood sign. But his familiarity of the roads and trails would be worth something, he hoped.

Coming back down the hallway, he bumped into Will, who still looked morose and seemed to have forgotten that the bungalow's little hallway hadn't been designed for two twenty-first-century men their size. They passed awkwardly, crushing Kaleo's gear against the wall.

"Change your shoes," Kaleo said, glancing down at Will's Birkenstocks, which he'd been wearing since the day he was born.

"I'm done for the day," Will complained as Kaleo kept going. "Stick a fork in me."

But Kaleo wasn't listening. He was glued to the TV screen, where a head shot of Serena Diaz smiled sweetly at him. The way those predators must smile at their prey, Kaleo thought. The banner under the news announcer caught his eye.

Mission Acres teacher suspended for alleged sex with student.

The report turned Kaleo's stomach. He picked up the TV remote and powered off the box with a thrust like that of a sword.

"Bring your night kit," Kaleo ordered. "We're going to the mountains."

TWELVE

IN ALL HER TWELVE YEARS, KIERA MARA HAD NEVER longed for her mother as badly as she did now, bouncing in the back of a dirty truck that smelled like bad BO. The man lying at her feet was bleeding. It was all over her shoes. She would never get it off. She would never forget this moment.

But she had already started to forget why it had been so important for her to get away from her mom. It had something to do with feeling unappreciated, with being asked to do too much for her little brothers while her mother worked graveyard shifts by night and then slept by day. Todd had told her she deserved something different, and said he knew a way for her to get it: Food someone else had made for her—and plenty of it. A place where she could have her own room. Easy work that didn't involve babysitting. And spending money to buy herself some nice things for once. Like these shoes, which she had seen on the billboard that topped her apartment complex. "What kind of know-nothings post stuff like that in a place like this?" her mother said every day. "Nobody here got enough for the laces." The shoes were her birthday present from Todd.

Now she would forever think of him as Toad.

Three days had passed since he dumped her in a room that felt like a jail cell, and she passed the hours in fantasies of him coming back full of apologies and good reasons for why he had just disappeared. From there she'd been hauled into a blackened truck with two other girls, both much older than she was. They spoke to each other and ignored her, except for when they would tell her to stop crying.

From the truck they were taken to an unstable house that looked like it would collapse on its fire-eaten frame at any second. They were pushed like cows up the stairs, where three more women already waited. All of them looked so old. Definitely high schoolers, maybe college students. Here Kiera endured a night without heat or electricity, and a day in full view of a shooting. She watched from the messed-up window. One of the girls cowering near the back wall accused her of trying to get them all killed.

By then she was out of tears. Besides, she'd seen shootings before, twice, in the projects where she lived.

Within minutes all six of them had been loaded into the back of a delivery truck, where the man who was shot lay stretched out on his side, dripping blood everywhere. The girls—some stoic, some blubbering—pressed themselves away from him as if he had a gross disease. Which was stupid. They didn't make room for her and she didn't care.

Kiera sat next to him, thinking of the time her mother was gone and her brother broke his arm trying to fly off the back-porch rail and the bone stuck out of his skin. She'd had to stop the bleeding until the ambulance arrived.

Now she worried about him. Maybe it had been selfish of her to leave with nothing standing between him and their mother.

The man's nerdy yellow hat was gone, and his curly hair was matted and sweaty against his head. His breathing came hard. His eyes closed with the effort. Kiera took off her sweatshirt and reached over him to hold it against his oozing back, worried about pressing too hard. She could feel his short, shuddering breaths and worried about suffocating him.

The gate on the truck rolled down, locked, and plunged them into darkness again.

"Your name?" she heard him ask.

"Kiera."

"Thank you."

They balanced their bodies against the rumbling vehicle, Kiera sitting sideways on one hip while doing the best she could to sop up blood that she could feel but couldn't see. She had second thoughts about contagious diseases then. She'd heard that blood was worse than a wet sneeze.

A pothole threw them sideways and he grabbed her leg. He held on.

When the road smoothed out again his fingers dropped to her ankle, then to her ruined shoes, and he shoved something hard and smooth down next to her sock. Whatever it was had been warmed by his hands, and the sensation of it tucked away in her shoe soon became unnoticeable.

The truck rumbled along roads Kiera didn't know for long minutes that she couldn't count. Then it slowed, and the sounds outside changed tones, and the truck came to a stop in a space that sounded hollow.

Someone unlocked a gate and threw it open on a track that clattered like a roller coaster. They were inside a large garage or a small warehouse. Cool air rushed in, and the man under the firm pressure of her hands exhaled. She thought she felt his breath on her face. Life was leaving him the way cars left the freeway off-ramps at rush hour, trying to speed away but being forced to wait. Harsh lights cast a white glare over the women who wanted to escape the dying man, but it left him and Kiera in black shadow.

A coarse man backlit by the lights ordered them out. Five of the women obeyed, but Kiera couldn't leave this man alone. Who would help him? She focused on becoming invisibly still.

The man who ordered the girls out was joined by another silhouette of a man who carried a flashlight. It bobbed into the truck and landed on the injured man's face, taking a long and unfriendly look. Kiera snatched her hands back into the shadows.

"Is this him?" the newcomer asked. His voice was smooth like a piece of Dove chocolate. Kiera immediately lost her taste for the creamy treats.

"Unless you've started recruiting thirty-something males."

"I heard there was a woman too."

"We called Phil about these two—he said she was one of his."

"Well, she's not."

The driver snorted. "He got himself another new toy? He gets around."

"I'll settle him down."

He withdrew his light from the truck while the gruff one marched Kiera's companions off to their next prison. Then Dove turned his back on them all and lifted a phone to his ear. For a few seconds, a cool blue glow lit up his skinny sideburn and longish hair that curled up around his earlobe. With his other hand he tapped the flashlight against his thigh, keeping rhythm to a slow tune playing in his head.

"I told you what would happen if you didn't stop this," he said to the person on the other end. "What was that woman doing at the handoff today?"

The flashlight bounced off his leg a little more forcefully as he paced in front of the truck.

"I don't believe in coincidences. You can't control her. You can't control the kid either. You'll ruin us in a day."

The flashlight and the footsteps were not in sync, but the steady rhythm of each never stumbled.

"The problem with you is that you're insatiable. So end it before I have to. Kill her tonight. Or don't show your face again."

The blue light of the phone display blinked out.

The bobbing yellow flashlight beam knocked around inside the truck's box again, striking Kiera's eyes. She flinched and raised her arm against the brightness.

Dove swore upon seeing her. "Did he forget you because he's stupid or because you're smart, little girl?"

She was smart enough not to answer a trick question. This man frightened her.

"Maybe I was stupid not to go with him," she murmured. Kiera turned the sweatshirt around and pressed the cleaner side against the man's wounds. The beam alighted on her bloody hands.

"Well, you're gutsy at least. Who made you nurse to this piece of trash?"

She set her jaw. He nodded as if pleased with her responses.

"This one stays with me," Dove called out to the other man without taking his eyes off of her. His voice echoed off the metal walls of the truck's box.

Kiera could feel her heart begin to die then, dropping petals like the stalk of cut lilacs she'd once put on her mother's tiny kitchen table. They died before the next morning came.

THIRTEEN

BY THE ORANGE AND PINK GLOW OF SUNSET, LANCE plunged tortilla strips into a bowl of seafood ceviche. The scent of fresh fish, usually so appetizing, turned Serena's stomach. She turned her back to the restaurant, face to the ocean view, as if giving all her attention to Lance when really she hoped not to be noticed.

Lance had insisted that the LAPD detective, one Harlan Scott, question Serena somewhere other than the station, to protect her from the outrage that was already rising like the tide around Mission Acres High School, her apartment complex, and the local precinct. Angry parents, shocked board members, and curious students were looking for her. Neighbors who never before even knew her name seemed now to have insights into the personal details of her life that they thought they needed to share with camera crews.

Which only made Lance's choice of meeting place more unsettling: the Sunset Room of Gladstone's Restaurant, which, while not terribly busy on a Monday night in October, lacked a certain humility.

As did Harlan Scott's fingernails. Trimmed and filed and clean, they were at first glance nothing more than a sign of a well-groomed professional. They reflected the same meticulous attention given to his pencil mustache—but then they reflected more: the fading sunlight outside, the ambient light within. Detective Scott wore clear fingernail polish, and this became a terrible distraction for Serena, a suspicion about his character.

The detective declined to eat. The trio spoke quietly, while Serena worried that the high ceilings and smooth floors would carry their conversation to places she didn't want it to go.

Discreetly, the LAPD detective pushed a manila folder toward her across the table, his shiny nails flashing as he opened the flap. One glance was all she could bear to offer. She turned away, hand on her mouth. Then she thought this might be disrespectful of Brock.

Brock as she had never seen him before: Brock, restrained. Brock, humiliated. Brock, crying. All with a woman who might have been Serena. All in the less-than-ideal lighting of a dim room and a hidden camera. They were video stills, the best images from the grainy efforts of a young boy desperate for a way out of a situation he didn't want to be in.

If she hadn't known with every cell of her own body that she had never, ever participated in anything like this, her own eyes might have indicted her heart. That curly black hair might have the same DNA as the strands on her head. That blurry face might be reconstructed to match her unique profile. Under a magnifying glass, that butterfly tattoo on the left hip might be identical to the one on her own.

"That's not me," she said, over and over and over. She was conscious of little else about the interview. Lance rescued her from having to say much more. "That's not me. That's not me."

But the boy was Brock. Without a question. Brock, with the pink scar across his cheek from a lacrosse injury that somehow made him more good looking rather than less.

Between spoonfuls of ceviche, Lance pressed hard on his position that the images were fabricated. If they weren't, he claimed, there was enough evidence here for the officer to make an arrest.

Detective Scott said something about Brock not having the knowledge or equipment to create something this good, this sophisticated, and Lance erupted with remarks about how out of touch the LAPD must be with today's youth, who were more tech savvy than the average adult. If Brock couldn't do it himself, he had the money and networks to find someone who could. Serena tuned out the rest. True or false, the photos would destroy her.

Her heart kept turning to her student. What in him was so broken, so pained, that he would turn to this false claim as a fix? She worried about him. She imagined that woman in the images, that not-her woman, taking advantage of Brock and then trying to harm him further. Blackmailing him, perhaps.

The table fell silent and Serena ignored the server when she brought Lance a second glass of wine. Her own broiled halibut sat untouched.

"Is there any reason for Brock to lie about you?" Scott asked the question and then pressed a sleek finger to his lips as if that would help him listen better.

"He doesn't like the grades he earns in my class."

"How would you characterize your relationship with Brock?"

"Until last spring, it was great. He was a dream student—a little mischievous outside of class, in my opinion, but always on a teacher's good side. Really, I think he just hit a tough spot. He's involved in so much outside of school—"

"You're aware of his extracurricular schedule?"

"It's not exactly top secret."

"He talks about it in class?"

Serena's eyes shot to Lance. "From time to time."

"During class or afterward?"

"The class starts right after lunch. The most dedicated kids come in early to work on their experiments."

"Kids like Brock."

Serena could only nod. She tried to get the conversation back to Brock's grades. "Everyone gets in a bind sometimes. Brock has a lot to lose right now, with his scholarships."

"You're surprisingly sympathetic toward this boy."

Lance leaned in. "Ms. Diaz respects all of her students similarly. She understands what they're going through. That doesn't mean she lets them get away with whatever they want."

Serena feared Detective Scott's expression was skeptical. Or perhaps inclined to giving Lance's words some twisted meaning. Just as she gave to that disturbing clear nail polish, which seemed designed for visibility and invisibility at the same time.

The detective asked Serena if she had a birthmark on the ball of her right foot.

"Yes," she whispered. She had always thought that the birthmark below her second and third toes resembled a flower. Her mother had often said it was proof that Serena had a love of the outdoors in her blood.

In the second before the detective withdrew a piece of paper from his file and gave it to Lance, Serena thought that the flower on her foot and the one on the worry stone she'd found at the Station Fire house were eerily similar.

Lance pursed his lips and held the paper out to Serena. It was a crudely drawn footprint. And right on the ball between her second and third toes was a hand-rendered duplicate of her poppy birthmark.

Lance seemed far more rattled by the amateurish sketch of her birthmark than by the photos.

"I can explain those away," he said as they drove down the dark two-lane highway alongside the blackened ocean. "But that sketch—you have to rack your brain, Serena. You have to tell me how Brock could know what that mark on the bottom of your foot looks like. Please tell me you have pictures of it on Instagram or you showed it off during a health science class or something. Anything."

Serena could think of nothing. She didn't even recall that mark most days. Out of sight, out of mind.

"You wear flip-flops to school some days, right?" he said hopefully. "Something bedazzled that still looks professional?"

Serena was professional, but never bedazzled. And even now, in her twenties, she couldn't rid her mind of her mother's admonishments that no student ever wanted to be distracted by his teacher's toenails, for better or worse.

"Cover them like they're cleavage," her mother always said. "And for goodness' sake, don't be a hippie teacher. It's so cliché."

"I can't think of a thing," Serena said.

"I need you to," Lance pleaded. "A beach trip, a pool party, a hit-and-run that knocked you out of your shoes. It doesn't have to be Brock who saw it. Anyone could have told him. So you review any and every moment you were ever without a shoe on in a public or semi-public place."

Nothing. Her mind was a blank slate. Lance let up.

Serena was afraid to go home, which didn't matter because Lance showed no sign of taking her there. He was saying that they ought to film the video as soon as they got back to his house—he had equipment in his home office already set up, very helpful for taping client statements.

"You're not the only one in Southern California who has reason to hide from the public," Lance murmured, and she felt embarrassed. Of course he was bound by privilege not to talk about his cases. She wasn't qualified to make assumptions.

"I'll do whatever you think's best."

"I want to preempt the possibility that Brock or whoever helped him produce that pathetic piece of porn may put it on YouTube soon enough to crush you."

"Isn't it evidence?" There she went, making assumptions again.

"Not the type the police can lock away in a plastic bag."

Serena shivered. There would be copies, of course. For eternity, digital copies floating around the intangible parts of the world, haunting her. And Brock.

"Would he post something in which he's so clearly identifiable?" she wondered aloud. "Wouldn't it crush his future as much as mine?"

"Can you explain everything teenagers decide to do?" Lance asked.

In her heart of hearts, she believed ninty-seven percent of what they did was connected to a universal human need for affirmation. They just didn't have the maturity to go about it the best way. Nor, for that matter, did many adults. She didn't say this. In her experience that point of view was hard for successful people like Lance to understand.

"I only need two minutes to put the statement on paper," he said. "Something that humanizes you, makes it harder for them to judge you." He glanced at her as he entered Pacific Palisades and offered the first confident smile she'd seen since those horrifying images. He tapped a finger to his temple as they accelerated out of a curve. "Already composed in my head."

At two in the morning Serena sat at the marble-topped island in Lance's kitchen, still fully dressed. The mug in front of her was full of herbal tea long gone cold, and the windows over the sink were black mirrors that cast her haunted gaze back at her.

Lance slept because she had begged him to. But she feared nightmares involving Brock Anderson, dying men with brown curls, frowning detectives, and lurid photos.

She was happy with the script Lance had written. It was only one minute long and easy to read without looking scared or defeated. It appealed to the goodness in Brock, in her, and in the community. But what had pleased her most was how Lance knew what she'd wanted to say without putting her through excruciating paces to extract it from her.

Today has been heartbreaking for everyone who believes in the sacred trust all students should be able to place in all teachers. I'm recording this message as a promise to the community: Though the accusations against me are completely, verifiably false, I'll cooperate fully with administrators and authorities to bring the truth to light as swiftly as possible. I care deeply for the welfare of the involved student and will do everything in my power to prevent further humiliation or harm to him, no matter what reason he has for telling these terrible lies. More than anyone else I want to protect the young adults and staff of Mission Acres High School, and to assure you all that I have not betrayed your trust.

She'd breathed a sigh of relief when he sent the file on to his legal secretary to upload it directly to a Vimeo account, then forward the link to local journalists. It was the right thing to do, to set a nonconfrontational tone. Everything would come to light. Everything would be explained.

Lance's house brimmed with the high-pitched tone of complete silence that she never heard at her bustling apartment complex, where neighbors kept their business but not their noise to themselves.

She thought of calling Brock herself, right now, without anything needing to be recorded. At this hour Brock might not be surrounded by hovering attorneys and parents and detectives. He might be staring at his YouTube account, his finger hovering over the Enter key, pondering whether it would help or hurt his cause to make the details of his humiliation a public event.

Don't do it, her heart whispered. *Think of your future.*

They could speak reasonably. She could find out why he was doing this—not to her, but to himself. She could appeal to all the strengths of his character: *We're all a mix of strengths and weaknesses,* she imagined herself saying to him. *Whatever weakness led you to cheat on that test is getting stronger in you, in your choice to tell this heinous lie. But it's not so strong yet that you can't stop all this. You can turn back. You're so young. It's not too late to turn back. We can wipe the slate clean. I won't hold this against you.*

Her phone was on the countertop, the same shiny black as the kitchen windows. Lance had programmed Brock's number into her contact list so that she could avoid any calls he might make to her. "Don't speak to him without being recorded," Lance had said. Serena wondered if that was the same reason behind Mr. Walter's recommendation that she not contact Brock at all.

She picked up the phone and tapped her way through the contacts list to Brock's entry. Serena thought of his mother. Brock was her only son.

The voice of an angry mother shouted down Serena's mind: *"What's a ratty doll to you, rich brat? Too spoiled to share your toys? Think my girl don't deserve half what you got?"*

Serena let the screen go back to sleep. She set the phone aside, but not because Lance wanted a recording of their call. Not because Mr. Walter had warned her away from speaking to Brock at all. She let the boy alone out of respect for his mother. If Serena were the parent, she'd want to be in on any phone call between Brock and the woman he accused, whether she trusted her son or not.

She wondered what this respect might cost her.

FOURTEEN

WEAK MOONLIGHT CAME IN THROUGH A BOOK-SIZED
vent where the wall met the ceiling, and lamplight squeezed in
through the crack under the door.

Kiera sat on a mattress that lay on the floor, a mattress without any covering to separate her from its grime. She wouldn't have
touched it had she not feared the crawling floor more. Something
brushed her exposed ankle, which she snatched up to safety. Her
body folded in on itself, tightening into a compact ball of dread.

"You get used to it," the voice on the other side of the room
said. It sounded like a woman. A tired old woman, rolled on her
side and facing the wall.

From her shoe Kiera pulled a little disk, a secret present she
hadn't been able to examine until now. But the moonlight was too
dim to see by, and when the thing slipped out of her fingers, she
heard it roll away but couldn't see where it went. And she wasn't
curious enough to pat the floor with her bare hands looking for it.

"What are we waiting for?" she finally whispered.

The shadowed lump that was on the other cot moved.

"Food," was the sarcastic reply.

"I'm not hungry," Kiera said.

The tone softened. "We're waiting for your turn," the lump
said.

"My turn for what?" she asked.

The other woman shifted and rolled, and the lump became a more human form. A person wrapped in a cocoon of blankets. Her hair shielded her face. She pushed it out of the way, then leaned into the narrow shaft of light that came down from the wall.

"How old are you?" she asked Kiera. Her eyes were red and glassy. There was a blister on her lip and an old bruise on her cheek.

"Thirteen," she lied. She thought the other girl might be eighteen, nineteen. Old enough to smell a lie. "I'm Kiera. What's your name?"

"No one needs to know names in here."

Her retort made Kiera want to cry. She was only trying to be nice.

"What's going to happen?"

Her roommate rubbed the blanket across her nose and passed through the light. She came to sit on the mattress, placing herself between Kiera and the door, and Kiera thought of the bleeding man who had put himself between that woman and that gun. He was probably dead by now.

"Do what he says. It'll go easier for you."

"Who? What will he tell me to do?"

"Does it matter?"

Kiera thought about this. She could think of many things she might not be able to do on command. Like eat cockroaches. Or kill a person.

"Do what he says. Don't think. That's your fastest way out."

"Out, you mean to go back home?"

"I mean out, back to this room, maybe out to a house where you get a window with bars on it."

"I hate this room."

"You'll learn to love it soon enough."

"Well, I don't want to love it. I want to go home."

"Look, you're here because Roman gets first taste of all his goods, and he keeps what he wants. So think of it like ripping off a Band-Aid."

"I don't know what you mean."

"Have you ever slept with a boy?"

The question made Kiera blush. She'd wondered many times what it would be like to sleep with Todd—Toad—but he never made a move and she didn't have the courage to do it herself. Though many other girls her age talked about their experiences, boasted about them, Kiera suspected many of the girls were not telling the—

And then the meaning of the question landed heavily in her stomach.

The other girl sighed. Kiera could feel her body start to shake.

"My name's Becca," she said gently. "And I don't think you're thirteen."

"I'll scream," she whispered. "I'll fight."

"All the screaming ends eventually."

Kiera thought of the dying man, of his courage. His reckless bravery. "I'd rather die."

"Death isn't an option. You're worth more alive."

The light under the door was eclipsed by the shadows of feet that paused outside the door. A key was inserted into the lock. Kiera grabbed hold of Becca's arm. The girl shook her off.

"Please," she begged. "Help me."

The door opened behind her, casting Kiera in shadow. Quickly Becca leaned over Kiera's ear.

"If you fight, fight hard."

TUESDAY

FIFTEEN

THE MAN IN THE TASSELED YELLOW HAT PULLED UP
a stool on the other side of the marble kitchen counter. He removed
the cap, exposing his mass of curly brown hair, and placed it on a
gourd in the centerpiece, giving the vegetable a cocky personality.

"You're surprisingly sympathetic toward this boy," he said. It
felt like a compliment. "We need fools like you."

Serena jolted upright and a blanket slipped off her shoulders.
Her thick black hair had absorbed the sunlight blazing across the
kitchen island and fell hot across her bare arm. The man she called
Chris was not there playing with the winter squash.

There was a note under her fingers, a sloppy scrawl on the
back of an envelope.

> Go back to sleep in one of the bedrooms. Quick trip to the
> office, back in a flash with breakfast. Chin up.
> —L

The immaculate kitchen was clean enough to belong in a model
home and large enough to encompass the entirety of Serena's studio apartment. For the first time she thought how strange it was
that a bachelor who could afford to run out for every meal of the
day and hated to cook should have a kitchen like this.

For catering office parties, she thought. And showcasing seasonal bowls of fruits and vegetables. She touched the acorn squash, expecting plastic. It was as real as the dream.

"We need fools like you."

Serena chewed on the backhanded praise and couldn't return to sleep. She fidgeted with her cold tea mug and considered that her normal morning routine might feel even more foreign today than something entirely new.

But what else could she do? She found a fresh change of clothes that she'd left in one of the spare bedrooms. She ran the grimy set she had worn all day and night through Lance's washer, showered, borrowed a robe, then put the items in the dryer. She made a cup of coffee in his Keurig, stood in front of his meagerly stocked refrigerator wishing for half-and-half, and drank the coffee black. It was only eight thirty. The day stretched out ahead of her like the Pacific in winter.

This was life stripped of everything that had been meaningful. Life in a grand house, sterile and empty, with no lessons to plan or papers to grade, no students to serve, nothing to accomplish.

Now she was the needy one. She felt angry at what Brock Anderson had taken from her. This loss of her career, of her reputation, of her peace of mind—it was only the beginning of her problems. She could sense it. And her first reflex in the face of this threat was to reach out and grab hold of what she could.

Hair damp, feet bare, she returned to the kitchen for her phone and discovered Lance had turned it off. She powered it on. She dialed the Mission Acres principal's direct number.

"Yes." Mac Walter wasn't typically curt, but caller ID could bring out a person's true feelings. Her name was inseparable from what was probably one of the worst days of his long career. And yet he'd answered, hadn't he?

"Mr. Walter, I'd like to make arrangements to get some personal items out of my classroom," she said.

"What? Who is this?"

The questions were like accusations. It took her a moment to recover from the surprise.

"Serena Diaz?" She put her name out like a question, a request for permission to speak.

His manner changed to irritable recognition. "It's not the best time," he said.

"I imagine it's inconvenient, but if I could get a list to you—"

"No. When the police release your classroom we'll box up whatever they don't want and send it on to you. That's all."

The paternal tone he'd taken with her yesterday while offering advice was gone. She imagined authorities pawing through her things in their latex gloves, covering every surface of her room in a layer of lewd theories. The invasion provoked her to insist.

"There's just one thing, then. Please. It would mean a great deal."

Mac Walter didn't cut her off.

"It's a bound book of my photos from the Station Fire burn area. I leave it out for the biology classes. I could send someone by for it."

"And this is something you need immediately?"

It wasn't, of course. The book was nothing more than something important to her, something she didn't want to lose to Brock Anderson, something that represented what she loved most—the natural world and teaching. Standing barefoot in someone else's house wearing someone else's robe, she felt almost desperate for that little book, which she'd compiled online and could replace. Mainly, she didn't want anyone else to have it.

She opened her mouth to answer Mr. Walter but couldn't.

"Do you need it right now?" His tone had changed from impatient to inquisitive, as if someone else was listening in and prompting him.

"We need fools like you."

Was she a fool?

She found herself mentally reviewing the book, page by page. She even tried to recall all the photos she'd ever taken in the burn area, including field trip shots. Brock Anderson had attended one of those events with her, but she didn't think he was pictured.

Let them look for whatever they sought. They wouldn't find it in those pages or anywhere in her classroom.

"Never mind," she said.

"Ms. Diaz." Her boss's words rushed in to stop her from hanging up. "I didn't mean to be short-tempered. This week has been unprecedented. And it's only Tuesday."

"I understand," she said tentatively. She found herself listening for background noise, heard none.

"I don't think you do," he said slowly. "While I have you on the line, a quick question—do you have a minute?"

"A few hundred of them, to be frank." Down on the lowest level of Lance's house, the dryer buzzer sounded.

"A quick question," he repeated, "a personal question. I guess you'll be getting a lot of those from now on."

His testiness exceeded hers by a degree.

"What did you mean when you said you'd do everything in your power to prevent further harm to Brock?"

Had she said that? Yes, in the video. She felt mild surprise that he'd already seen it. The change of subject warned her to be cautious. What did they think she had meant?

"I think the statement is clear enough."

"Are you acquainted with a young man, early thirties, curly brown hair, about six feet?" It sounded like a million men in the greater Los Angeles area, so Serena waited for him to go on. The curly brown hair snared her memory, though.

There was a light rustling of papers on Mr. Walter's end.

"He has a surgical scar along his left elbow."

Serena didn't realize she had been holding her breath. She hadn't noticed a scar on Chris. "Except for that last bit, he could be almost anyone. What's his name?"

"We thought you might know. He doesn't have any ID."

Serena was having trouble understanding. "Why do you think I know him?"

There—in the background was the mumble of another male voice. Serena rubbed her brow.

"You'll have to explain."

Another mumble, then: "There's a dead man in our football stadium wearing a winter hat and swim trunks. He's propped up in the bleachers with a bullet through his back."

There was that high-pitched whine of silence again, ringing in her ears. She waited for them to explain why they thought she knew him.

"Ms. Diaz?"

A bright yellow tasseled cap that had collected twigs and leaves.

Fading brown eyes.

"Run."

"There's a name written in spray paint across the front of his chest." Mr. Walter said it like he was reading the minutes of the last school board meeting.

"Then maybe that's his name," she said, because she couldn't think of anything else.

"The name on the shirt is Brock."

"Then maybe you should ask Brock who he is," she heard herself say.

"I suppose they will," Mr. Walter said. "But the pictures in the guy's shirt pocket were of you."

That's not me. That's not me. Brock, what are you doing?

"I don't know any dead men." Maybe the truth of it was what lent her voice confidence. That man at the house, Chris or whatever his real name was, he was a total stranger to her. She didn't know his name, though she recalled that he knew hers.

"These people will kill you."

The same people who had killed him?

"I have no idea," she said. It was her answer for so many questions right now. "Who he is," she added, fearing she'd been mumbling aloud. They let the silence stretch out until she plucked the tense string. "Can I help you with anything else?"

"Thank you for your time."

She hung up her phone and wondered if they knew she was at Lance's and if they'd send someone for her, take her in for more questioning and lock her up until she confessed to murdering a man and abusing a boy.

Who was the dead man and what was his connection to Brock? It felt as if no one else in the world would think to ask that question. Their minds were too busy chasing her. Even Mr. Walter had lost his trust in her, with all those other voices in his office casting doubt and shadows on her reputation. *Who is this Ms. Diaz? How long have you known her? Have other kids complained?* If she's connected to a murder, it would be easy to see how she might not have any conscience when it comes to abusing her students.

Serena sank to the kitchen floor in a pool of morning sunlight. The rays bounced off the surface of her phone screen.

Her thoughts turned to Chris trying to help her in the tangle of toyon and burnt scrub oaks, trying to tell her something important. In her mind Serena put Brock and Chris together, looking for a connection. He was too young to be Brock's father. Too old to be the boy's peer. Too haphazardly dressed to shop at the same stores proud to carry Brock's lines. She couldn't make the pair work no matter what background she tried: a yacht, a dive, an artfully grafittied freeway underpass. Brock was too calculated, centered in the frame of her mind. He was always posing as if for a camera, and she wondered if he had done this in her classroom too—posed for her, tried to make her think he was something that he was not. An upstanding young man, a student elevated to the top of the class by his own brains and good character.

In the same settings Chris loitered at the periphery like a man who didn't care if anyone ever noticed him. At first she thought his crazy outfit might have been designed to attract attention, but now she wondered if it was just a sign of how little he cared about others' opinions of him. Her thoughts wandered to his eyes, which unlike the rest of him were clear and straightforward. She spent a long time thinking about his eyes, and what happened to them when he was shot.

Without thinking, she called Brock Anderson, formulating a calm set of questions to ask his voice mail. Her mind went blank when a living rather than recorded voice answered after four rings.

"Yeah?" The carelessness of his tone pricked her.

"What are you doing to me?" she demanded.

There was a moment's hesitation. "Serena?"

"No, it's Ms. Diaz. What's going on, Brock? What do you have against me that you would make up these stories and hurt so many people?" This was not the calm conversation she had imagined.

"I haven't hurt anyone," he said slowly. But she thought she heard a tremor in his voice. A hesitation that didn't suit a self-assured teen.

"You've hurt me beyond words. And my family. And that man!"

"What man?" It was nearly a whisper.

"How are you connected to the man who showed up dead at school?"

Behind the continuing silence she heard another voice in the background: "Are you getting this?"

She was being recorded. Yes, the truth was irrevocable: she was a fool for calling. Would hanging up now only make it worse? She thought it would.

Brock's voice was unnaturally slow. "Oh yeah, we were just talking about that." He cleared his throat. "I was saying you must be really, really mad to have killed a guy."

"I did not kill that man."

"Well, that makes two of us."

"Why is your name painted across his chest?"

"I thought it was a warning."

"What kind of warning?"

Brock didn't answer right away. Then in a rush: "Like, maybe you telling me I shouldn't have said anything. About us."

Serena blinked. "There is no us."

"I can understand why you'd want to end it now."

"End *what*? We never began anything. There's a dead man at our school—"

"You know there was a time when I would have done anything for you." Brock's voice cracked. Was he crying? Serena felt the blood drain from her head. "I just couldn't go on that way . . ."

Foolish or not, she ended the call. Regret was a swift river that might drown her, and she hadn't even thought to ask him how he'd made those horrific photographs of the two of them.

Where was Lance? Why wasn't he back?

When she dialed his number she got his voice mail and couldn't think of what to say. Anything she said might be used against her. Even by Lance, she feared.

What if the detective appeared on Lance's doorstep before Lance came back to advise and defend her? What if they'd traced her cell phone when she called Mr. Walter and even now were headed down to Pacific Palisades to haul her in for murder and who knew what else?

If she was in jail, who would investigate the real questions?

Serena left her clean clothes to wrinkle in the dryer and dressed in the spare jeans and long-sleeved T-shirt. Though it wasn't hot, she was perspiring as she laced up her dusty hiking boots, wondering if Chris's car was still sitting in the road behind where she had parked yesterday morning. She had to find out his connection to Brock.

She carefully composed a note to Lance before dashing out the door.

Had to go. Call me.

Then it seemed best to leave her phone behind, to separate herself from anything that could be traced. She crumpled the note and rewrote it:

Back soon. No worries.

On the Santa Monica Freeway, her heart caught in her throat: she had asked Mr. Walter for her photo album. They were no doubt examining it page by page that very second. Eventually they would come to the one image she now wished she'd left out: the abandoned stone house where Chris had been killed, photographed more than a year before their strange meeting.

Serena accelerated. She'd return to the area one more time, then never again.

SIXTEEN

IF FIRE FOLLOWERS HADN'T SPENT SO MUCH OF their time conducting awareness assemblies at Los Angeles area high schools, Amber Larsen might not have learned of her brother's death for days. But the student who found Christopher's body when he arrived at the track for an early training practice couldn't resist the bragging rights of having been first on the scene. After calling police to report his find, he snapped a picture of Amber's beloved brother and posted it to social media sites with a crude caption:

Mission Acres fans are more stiff than first believed.

Amber didn't learn about any of this right away. All she knew in the beginning was what showed up in her own feed, information sorted and placed there for her by algorithms she didn't really care about. She was the face of Fire Followers, and so her page was as public as it could be, open to the broadest possible swath of people and institutions who might need to know about the Larsens' organization. It might have been a combination of the "Mission Acres" tag and the popularity of the post, which passed through the two-thousand-member student body like a plague. The gruesome image of Christopher topped her feed with more than five hundred comments, but she read only the latest remark, because her eyes took it in against her will:

> Dude, can you hang this dummy from the tree in my front yard when you're through with it?

But Amber's heart was already seizing with grief, so much of it that she didn't have any thought of being offended—that would come later, with the details of how the photo had come to be delivered to her in this despicable way.

It was the hat that caught her eye, that crazy knit cap she had brought back for him from Tanzania. Red and green and black but mostly canary yellow, it was from a native woman who owned her own business. Amber had purchased hats for William and Kaleo as well, though theirs were far tamer: green for Kaleo because it was the Hawaiian's go-to color, and blue for William, because redheads in blue—this redhead in particular—made her insides go soft.

Christopher, who was always first to make purchases from such enterprising women, appreciated Amber's gesture but found the item itself amusing. He had accepted it with a laugh and a question: "What do they do with these in Africa?" He tied the tassels together at the ends and threw it over his shoulder like a purse, smothering it in his armpit. She had wrestled him for it, and because he adored her and always let her win at everything, she got it back and wrangled it onto his curly-haired head. She tugged the narrow plastic visor down over his eyes and tied the tassels under his chin like a bonnet and said, "They sell them to tourists from California."

In the terrible photo the hat sat on his head like a mockery rather than an endearment. Why was he wearing it at all? William was the only one who actually wore his, and Amber liked to think this was because it was the only way he knew to say how much he really cared about her. But even then he saved it for the rainy season.

Amber stared at the picture of Christopher but couldn't see anything but the hat. The rest was too horrendous for her mind to consider. Until her mind concocted a reasonable explanation.

It was a hoax. Yes, one of Christopher's usually brilliant stunts to get under a trafficker's skin. One named Brock this time. *Usually* brilliant, she thought. He hadn't consulted her on this one or she would have put her foot down. She was a little surprised it didn't violate even his own standards, which tended to be daring but on the safe side of good taste.

Disgust freed her eyes to wander over the picture, which was suitable for a Halloween shop-o'-horrors. Some Hollywood buddy who knew a thing or two about realistic makeup must have had a part in it. That guy from Studio City. What was his name? No wonder Kaleo and William hadn't been able to track her brother down last night—this must have taken hours.

Really, Christopher? This Brock guy needs such drastic measures?

She picked up her phone and tapped his contact icon. The grief that had pooled around her throat rushed away like bathtub water and was replaced by irritation. Amber didn't irritate easily, but this emotion was the close cousin of embarrassment. She'd give him an earful for failing to warn her of this. She scanned the comments while his phone rang and found that most people believed it was a Halloween stunt.

What'd you use for blood?

and

Shot for criminal fashion.

and

Sharing!

A scattered few were offended.

When I was in high school we shot baskets, not people.

Christopher's phone rang until the voice mail kicked in. "You've reached Christopher Larsen's virtual self. Do your thing."

The very sound of his voice made the photograph that much less real and that much more juvenile. The words she really wanted to say belonged in his ear, not on a recording. *I can't believe you'd do that without telling me, after everything we've been through. Did you think I wouldn't see it? It's cruel, Christopher, not to mention sick. Don't be cruel. It doesn't suit you.*

She said, "Call me when you get this?" and then added, because there was a silver thread of fear woven into her anger: "I love you."

Her browser automatically refreshed the page and a new comment appeared at the top.

Police arriving at Mission Acres High School now.

Posted just a few minutes earlier.

Amber muttered, "If you've done anything to jeopardize our work, buddy—" and then put her cursor in the comment box to ask a question: Why police? She typed but no letters appeared in the box. She refreshed the page herself.

The picture was gone. She scrolled, searching for it, but it was no longer there.

She went to the page for Mission Acres High School, but there was nothing there either except for a spectacular panoramic shot of the campus on a shining day and announcements about the fall football schedule. She couldn't remember the name of the original poster.

The police were at the high school, and someone had taken down the fake photo of her dead brother. Maybe because she wasn't the only adult who thought the fake was offensive.

Maybe because it wasn't fake.

Amber sat for long seconds hunched over her computer, paralyzed by a terror she'd only known once before in her life, when she needed the one thing she had willingly given away: her own safety. It was like a slow and torturous suffocation, until Christopher had rescued her.

What if there was no rescue this time, for him or for her?

She grasped for her phone and dialed the only person she loved as much as her brother, though she was too damaged and cowardly to tell him.

He answered on the second ring.

"William," she whispered. And then she couldn't say anything more.

SEVENTEEN

KALEO HADN'T EXACTLY OVERESTIMATED THEIR ability to search the Big Tujunga Canyon Road after sunset Monday night. It was more accurate to say he had underestimated the reach of Los Angeles' city lights. The road cut straight through the Station Fire burn, and the majority of the area still bore the scars. He and Will searched the twelve-mile road for four hours, driving a piddling five miles per hour and turning off each driveway into campgrounds, trailheads, and residential areas. Soon their eyestrain turned to headaches, and at two a.m. they admitted their need to wait for sunlight.

They found a wide shoulder near the reservoir and reclined their seats, cracked the windows, and locked the doors, each man examining his own thoughts. There was no reason to believe the Big Tujunga Road was Christopher's ultimate destination. It was simply the last place they knew him to be. Kaleo guessed Will was thinking the same thing.

The forest seemed impossibly large in that moment.

Kaleo felt as if he slept with his eyes open. Will's breathing never reached truly restful depths. Daylight arrived on wings of wind and fog that lifted quickly but promised the kind of California day that slouched: untidy, begrudging, grim, and gray. The sun rose on the east face of Mount Gleason. The landscape, which

Kaleo had always thought of as sparse, seemed wiry but spunky. Undead. He didn't come up here much. The acres hit hardest by the burn were behind them and to the east, still restricted to the public.

When the gray was light enough to see the full width of the road, Kaleo pulled back out and headed west. Will stirred and righted his seat, repositioned his red-framed glasses. Silently, the men retraced their route of the night before, scanning the sloping hillsides and examining each side road in search of Christopher's blue Kia.

"Should we get out and walk around?" Will suggested at one campsite.

Kaleo kept driving, needing some sign that Christopher's wheels had been nearby.

"We should call the police," Will offered.

"Not yet."

"Our contact at least, if not missing persons."

Kaleo wasn't ready to admit that Christopher might be doing anything but chasing a good lead with a dead cell phone battery.

They were nearing the Stonyvale homes, so many of which had been leveled by the blaze, when Will's phone rang. He reached for it on the dash and answered without taking his eyes off his surroundings.

"Yeah." Then he turned away from the window and looked to the floorboards. "Amber?" And after a few seconds' pause: "What is it?"

Kaleo slowed to take in both sides of the road while Will was distracted. Then he became distracted himself when the man started repeating, "Okay, okay," every five seconds in a tone that made Kaleo think nothing was okay.

The wait for an explanation was almost as excruciating as the explanation itself. Will kept Amber on the line and repeated her news to Kaleo.

One minute later Kaleo was blazing down the Big Tujunga, crossing the center line as needed, toward North Hills.

"Why don't you let us come pick you up?" Will was asking Amber. "At least stay on the line until we meet you . . . Okay, okay," he said, again in that way of suggesting that it was not, and then he closed his phone.

"She has to get dressed," he said. Then after a moment's paralysis he unfroze and pulled up his navigation app to help get Kaleo to Mission Acres High School.

"Has she spoken to the police yet?" Kaleo asked.

"No. Couldn't do it alone, she said."

"So there's a chance this is all a mistake."

Will focused on his phone. "Yeah. A chance," he said. Like *Okay, okay.*

"Stop doing that," Kaleo said.

Will looked at him from the corner of his eyes without moving his head, then resumed his search for driving directions.

For Kaleo, the murder of his good friend in a high school football stadium was as likely as the Lakers winning the NBA championship this year. Sometimes, the best a man could do was believe certain things were *im*possible.

"What high school again?" Kaleo asked.

"Mission Acres. North Hills."

"Why have I heard of it?"

Will's tone was flat. "Serena Diaz teaches there."

Kaleo swore. He came around a curve and had the good fortune to be on the outside because the driver coming up on the inside was in just as big a hurry and drifted into his lane.

Kaleo hit his horn. Will looked up.

"Get the plates," Kaleo said. "I'm in the mood to sue someone."

Will twisted like a contortionist.

"I wasn't serious," Kaleo muttered.

"Was that her?"

"Who?"

"Diaz. Silver Volvo."

He slammed the brakes and Will braced his arm on the dash. Kaleo craned his neck to see; the other vehicle was already out of sight.

"I would have noticed," he said. He was the one who had taken the pictures of her car, who had made the notes about her work history, who had downloaded everything to Will's super-meticulous electronic files. But the truth was, what Will saw at a glance often took Kaleo long minutes of study.

Will didn't respond to Kaleo's not-so-subtle plea for confirmation. He was facing forward again, looking at the road.

"C'mon!" Kaleo snapped.

"You're the one who took the pictures," Will said.

"Well, you're the PI!"

"We can't let Amber walk onto that football field all by herself."

Will had slept on the side of his face, and his reckless red hair formed a mountain slope of its own that gave him a lopsided, genius look. Underneath all his street smarts, the guy had a soft spot for people who needed what he could so easily give.

But Kaleo was at the wheel this day. He yanked it hard into a one-eighty and peeled back out onto the asphalt road.

"Amber needs us," Will said.

"Amber's a big girl," he said. "But Serena Diaz might be our only link to justice right now."

"You don't know she's *in* that car. Anyone could be driving it."

"Right."

Will sniffed and frowned. Kaleo wasted no time. Already, she might have zoomed beyond their reach. But she hadn't. In a very short time Kaleo spotted the compact car scurrying like a squirrel over the road. He leaned forward over the steering wheel.

"What's your plan?" Will said.

"You sound like you don't want to know."

Will sighed. The Volvo slowed just enough to pull off the paved road and make a narrow turn onto a dirt lane that Kaleo hadn't seen last night in the dark.

"Amber would want us to do this," Kaleo said, following Serena.

"*I* want us to do this too," Will said. "But priorities, really! She asked for my help. We found Christopher, and he might be dead. Right now I don't give a rip about the teacher."

"This will only take a minute."

Will turned his face toward the passenger window and stopped speaking. Which was just as well. He wouldn't like Kaleo's plan. In fact, he'd hate it so much that he might be able to talk Kaleo out of it if he tried. And he would try.

Kaleo pursued, his mind growing loud with all of Will's unspoken arguments for why he shouldn't do what he was about to do. It was irritating, the way a man's character could be so loud without him having to say anything at all.

"Stop doing that," Kaleo muttered.

This time Will didn't even look at him.

Who was Chris?

He was a dead man.

He was a hero made larger than life by mystery.

He was, possibly, the solution to Serena's problems. If she could find the stranger's car, she might be able to learn his real name, and then find his connection to Brock, and maybe even figure out why these things were happening to her. Maybe solve the real crime before a false one was pinned on her and the case was declared closed.

She had no fantasies of being a detective, though, and the prospect of how difficult all of this would be for her sat in her empty stomach like the flu. The LAPD probably had already impounded his car and identified him. Mr. Walter's inquisition was probably some effort to trap her into a confession. They probably had some kind of big-brother-in-the-sky satellite imagery of her running into him right after she was dismissed from school. Right *before* Chris was murdered. At that distance it probably even looked like she was the one who'd shot him.

The last person they would disclose his identity to would be Serena Diaz. She was Mary Magdalene. She was Hester Prynne. She was Sarah Good. The latest in the line of outcast women who were "guilty" of unspeakable things they might have never done.

Serena rattled down the dirt turnoff at too fast a pace, bracing herself for the likelihood that there would be nothing left of the little rusty blue Kia this morning but tire tracks. So when she came around the bend and saw it parked in its identical spot, she indulged in the idea that she would wake up from this nightmare much sooner than she'd dared to hope.

She parked in front of the SUV, where she had been yesterday, and grabbed a fast-food napkin out of her glove box. She might have to leave shoe prints in the dirt, but she wouldn't leave fingerprints on his car, which she soon learned was unlocked.

The contents were messy but not slobbish, the organized chaos of a responsible-college-student-meets-adventurer. On the front passenger seat was a backpack unzipped at the top. In the footwell was a mass of clothing—jeans, T-shirt, athletic shoes, as if he often changed clothes on the run.

Serena walked around the outside of the car, aiming for the driver's side and the chance that the car was registered in his name.

In the backseat, a wadded jacket. In the cargo area, boxes of some kind of flyer, a roadside emergency kit, a blanket, several paperback travel guides to locations in Eastern Europe and Asia, three battered Frisbee golf disks, baseball hats, and a gallon jug of water.

With her fingers tucked into the napkin, she opened the front door and dropped onto the seat and began to search for the car registration. There was a slip of old CDs above the visor, many of their labels too worn to be read. The door compartments appeared to be makeshift trash bins. The glove box was a tangle of receipts, maps, and spare fuses. Where on earth was the registration?

She flipped down the passenger visor, and a small stack of glossy photos rained down on her. Pictures of her—walking onto the high school campus from the parking lot; speaking quietly to Lance at a restaurant; driving into her apartment complex. There were other pictures of Lance, mostly with her, all in public places. There were pictures of other men she didn't know.

She clutched the pictures so tightly that their edges met and formed a tube. Then she flattened them out and bent low across the seats to ensure she'd found every last snapshot that fell. The last thing she needed was for authorities to find this car and these photographs in it. She shoved them into the rear pocket of her jeans.

No registration papers probably meant whoever owned this car—or didn't—wasn't so up-and-up about the law himself. She turned her attention to the backpack and reached out to lift it into her lap. The poppy stopped her.

It was an orange poppy on a white background, a colored image with minimalistic lines filling a circle about three inches in diameter, mounted on a button pin. It was the same as the flower on the worry stone that Serena had found in the abandoned house, only this one was encircled by red letters that spelled Fire Followers. And it was pinned to the top of the backpack.

She pondered this coincidence for just a few seconds. Already, she had too many dots that needed connecting, and this one seemed like the least important. She resumed her search for some kind of ID and closed her fist around the top strap of the backpack.

The door beside her opened. It was a forceful, violent jerk followed by yelling, loud demands that Serena couldn't sort out right away. Her heart was knocking in her ears and her startled yelp seemed louder than the man blocking the way out.

". . . you're doing!" he shouted. The man—tall, tanned, with bold Hawaiian features—grabbed hold of her upper arm and began to tug her out of the car.

She moved the other way, twisted out of his grip, scrambled over the emergency brake between the bucket seats, and reached for the passenger door. Her boot lace caught on the seat belt latch. He threw himself onto the driver's seat, pinning her ankle between the console and his thick body. Serena kicked. At the same time, her fingers found the handle and pulled. The door winged open. The man grabbed her hair and yanked. She cried out, face pressed against the headrest, ankle bent behind her at a terrible angle, her twisted knee sending stabbing pains around her thigh. The backpack was a pillow she clutched with one hand while she scratched at his grip on her hair with the other. The blades of her nails drew blood.

He released her. He recoiled just enough to free her foot. She pushed off and went out the door, falling atop the heels of her hands and the backpack.

While he shouted, she was already scrambling away. He wouldn't let her go so easily. She was sure of that much. Serena fled, keeping hold of Chris's backpack, her body not fully balanced over her feet. A scrawny branch, brittled by fire and autumn, reached out and caught her cheek as she stumbled by.

She had nothing on his size. Probably nothing on his speed. And certainly nothing on his physical strength. So she put all her chances into one fragile basket and hoped that she knew the area better than he did.

EIGHTEEN

SERENA HAD NOT HEARD ANY SIGN OF PURSUIT FOR nearly ten minutes. Rather than take a direct line to the abandoned house, which he might know about, she had chosen a path that resembled a lopsided star, hand-drawn by a child without lifting the pencil from the paper. She believed she lost him at the star's third tip, which traversed a small canyon. The gap wasn't impassable, but the descent was tricky for those unfamiliar with the way.

From the bottom of the steep grade she watched him try to find a surefooted way down. While he was preoccupied, she made her way in bursts of short moves two hundred yards downwind, where she hid behind a boulder. When the matter of his own safety commanded all of his concentration, she made her way back up, one eye on him until she could no longer see his progress.

At the top of the ridge she broke into a run, Chris's pack smacking the small of her spine with every loping step. There was something knobby in the compartment that poked her, but the real pain came to her feet. Her sturdy boots weren't made for this kind of activity, and blisters bloomed in the soft pads under each of her big toes.

Running on the outsides of her feet, she veered slightly off course and headed back toward her car. She only needed a few seconds of lead time to drop into her seat and lock the doors, then drive away. The man who pursued her was at least five minutes behind. At least.

She broke onto the narrow road and came up short. Dropping her hands onto her knees, she gasped for air and willed her mind to overrule the blisters' complaints. They were instantly overcome by a worse reality: her car was gone.

Chris's backpack pressed her sweaty shirt into her back.

His car was still there, as was another one parked directly behind it, this one an old-model Toyota sedan the color of champagne. This might have been the vehicle the big Islander had brought with him, though Serena should have noticed it creeping up so close.

Where was her car? Instead of an answer, the memory of leaving her keys in the ignition came like a smack on the forehead.

If they could take her car, well, she would take one of theirs.

She would have, but both were locked, perhaps anticipating she'd think of this option. Running her fingers under the frames of the cars yielded a lot of black soot, but no spare keys.

Serena might have been able to ignore the pain in her feet if she'd only kept running. But now every step was an agony. She'd only been at this for forty-five minutes, maybe an hour, and she had to get out of this spot. Evading her attacker would be pointless if she was here when he returned.

She turned her sore feet toward the abandoned house and headed there directly this time, hoping no one was there, hoping no one would show up if she had to shelter there for the night. But with no car and no phone, she didn't dare brave the hike back to the Big Tujunga Road until after that bubbly Toyota and rusty Kia were gone. It would be too easy for them to see and overtake her on the road, where there was virtually no brush to hide her. She wondered if Lance would think to look for her here.

He had a head for details. He'd remember what had happened

to her here yesterday. He'd quickly realize she'd left her phone behind.

The walk took all her concentration. Mind over blisters. Like walking on a cheese grater. But she had to spare some of her attention for sounds of pursuit. The divided effort exhausted her. That man was no friend of hers—but was he a friend of Brock, or of Chris, or of the man who had killed him?

Was Chris her friend, though they didn't know each other? Why else would he have helped her, and at such a high price? In her memory, the stranger stood before her and said her name, *"Serena Diaz,"* and then the gunshot, and then the fading brown eyes.

The word *friend* took on new and difficult meanings that preoccupied her for the rest of her limping walk.

Phil Lancet turned into his driveway and slipped into the far left slot of his four-car garage, grabbed the drink carrier crammed with coffees and pastries off his passenger seat, and made his way into the cavernous house.

"Serena!"

No answer. His kitchen was empty. He leaned his head out into the foyer and directed his voice down the hall that led to the master bedroom.

"Are you starving?"

He wondered which bedroom she'd chosen to sleep in. His, he gambled, returning to the kitchen and setting the takeout on the island. If he was right, he'd join her. If wrong, he'd drag her out of bed boot-camp style and subject her to all the grotesque developments of the morning. Then, when she was reduced to a blithering mess, he'd comfort her with charms and promises until she realized that he was, truly, her savior. Win-win.

Phil shucked his jacket and saw the note on the counter.

Back soon. No worries.

He briefly wondered if the nail-gnawing John Roman, who liked guarantees and hated risk, had lured her away to kill her himself. Annoying.

Phil withdrew his phone from his pants pocket and dialed Serena's number. The bowl of squash on his kitchen counter rang. He fetched the phone, pulled up her call log, and saw that she had called Brock.

Well, if she kept that up he could drop the whole attorney charade. He wouldn't even have to pretend to be a *bad* attorney because Serena would seal her coffin all by herself.

Her self-starter behavior was beginning to annoy him. But this was what he'd signed up for, wasn't it? A new challenge? A change of pace? Someone to save him from the boredom of ruining lives that were already pretty much ruined?

After Brock's unwitting suggestion, when Phil decided Serena Diaz would be a deserving but desirable target, he inserted himself into her life via a school district board meeting. He found her in a fight with a board member thirty years her senior, during which she upended a bucket of disturbing statistics about the present state of education and the need to revolutionize local and national models all over the microphone without consulting a single note.

"I have never met a stupid child," she remarked. "I've only met children who have been chewed up and spit out by the system and told so often that they are stupid that they have come to believe it."

A different kind of trash, Phil agreed.

"I became a teacher to help put an end to our failure," she announced. "I might have to start by playing the rules of this particular game, but don't misunderstand me: by the time I've been in this career as long as you have, sir, I hope to be teaching in a world I've helped to change."

Phil waited until she had been marginalized at the back of the room under a flickering fluorescent light, sent there by cynical eyes that had placed a figurative dunce cap on her head.

"So you think we should turn children out into the jungle to be educated à la Mowgli?" Phil said to her. He offered a small cup of water while he sipped from his own.

"*Some* children," she said warily, taking the cup. "But most kids would be better off in an educational system that wasn't set up like a factory production line. I teach biology. I favor a model that's a little more organic. An English garden instead of a field of Astroturf."

"They're just scared." He nodded at the room in general, allying himself with her viewpoint.

"I hoped for more support," she said.

"You can't eat an elephant in just one meal," he said sympathetically, and her smile was quick.

"I know. I have a lifetime to change the world, right? I just didn't want to do it single-handedly."

"Oh, a lot of people agree with you. They just don't come to these meetings anymore."

She looked surprised. "This is exactly where they should be."

"How long have you been a teacher?"

"I just finished my first year."

He shrugged as if she'd figure all this out on her own soon enough. It had the desired effect of embarrassing her but not shutting her down. Her cheeks flushed.

"And you?" she asked.

Phil took a sip of water, then shook his head. "I haven't been inside a classroom since the day I passed the bar. Do some work for the CTA, so I try to drop in from time to time."

"Ah. A union lawyer. I suppose I should make friends with someone like you." There was a tease in her voice that was part self-deprecating and part flirtatious. "You might come in handy next time I get . . . animated."

He held out his hand, "Lance Liebowitz."

She took it. "Serena Diaz."

He lifted his cup and held on to her fingers. She didn't pull away. "May I offer you something a little stronger?"

She lifted one brow. "If it's black and contains caffeine."

She was a good girl. So good.

"I won't even charge you for my time," he said.

So good she didn't catch the innuendo. Didn't even blush as he held out his arm to suggest that she should go first out the door. He followed her, admiring the view.

Now Serena Diaz had swum alone from shore into an undertow of trouble. He would dive into the roiling seas after her, while a crowd gathered on the beaches of her life, calling for a drowning. It was entirely possible Serena would take him below the surface with her.

This was what John Roman feared: the public exposure of their enterprise.

The very same thrilling risk that Phil craved.

Because Roman was right. Phil was insatiable, and ordinary success, as defined by his tedious line of work, no longer satisfied.

The contents of Chris's backpack didn't shed any new light on his true name. She'd spread them out in a closet under the sawdust-strewn pine staircase, where she could both hide and make a quick exit out the doorless front entry should anyone arrive via the driveway at the back.

An electronic tablet with a dead battery.

A smashed peanut butter Cliff bar.

A pair of small and expensive-looking binoculars.

A wrinkled but still sterile Band-Aid, which she immediately applied to the largest of her blisters, then wished she hadn't, because putting her shoe back on was a punishment.

A pair of mirrored aviator sunglasses.

Something that looked like a lock-pick set nestled in a zippered pocket, loose change, a gift card to a fast-food restaurant, and a few random paper clips.

The poppy button pin on the top of the backpack pricked her thumb when she yanked the sack open, searching for a name penned into the inside lining, a note addressed to him, a library card.

She even looked at the back of the button pin to see if his name had been written on it, chiding herself as she did it. This didn't belong to some schoolboy whose mother had marked his every possession. But she couldn't help herself. Chris and Brock were connected, and by something other than her. She would find this thing if she looked hard enough.

There was something taped to the back of the pin. Ruffled orange poppy and red fire followers on the front, itty-bitty plastic zip bag on the back—the kind that sometimes held spare buttons and mending threads for new sweaters. Inside was a tiny capsule about the size of a grain of rice.

She stepped out from under the stairwell where the light was better. It seemed the device was a chip of some kind. The electronic pieces were visible through the skin, just three little silver- pronged thingys that reminded her of old circuit boards that her brother used to tinker with. A data device? What came to mind was a trip to the vet with her mother, years ago, during which the doctor had shot a similar device into the fleshy skin of their dog's neck, because he had a habit of digging under their fence and inviting neighborhood pooches on wild escapades.

Her sister, Natalie, had been opposed to chipping the dog, saying, "Wouldn't it be nice to be able to deny he's ours next time?"

Even with her limited knowledge, Serena knew that she needed a special device to interpret the chip. Her vet used a type of handheld scanner that could read the data. But it was only a wild guess that this was the same thing. Where on earth would she find something like that? And what if it wasn't a data device, but something more high tech, like a tracker?

One end of the piece had a colored tip on it, a reddish-purple color. Serena untaped the bag from the back of the pin and opened it, tipping the chip out into the surface of her palm.

The moment it hit her skin the thing burrowed into the pad of her thumb, purple end first, like a parasite. Serena screamed and tried to brush it off, then shake it, a frantic defensive dance. But it had entered her hand the way a dolphin cuts through salt water. There would be no grabbing that beast by the tail and hauling it out.

She heard the metal button pin glance off the wood floor somewhere with a ping. Dizziness filled her head and nausea coated her empty stomach. She reached out to brace herself on the stairway railing, forgetting that it had none.

But there it was: a glossy banister rail with a common walnut finish, framing carpeted stairs that rose to a loft filled with light and laughter.

There were people in the house. She startled and swung around to take shelter in the shadows of the alcove, when the cabinet door opened from the inside and banged into her face. Heat immediately radiated from her nose, the warmth of blood vessels under her eyes splitting open and forcing hot tears into their ducts. The cupboard was also glossy. Also walnut stained.

A hand reached out from the closet and grabbed hers, pulling her inside.

Serena thought of Alice in Wonderland falling into that rabbit hole, dark and dizzy, and wondered how the girl had done it without being injured. But maybe that wasn't the real reason she thought of Alice, who was also misunderstood and falsely accused of crimes.

She crashed down onto her backside and the side of her head bumped one of the stairway risers. The space was utterly black. A large hand completely encircled her upper arm.

"Hi, Serena."

NINETEEN

KALEO HAD LOST HER, AND THE ONLY EXPLANATION could be that she knew this area much better than the average bear.

It took him too long to get out of that ravine. He was not a murderous man when he went into it, but he emerged transformed and ready to shoot something through the heart. Preferably a pretty coal-haired sprite.

This desire was tempered slightly when he stumbled back onto the path where Christopher's car was parked. He noted the light tracks in the dry ground where the teacher had pulled out into a three-point turn. He saw, around a slight bend in the road, the tan-colored hood of his Toyota sedan. The silence of the scene struck him as odd, but he wasn't immediately sure why.

Then he knew: Will wasn't here. He'd stayed in the car as Kaleo leaped out. The two had bickered with their eyes, Will unspeakably furious that Kaleo had chosen this woman over Amber. Serena had been visible in the driver's seat of Christopher's car, and he feared she'd quickly find the keys their friend had probably left tucked under the floor mat. All three of them left their keys under the floor mats, because it was the nature of this particular volunteer work that any one of them might have to dart off in any available vehicle. The agreement they'd made together more than ten years ago, to never begrudge each other the use of their wheels, had become a way of life that they all took for granted.

On his return Kaleo read his first glance of the scene like this: Will had finally hauled his butt out of the car to help make chase. Serena had outwitted them both and returned. Then she had disabled their cars and driven off in hers.

But that was something Kaleo would have done. If this woman also knew enough about mechanics to prevent a car from starting, he just might go off the deep end. And in all truth, unless Will was injured, he'd have made it back here before Kaleo. He was the better outdoorsman, the better navigator.

"Will!" he shouted.

Kaleo approached Christopher's car to see how much damage she had done. None visible from the outside. The doors were locked. He quickly passed the Kia and aimed for the Toyota, having the fleeting thought that Will had been beaten over the head with a tire iron behind the trunk. If Serena Diaz, in cahoots with Phil Lancet, could shoot Christopher through the heart, what else was she capable of?

He found no evidence of Will's behavior until he noticed a slip of paper tucked under the wiper blade. Kaleo pulled it out and read Will's precise block lettering, the unhurried, consistent print of a man who lived by good methodology.

I've got her car. If ours are still here, so is she.

Brilliant. Really. In the space of two sentences Kaleo was reminded of all the reasons why their team had stuck together, enduring each other's quirks, for so long.

Kaleo laughed and ran his hand through his hair. Will would probably criticize him later for having taken the Toyota keys with him when he went after the teacher. He hadn't meant to, but Will was the one who thought of those things. Kaleo patted the pocket of his jeans to make sure he hadn't lost them.

When he found her, he'd spare her life. And Serena Diaz would have Will to thank for that.

The closet under the stairs should have been oppressive, hot, and hemmed in by threat. But the first thing Serena noticed after the shock passed and the throbbing in her nose faded to a gentle pulsing was that the grip on her arm was protective.

The breath on the side of her face was sweet.

The laughter from upstairs rained down from above through the floorboards and over her head like a warm shower at the end of a hard day.

The cupboard wasn't as dark as she'd originally thought.

"What are you doing in here?" the man next to her whispered.

A funny question.

"You pulled me in." She whispered too, because maybe he knew something that she didn't.

"But this is where you wanted to be."

Not a straightforward beginning.

"Who are you?"

"I'm a what," he said. "Not a who."

"You mean a figment of my imagination."

"More and less," he said in her father's voice. Then he pushed the cupboard door open with his foot, which was first to enter the light. He scrambled out, leading with flip-flops that she'd last seen tangled in the undergrowth of toyon bushes down the hill, then bent down and extended a hand to her. A knot in the wood snagged his yellow knit hat and almost pulled it off, but he separated the two and sat the hat squarely on his head once again.

She allowed him to take her hand. His thumb applied firm pressure to the spot where the chip had buried itself, but there was no pain. This time the sensation of his touch felt less human and more like the weight of a comforting blanket. Still protective.

The room was finished and sawdust free. Warm blue paint covered the walls. Cheerful sunlight cut through clean windows and gauzy curtains. Thick carpeting yielded to the stiff soles of her boots. New furniture was arranged as if for a big family that enjoyed talking together over watching TV. In fact, there was no TV that she could see. Maybe it was tucked away in that broad cabinet on the wall opposite the stairs.

A wide door that was a large frosted glass panel framed by the same walnut wood of the banister replaced the windy gap that had been there a moment ago. It had matching sidelights, as if to insist this old house would never be completely dark. Even at night the porch lights would shine in.

Serena couldn't see the kitchen from where she stood, but she imagined spotless floors, shiny appliances. Skylights.

"I like skylights," he said behind her. And if he could read her mind, that was no less odd than a house that could go from condemned to renovated in a blink.

"What's your name?" she asked him.

"Chris," he said. And what could she say to that? Of course his name was Chris. Everything here was rooted in her own mind.

"Not everything," he said, winking.

She wondered if the device that had penetrated her palm contained a drug.

"Aren't you dead?"

"How could I be dead? I'm not a who, remember?" He grinned at her and inclined his head toward the stairs.

Happy voices of young women continued to tumble down, and the sound was full of everything that the past twenty-four hours of Serena's life had lacked: carefree joy. Serena moved toward the amazing noise, imagining dozens of women crammed into the loft like a sorority party.

The loft was decked out like an expensive bed-and-breakfast, with soft curtains and downy bedspreads and thick area rugs and, yes, skylights. The place was cluttered with books and candles and coffee cups and the scent of sun-dried linen. No five-gallon buckets full of stench anywhere in the room.

There were only four of them, making all that noise. Three women sat on the floor in front of one of the windows, no longer warped by fire but smooth like the glossy cover of new textbooks. They bent over something that Serena couldn't see. Whatever it was gave them fits of laughter.

The fourth lay on her stomach up on her bed, drawing in a sketchbook, her figures dancing off the page—rising off the surface, figures that seemed animated by the girls' magical joy, dancing together across the bedspread in a goofy ballroom spin, then falling off. A young man with spiked hair and coattails. A woman in a pretty black dress and heavy boots. A doe-eyed girl in pigtails who blinked every time someone guffawed.

Their plunge off the edge of the bed put the foursome into another fit of giggles. Serena stared at the scene, disbelieving.

The artist looked toward Serena, but if she'd seen Serena and Chris ascending, she didn't object. Serena gasped in recognition of the young woman: this was a girl from the first class she had taught as a high school teacher, a human health unit for freshmen. Becca was the girl's name, and she left school before her sophomore year. Becca was a soft-spoken blond with fair skin that was always a little burned on the cheeks, legs long and slender like stilts, and a torso shaped more like a cell phone than an hourglass. But so gentle, such a lovely person.

Serena's gasp was also from shock: Becca's face was scarred as if a bear had dragged its horrible claws across her nose and mouth from hairline to jawline. The damage itself was grotesque, not a new injury but an old one, as healed as it would ever get. Uneven white and pink welts left crude tracks where the skin had tried to repair itself without the aid of early intervention.

But the girl was smiling, laughing hard, enjoying the sight of her drawings falling off the bed so much that she squinted and threw her head back. Becca held her black pen suspended over the paper, as if she had much, much more to draw when her body stopped shaking.

"What is this?" she asked Chris.

"They are not whats, but whos," he said. "Four young women."

"I can see that."

"You know them."

"I know her, Becca." Serena looked at the others and didn't recognize them at first, but a closer look tapped her memory. The one closest to the window might be the same woman—not a woman yet, but still a girl—who had stood behind the bubbled glass the day before. The one who might have placed the little poppy disk in the windowpane.

Next to her was a woman holding on to childhood in the form of a black-haired baby doll in a frilly pink dress. A woman clearly older than the other three, Serena's age. Chris was right: Serena knew this one too. She had no doubts about who the nameless woman was, tall and elegant with silky smooth brown limbs like a manzanita's. The child who was only six years old the last time Serena had seen her was aged beyond her years and also frozen in time. But today, she smiled.

These women also had devastating scars across their stunning faces. Both were also tragic but made beautiful by joy.

The fourth face was turned away from Serena, but she could see the burn scars exposed by the girl's halter top. Boiling skin rippled the width of her shoulders and down the backs of her arms.

Serena wanted to cry but couldn't. There was just too much happiness in the room, joy like wide push brooms able to sweep grief to the dim corners. The women laughed like children, far too long, far too loud, over something that couldn't possibly be funny anymore, whatever it was. Becca clutched her stomach and rolled off her back onto her side, giggling so hard that tears squeezed out of the corners of her eyes. The silhouette dancers that had fallen off the bed ran over to the little circle to see what was so funny. They hopped up on the molten-lava shoulder and leaned in. The boy with spiky hair fell off, tumbling headlong into the cause of everything, and the doe-eyed pigtail girl started to laugh too.

"This isn't what it was last time I was here," Serena said.

"No place ever is."

"I mean, this isn't real."

"A possibility is as real as anything that you can touch," Chris said. He nodded at the foursome. "This is what's possible—if you choose it."

"Choose what?" Her eyes darted to the doll, which looked fresh out of the box and not two decades old. "This is *im*possible. This is some kind of hallucination caused by that thing."

Serena looked down at her hand and balled it into a fist. With her fingernails she probed the spot where the rice-sized device had burrowed into her skin. It wasn't there. There was no evidence of it at all, not even a tiny knob or tender bruise.

She turned to look Chris in the eye, to demand some answers for all the questions of this scene, even if he was a by-product of her stress. She thrust her balled fist out toward him and realized that he was standing much closer to her than she realized. He seized her wrist and she took a sharp breath. Her strong nails bit into the fleshy pad of her palm and she felt the sting of skin splitting. A bubble of blood appeared on the surface. With his other hand Chris tried to pry her fingers open. Involuntarily, she resisted.

She blinked, and the world changed.

It wasn't Chris who had her by the arm, but that man she had evaded in the ravine. She flinched, and all the laughter vanished as if she'd slammed a door on it. Everything went away: the comfort, the natural daylight, the beds, the books, the scent of fresh laundry. She stood in sawdust at the top of unfinished pine stairs, her only way out blockaded by a man huffing anger out of his nostrils. Dust coated his clothing and powdered the sweat at his hairline.

He would break her fingers if she didn't open her hand, she thought. She allowed them to flower open.

The tiny device with the purplish-red tip sat in the nest of her hand.

He pinched it out.

"First you take his life, then you take his things," he accused. The hard lines of his face and the jolt of moving between experiences that she didn't understand stole her voice.

He shifted his grip to her upper arm and yanked her back down the stairs and through the haphazard renovations of the burned-out house.

TWENTY

WILLIAM AND KALEO WEREN'T AT THE MISSION
Acres football field when Amber arrived, and since waiting alone
seemed worse than going alone, she went in by herself. Her legs
felt disconnected from her mind as she approached the police
officer who stood at the barricade, a simple strip of yellow tape
stretched across the wide blacktop slope where the parking lot
rose to the fenced-in hilltop field. The officer was a woman in
uniform. She wore a dark jacket, arms crossed, eyes scanning the
area, alighting on Amber because she was headed toward the yellow tape rather than away from it. Amber's mind ran through the
exchange she hoped for:

"*I'm sorry, but you'll have to come back another time.*"

"*That's my brother in there—the dead man is my brother.*"

"*Dead? No one's dead. But since a death was reported, we do have
to file a complete report . . .*"

And the officer would point to the end of the parking lot where
Christopher, in his senseless outfit, was wringing his knit hat and
being interviewed by a detective in a trench coat and admitting
what a stupid idea the whole thing had been.

Sometimes he acted like he was still in college. It was the only
fault Amber had ever found with his choice to bring William and
Kaleo aboard as cofounders of Fire Followers. College buddies

were prone to forgetting they'd left those years behind them. But the occasional flare-ups of immature boyishness were nothing compared to their devotion to the cause. She loved them all like brothers.

William more.

Her anger with them now was really about the fact that they weren't here. They'd left her alone.

"The field's off-limits," the female officer said, stepping out from the tape. Someone carrying a boxy black kit stepped through the opening the woman guarded. The person's fingers were unnaturally white. Deathly white. Covered in latex. Amber couldn't take her eyes off the gloves. She couldn't look into the police officer's face. She couldn't allow anything about this abstract and terrible moment to become concrete, tangible.

"My brother," she said, and the rest caught in her throat. But her focus followed the latex gloves.

"I'm going to have to ask you to leave."

"He's my brother," Amber whispered, looking up at the fence, at the field, at the gloves, at the box knocking against the man's thigh as he moved toward the stands. "You don't understand."

The officer put a firm but comforting hand on Amber's arm. Did she look so upset?

"Who's your brother?"

It was the touch that caused Amber to come undone, that gesture so fundamentally human that it didn't matter if these two women didn't even know each other's names.

Words bubbled out of Amber's heart. "He's so strong. He came for me. He was wearing a Bruins sweatshirt and he and William got four of us out. It was blue and yellow. He likes yellow. The hat was a joke, see? He can't be dead. You're supposed to tell me this is just a prank." Amber looked at the woman finally as if eye contact might force her to tell the truth. "We have so much work to do," Amber said, and she felt her fantasies cracking under the weight of the woman's compassionate expression.

The police officer turned her cheek to the radio at her shoulder and requested someone with *Detective* attached to the name.

Amber started to cry. "He's late for our work. Christopher's never late for work. The girls are counting on us. He always says they could die if we're late for work. I almost died, but he wasn't late. We can't be late."

Serena regretted not putting up more of a fight by the time the broad-shouldered Islander deposited her in his lair. It belonged to a serial killer—this was the only way to explain the house, which might have been a typical Santa Monica post–World War II bungalow if not for the creepy stalker photographs tacked up over every inch of available wall space. It would also explain why he didn't seem to care how much she studied his face, why he hadn't bothered to blindfold her before bringing her here.

It would explain the girl in the window at the abandoned house, and the reason why the guard there tried to kidnap her, and Chris's interest in the forgotten place. They were misogynists bent on ridding the world of women, one at a time.

Were those four women she had seen in her hallucination victims these men had killed there?

But this theory flew in the face of a man who would die saving her life. And it didn't explain why this man seemed to know Chris but would sooner kill her than tell her what was going on.

Serena thought Chris might have disapproved of this guy's threatening demeanor. Her mind formed a mental picture of the men arguing there, in the nook that was the tiny kitchen, with Chris casting protective glances out toward her. For some reason this held her fear of death at arm's length. She liked the idea that Chris was shielding her, but her mind scoffed. He was a what, not a who anymore.

Serena sat at a makeshift desk, a small table just the right size for four people in a breakfast nook. But this one sat to the side of the living room, where no woman with any sense of order would have put it. Her wrist was cuffed to the table's leg. Five or six snuffed cigarette butts filled a dirty ashtray in the center, next to a stack of mail. The envelope on top was addressed to a William Brenner.

"What's your name?" she asked.

He was standing at the sink, filling a glass with tap water. Undrinkable Los Angeles tap water. "Kaleo," he said. The silent drive out of the Angeles National Forest seemed to have defused his temper slightly. He brought the cup to the table and set it in front of her, then seemed to notice her eyes on the mail. He sighed, picked up the stack, flipped through it, then pulled out an envelope and showed her a credit card offer for one Kaleo Iona. "Want to know my credit score?" he asked.

Serena averted her eyes. Kaleo put the stack of mail on the wide windowsill behind him. He sat opposite her and placed both hands flat on the dull wood of the table. Sunlight caught the face of his cheap watch.

"You think I'm going to kill you," Kaleo said. He sounded apologetic. Was this part of his routine?

Serena couldn't stop her eyes from darting to the pictures on the walls.

"I don't kill people," he said.

"Like you don't kidnap them."

"You got into my car all by yourself."

Serena took a long breath. "Then what is it you do?" she asked.

"We rescue women from pimps and traffickers like Phil Lancet."

She'd never heard of Phil Lancet. Kaleo's tone raised images of

159

a fat middle-aged man dripping in gold chains and a half-buttoned silk shirt.

They rescued women?

Kaleo cleared his throat. "My friend is dead. My friend Christopher. I want you to tell me how it happened. Please."

His name *was* Chris—Christopher. Kaleo was his friend, and it was their work to save women, and everything would be okay. Somehow. No matter how bad this misunderstanding got. Because Christopher wouldn't have stepped between Serena and a bullet if he didn't think her life was worth saving. Christopher wouldn't have done it. Not the man whose name brought to mind the patron saint of travelers and also the best friend of a stuffed-with-fluff bear. A holy man and a gentle child. Legendary, fictional—perhaps. But to Serena, Christopher was as real a hero as they come. And no longer a stranger.

"Tell me everything about him," she said.

She opened her eyes. Kaleo was watching her, glaring.

"What were you doing up off the Big Tujunga yesterday?"

Christopher hadn't asked her that. She felt defensive. "It's a public road."

"You're a teacher. You should have been in school."

Of course he knew who she was, after the story that broke yesterday. Even Lance had said her picture was everywhere. And there was the video she had made last night. Still, she felt violated and wondered if this was how it was going to be for her for the rest of her life, with people who didn't even know her having hateful opinions of her.

"If you know who I am, you also know why I wasn't at school yesterday."

"I guess it was a bad day for you, all in all," Kaleo said. He leaned in. "But I want to know why you were in Angeles National Forest, on that particular road at that particular time."

"I want to know the same thing about Christopher."

"But he's not here for us to ask, is he?"

The humanitarian voice of Serena's father and the legally informed voice of Lance collided in her head then. The truth is the only thing that ever got anyone out of trouble, her father always said. The urge to tell Kaleo everything, including her belief that he and Christopher were working with Brock, was strong. Was it so bad to want to explain things? But Lance's voice reminded her that, while she should never perjure herself, it was sometimes wisest not to say anything at all. What if Kaleo, holding her truth in his hands, might twist it beyond recognition?

"It's a place I often go. Into the Station Fire burn scar."

"With Phil Lancet?"

That name again. This time it made her think—unwillingly—of Lance.

"Who's that?"

Kaleo stared at her as if silence could give her facts.

"I go with students," she continued, "or I go alone. I have a couple of friends who don't mind tagging along with me from time to time."

"To do what?"

"I'm documenting the recovery of the area. I have pictures. I can show you online if you want to see."

"I'm not really interested in a slide show." He took a drink from her untouched glass. "I think you lured Christopher up there and killed him, then moved his body to the high school."

The accusation was so startling that for a moment she couldn't speak. Then she managed, "Why would I do that?"

"Because you work for Phil and Roman."

"Who?"

"They must have found out that he was on to their new delivery, and they sent you to get him off their scent. Christopher got an anonymous tip from someone yesterday morning, telling him that an exchange was going to go down somewhere off the Big Tujunga Road. Even if you didn't make the call, you could still be the one to reel him in."

"What? Christopher followed *me*. You guys seem to know how to do that." She nodded at all the photos. "I didn't even know he was there until he walked out of the oak."

"And why did he do that?"

"Because another man there was about to shoot me!"

"Someone else met you there to loan you some muscle, in case Christopher got out of hand."

"No. There was someone at the house. They surprised me! Several people."

"Who were they?"

"I honestly don't know."

"I think you do, but let's play: they're men who pull little girls out of their pathetic, miserable homes and sell them into the worst kind of life you could ever imagine in one of the fastest-growing industries in the world. They work for Phil Lancet, a trafficker who works for the pimp John Roman, who is a grease-coated snake."

"I'm telling you, I don't know those names."

"Yesterday there was a point of sale to take place in the forest. We didn't know where. Christopher went to scope out vehicles on our watch list. Instead, he ran into you."

"Why would he be interested in me?"

Kaleo slammed his palm on the table and Serena flinched. Then he rose and stalked across the straw mats to a particular photo taped to a whiteboard. He snatched it off and brought it back to her.

The photo he put in front of her was a copy of one she had taken from Christopher's car. She stood next to Lance Liebowitz outside a restaurant in Malibu, where they waited for a table. He was inclining his ear toward her. Serena couldn't remember what they were talking about. Holding the picture closer to the window's daylight, she realized she was studying the background for a sign of Brock, or for some clue as to why and how he'd engineered the events of the last two days.

Kaleo took the snapshot back and pinned it down with his forefinger. The pad of his fingertip covered Lance's face.

"Phil Lancet," he said.

"No, that's Lance Liebowitz."

"Don't lie to me."

"I'm not. He's an attorney for Strauss & Liebowitz in West Hollywood. Look him up."

"I don't have to look him up. He's not an attorney and he has no reason to be involved with a high school teacher like you unless he's getting something out of it. And here's what I think he gets: a whole student body full of vulnerable young women for his pickings. Girls who trust their nice teacher, who's really a hungry wolf about to eat their sweet little red riding hoods. You get a cash bonus on the side to supplement your pathetic income, and you think, why not take a few boy toys of my own while I'm at it? Can't let Phil have all the fun, now, can you?"

"That's sick." Her heart was clogging her throat.

"Is that what you do for your parents? Take women to a place that looks safe but's really a slaughterhouse? Make it a family operation?"

Serena's voice was brittle. "The Safe Place is a legitimate program. They've been around for thirty years."

"You shouldn't have got greedy. Here's what's going to happen to you: someone found out about your little moonlighting venture—"

"Brock is lying."

"Brock?" Kaleo leaned back to chew on the name as if it was

new to him. And of course it was. Only people on the inside of the case would know the minor's name. Except—

"The name plastered across Christopher's chest?" Kaleo said. "Was that you warning other boys not to mess with you?"

"There are no others. There's not even Brock. Brock Anderson."

"Why would he do this?"

"He earned a bad grade. This is his idea of getting revenge."

Kaleo scoffed. "Now that you're in the spotlight you're a liability to Phil, which makes you a roach in Phil's kitchen. If he doesn't squash you, I will."

Serena was dizzy with false accusations. She couldn't defend herself against something she couldn't understand. "Who is Phil?"

"Let's try this again," Kaleo said. "I think you killed Christopher and set him up for Phil and Roman and all their buddies and all your victims to see. Don't mess with the teacher, she's still willing to do the dirty work, taking out the good guys, and if that's not enough she can turn on the bad ones too."

Serena covered her eyes with her uncuffed hand.

"Then you should take me to the police," she said. "If you think I killed him."

"You'll get to the police eventually."

"Take me now." At least in a cell she'd be safe from crazies like Kaleo, and she'd have access to Lance. He'd be so upset with her for leaving the house. "I want to go now. Please."

"The cops and the media are a little preoccupied with your new bad-girl side, which is just what Phil and Roman need: a scapegoat to steal the show for even a few days while they burn all bridges connecting them to you and slip off the grid again. I can't afford to lose them. Do you understand me? We lost Christopher today, which makes me a desperate man. Who knows what I'll do? So give them to me now and I might think about turning you loose down a dark alley where you have a chance of slipping away."

Serena jerked hard on the handcuff chain and yelled her frustration. "I can't give you something I don't have! I don't know a Phil Lancet. I don't know anyone named Roman. I didn't hurt Christopher! I walked into a bad situation blind and he came out of nowhere. I didn't recognize him, I didn't know what was going on. But he was just *there* and he got me out. He didn't have to, you know. He could have stayed hidden. That shouldn't have even cost him a guilty conscience—what am I to him? But he chose to help me. It should have been me who died but it wasn't, and I'm so sorry."

Kaleo kicked the wall. Put a hole in the Sheetrock with his boot.

"Kaleo, stop." The new voice drew everyone's attention to the door. A young woman stood there, pale and washed out in a drab gray T-shirt and sweats that didn't hide her few extra pounds. Her hair had been pulled back from her face hastily, so that its thick waves created a bumpy path to the ponytail in back. In a glance Serena saw the grief in her brown eyes.

These were Christopher's eyes exactly. And something else, a detail that made Serena's heart trip over itself.

"Leave her alone," the woman said, again to Kaleo.

Another man entered behind her, tall and slight and covered in strawberry hair. Fatigue dragged down his posture and his eyes, framed in thick red-rimmed glasses.

Kaleo thrust a finger at the middle of Serena's forehead. "She killed Christopher."

"I haven't killed anyone!"

"You're working for them," Kaleo persisted. He looked at the man and woman. "She's working for Lancet. I have pictures. She has connections. Amber . . . she's working for *Roman*."

Serena shook her head, felt Amber's sad eyes on her.

"Christopher would have saved her anyway. You know that, Kaleo."

"Not *her*," Kaleo said. "Not if he knew about her connection to Roman—"

"He knew it was possible, didn't he?" Amber asked, glancing at the redhead. "William filled me in. Listen to what she's saying, Kaleo. She's describing him just right. She's describing exactly what Christopher does. Has Christopher ever asked for the résumé of any woman he's tried to help?"

Kaleo looked out the window.

"So what are you doing? You abandoned me for this stupid inquisition? Do you think that's what Christopher would have done?" She turned on the redhead. "He would have made sure no one had to be alone when her life came undone."

Silence came over the room for a brief moment before Amber continued, "Why does she seem to know him better than you two do?"

Neither man answered. And the detail Serena had been trying to pinpoint popped into her mind in full color.

Amber was the fourth woman in the Station Fire house, laughing with the other girls while drawings danced on her shoulders. She was the one bearing the scars of painful burns all the way across her back.

"Then take those cuffs off," Amber said. "Things like that make us worse than the real criminals."

TWENTY-ONE

AMBER SPLASHED WATER ON HER FACE AND STARED into the bathroom mirror, water dripping from her jaw onto the sweatshirt. Behind her Serena sat on the edge of the bathtub, staring out the tiny window, which was too small for an escape. Kaleo was parked on the outside of the door in the hall, the compromise he had agreed to after Amber insisted on the chance to talk with her privately. Kaleo might have had training as a police officer, but he had zero experience as a woman.

Of course Serena didn't know Christopher better than Kaleo and William did. It was an unfair accusation, and Amber already regretted the way her sadness came out of her in bursts of flame that burned the people standing closest to her. When she was done here, she'd apologize. William would forgive her. Kaleo would forgive her eventually. He'd only been acting on his grief too, in his own way. In fact, what were they all doing but clawing the lip of a pit, trying not to fall in?

Christopher was dead. Now what?

The question was too massive. Amber had to start small.

"Why are you a teacher?" Amber asked.

"Was a teacher," Serena said. "Because I'm good at it. Was good at it."

Amber reached for a towel and blotted her face.

"Not because you love the kids?"

"Of course I love the kids. But I could love kids and be a pediatrician. It's just I have this really awful gag reflex. Blood, snot."

"Ear wax," Amber offered, turning and leaning against the sink.

"Diapers. I'd make a terrible mother."

"What are you going to do next?"

Serena shook her head, and Amber thought the woman's heartache looked a little bit like her own. *Now what?* Amber took a seat on the closed toilet.

"Did you do what they're saying you did?"

"Which thing? Molesting a boy? Murdering a man? Trafficking girls?"

"Any of it."

Serena lifted her eyes to meet Amber's. "None of it. *None.*"

Amber nodded. "I believe you."

These three words reached into Serena's confusion and lifted her chin. Amber suspected no one believed much this woman had said in the last twenty-four hours.

"Why?"

"Because I think you really believe Phil is Lance Liebowitz. But we can prove he's Phil Lancet." She'd have to withhold judgment about all the rest. But an idea had begun to form in Amber's mind the moment she walked into her childhood home and saw this woman sitting at the table where her brother ate breakfast every morning. This woman, who had been on the news for crimes that disgusted the average person. It was a test that would answer Amber's question about character and, if Serena cared about her brother's life, possibly help them advance Christopher's cause.

"Lance isn't an attorney?" Serena frowned.

"Have you seen his licenses? Been to court?"

Serena hesitated. "He's never seen my teaching certificate, never been to my classroom. Doesn't make me less of a teacher."

Amber shrugged. "For all I know, Phil is a Supreme Court judge. Maybe he's an attorney. For sure he can swim through sewers and stay invisible to authorities. He might just know the law well enough to do that."

"I've read his website."

"Anyone can make a website."

"How can you prove that he's . . . not Lance?"

"Eyewitness accounts of girls he groomed and then sold to Roman. We've got a few out who can identify him from a photo lineup. But that was in his early years. He's got other men doing that job for him now. He divides and conquers like a cancer."

"Are we talking about human trafficking?"

Amber nodded.

"I've known Lance for a couple of months. The description just doesn't fit."

"Most girls who fall in love with men who are plotting to ruin their lives would say exactly the same thing."

"I thought I'd stumbled across some kind of drug house, and the guy running it wanted to keep me quiet. It all looks different now."

"The house Kaleo found you in?"

Serena nodded.

"Did Christopher go inside?"

"Not while I was there. But I had the impression he'd been there before."

Amber shook her head. "He would have told us, especially if he suspected it was a transfer point."

"There was a small stone in the upstairs window. About the size of a quarter, with an image of a poppy on it. The same flower I saw on the top of Christopher's backpack."

Amber stretched out her leg so she could reach into her pocket and she withdrew a stone that fit the description.

"That's just like it," Serena confirmed. "What is it?"

"This," said Amber, holding the small piece with both hands, "is a story."

By the time Amber was fourteen and emerging from the all-consuming dramas of middle school, she felt like a person gone missing and presumed dead by her family. Not literally, of course, but in every way that mattered. Her older brother, Christopher, was off to college, and her older sister, Gina, was off to any location where her friends were and her parents weren't. Her father was off to work (more and more often to work out of state), and her mother was making her way off some mental plank into the deep end of the mind's troubled waters. Amber saw this clearly. Everyone else seemed to think the woman was merely preoccupied with the waters in the pool of her country club.

Every day Amber made herself breakfast and got herself to school, remembered her homework and forged her parents' signatures when necessary, avoided the mean girls frozen in their middle school time warp, skipped lunch and saved money and was never sick, having no one to share germs with. It was a solitary life but an orderly one with tidy boxes lined up inside of it, one for containing her misery.

She wasn't looking for anything more than what she had. She didn't dream of a life more exciting, more unpredictable, more reckless, more likely to appear in a movie script. So no one was more surprised than she the day that John Roman, a staggeringly gorgeous half-day senior, invited himself to eat lunch with her on the concrete slab of the outdoor handball courts, even though neither of them had a lunch.

Roman, who got Amber to agree that his last name was nicer

than his first, was stunning and had his own car. Within less than a week he'd also talked her into sneaking off campus at lunchtime for a ride in it. She made him promise to get her back before the bell for fifth period rang, and he did, and that was the point at which her curiosity in this man (if he forgot to shave he turned into a porcupine) became an insatiable crush.

Amber had no idea what the other girls thought of him, not being invited into their circles of gossip even after receiving Roman's attention. But it privately thrilled her to know she was at the dead center of their chatter now. It made them easier to ignore.

She grew a foot in the two weeks that she was with Roman, just by the straightening of her spine. She thought herself prettier and wondered about that, having done nothing different to her hair or her simple makeup. Roman said it was because she was finally able to see herself as he saw her, and Amber agreed that this was the most important thing. Not how her parents saw her (slow to grow up and get out because they were tired of parenting already), not how her siblings saw her (a pest), not how her peers saw her (pathetic), and not even how she saw herself (invisible). But how Roman saw her: smart, interesting, pretty, funny.

He bought her lunches. He took her to the beach and to the hills. He compiled the most amazing playlists for her. He told her about all the places he'd been and all the places he was going to go when he finally had enough of school and could really get started with living. He had plans to travel the world with this really cool aid organization dedicated to building wells in places where there was no water. They sat by the Pacific Ocean and tried to imagine living in a place without water.

He listened to stories about her stupid family and said helpful things like, "Well, what do they know about anything?"

The day he kissed her for the first time, Amber stopped caring about her orderly life with its tidy boxes: homework, chores, meals, pain. They sat on the top of a hill in his car overlooking the Los Angeles basin, which was too full of sunshine and ocean air that day to make room for smog. And Amber thought, *This is the life I want. What is my other life worth? Nothing but organized shoe boxes. I want to dig deep wells.*

Without realizing it, she spoke the words aloud.

Roman clasped her hand and lifted her fingers to his lips. Tiny porcupine quills scratched her knuckles.

"Let's go to San Francisco," he'd said, and she laughed. "What's stopping you?"

She couldn't think of anything at all. She'd been living on her own already for months, figuratively speaking. She was responsible, mature, hardworking, and could take care of herself if need be—but she wouldn't have to, ever again. She was with a man who appreciated her. Who would take care of her.

"I guess no one will miss me," she said, and he laughed.

Amber ignored the gaping hole that laugh opened up in her heart. He was only agreeing with her.

They left three days later, windows down on the Pacific Coast Highway, butterflies knocking around in Amber's stomach, cup holders full of massive sodas pumped full of cherry syrup from the Arco station.

She reclined the incredibly soft leather seat all the way back and closed her eyes, took off her sunglasses so she could feel the heat of the sun right on her lids. She crossed her ankles and propped them on the dash, feeling like a starlet. Roman ran his rough hand along her smooth leg.

She felt sleepy, which surprised her, considering that her heart was pumping excitement into every fingertip, into the very ends of her hair. It would be the first time she'd ever been to San Francisco.

"You said you found an apartment?" she asked.

"With a view of the bridge," he said.

The moment was as perfect as the world could ever become. She remembered thinking so in those quick seconds before she fell asleep, and in the years that followed, when the perfect moment was followed by a free-fall into hell.

"He drugged you?" Serena asked. The bathtub rim had become uncomfortable and she slid down to the floor mat, her mind only half on Amber's story. Lance would be back at the house by now, fielding calls from detectives about her connection to the dead man. Lance, who might not be Lance.

"All the way to Las Vegas," Amber said. Then she looked down at her hands, her nails trimmed short. She picked at a cuticle. "Though I didn't figure out where I was for two years."

Serena wasn't sure she'd heard correctly. "How does that work? Las Vegas isn't too easy to mix up with other cities."

Amber caught her eye and tilted her head to one side as if deciding how much more to divulge.

"Of course, Roman was far older than nineteen. Far wealthier than any high schooler I've ever known."

"Why Las Vegas?" Serena prodded before she put everything together. And then she thought she didn't really want to hear this story. She wanted the sordid tales that involved fourteen-year-old girls to stay at arm's length the way they did in the papers, or in her parents' safe house. She wanted them to remain trapped at a safe distance on digital screens, where she didn't have to look a victim in the eye and find she had no idea what to say. She cleared her throat. "I thought you were going to tell me about the poppy."

Once again Serena was struck by how similar Amber's eyes were to her brother's.

Amber nodded. "I'm sorry for what Kaleo did to you. I can imagine how scared you were."

"It's not like I was drugged and hauled to another state." Serena found it hard to look at Amber, that old familiar shame standing between them. It was a type of survivor's guilt, her mother had tried to explain, the result of having gone so far through life relatively unscathed.

"You should go soon," Amber said. "I expect police to come around in the next few hours with more questions about Christopher. They'll want to see his things, and where he lived."

Serena closed her eyes. "Kaleo thinks I killed your brother."

"And Kaleo, a guy with ties to the police department, kidnapped you. Trust me, he won't want you here any more than you want to be here. But tell me: Did Christopher really die saving your life?"

"Yes."

"Then I need you to do something for me before you go."

Hope and fear mingled in Serena's chest. This woman might ask her anything. She resisted the sense of obligation. "What is it?"

"Ask me a question about Christopher. Anything. Tell me what you want to know about him. I just want to talk about him."

It was the oddest request ever put to Serena, the last she would have anticipated in this situation. "Why did he help me?"

The corner of Amber's mouth turned upward.

It was much later when Serena thought of the question she probably should have asked: What is Christopher's connection to Brock Anderson? But it too was an imposter that masked the real question, the question that might have no answer at all: How was she supposed to live with his death?

TWENTY-TWO

THE FIRST ILLEGAL BROTHEL CHRISTOPHER EVER entered was underground. He entered from a casino street so brightly lit that it might have been two in the afternoon as easily as it was two in the morning. He wouldn't have found the place if there wasn't someone to guide him there, a woman who seemed too eager to take him into the pit. No light could reach the downward steps. They were sticky with stuff Christopher was glad he couldn't see. At the bottom he found himself in a concrete well with an unmarked door and a metal grate that covered a drain. The woman knocked and was admitted. He was allowed to follow after he showed his cash.

It was the only thing the woman cared about, it seemed: his cash, and his preferences. "Underage," he'd said. "Fourteen or fifteen. White. Blond, brown eyes, pretty. Round cheeks—"

"We're not a pizza parlor," she'd said, laughing. Harsh yellow lights reflected off her sallow skin and her wrinkles cast shadows. She was repulsive, age masquerading as youth, but acted as if he'd said he found her beautiful. "Come, see what we have. We'll have something you like."

Christopher went, worried that he might actually find Amber. Worried that he wouldn't.

He had been in his fourth year of law school at UCLA when Amber vanished, leaving only a note that said,

Look me up in San Francisco when you have the time.

But they couldn't find her in San Francisco and she never called.

An apartment near the campus had become more home to Christopher than the bungalow his parents still lived in. He walked away from his lease and his exams and the requirements of his scholarships in a wild state of disbelief, and then he joined his father and the detective assigned to Amber's case in unraveling the mystery of her whereabouts. How far could a fourteen-year-old girl go with two hundred dollars withdrawn from her savings account?

It took them four months to deduce that Amber was not in San Francisco, and that the boy who was apparently her closest friend had been enrolled at the high school under a false name and address. There were no photos of him on file. The so-called John Roman drove an expensive car and was unpopular insofar as he was untouchable. The boys described him as irritable and arrogant; the girls, dreamy and charming. More than one claimed to have slept with him, then been dumped. He was universally thought to be older than he claimed and got what he seemed to ask for: to be left alone. Rumor was he worked for a local telemarketing firm, but this too turned out to be a lie.

It was a mouse of a girl named Angelique Renaud who pointed them toward Nevada. Her locker sat two rows beneath and one column to the right of John Roman's, and she'd often felt her skin crawl under his gaze, though he never spoke to her.

Until two weeks before he and Amber vanished.

"You ever been to Sin City?" he asked her, and when she

noticed that he was speaking to her, she blushed. She had no idea where Sin City was. He handed her a postcard and said, "I think you'd like it there."

Angelique had put the card in the back of her locker, both repelled and fascinated. The postcard bore a phone number that, by the time the LAPD got to it, turned out to belong to a pre-paid and discarded cell phone. The image on the card belonged to a brothel in Nye County outside of Las Vegas.

"Prostitution is legal there," the detective told Christopher.

"Not for underage abducted girls," Christopher challenged.

"I only meant that it gets trickier now."

It did. The case became stuck in quickly hardening cement at that point, requiring the fresh involvement of the FBI and Nevada's law-enforcement agencies, both of whom broke the not-surprising news that finding a girl across state lines in a prostitution ring, whether legal or not, was next to impossible. The lucky ones would be caught in the wide nets of the occasional raids. The not so lucky, well . . . And here was where the helpless side of everyone's good intentions showed. The human trafficking industry, not just a Eurasian problem, was thriving in the United States.

In the twelve months between Amber's disappearance and the dreadful anniversary date, the Larsen family eroded like an untended coastline. Christopher's mother fell into a deep depression and then experienced a swift mental degeneration into early-onset Alzheimer's. The medical professionals didn't believe the two were necessarily related, but the middle sibling, Gina, did and she held Amber fully responsible. This created escalating conflicts in the small house where Mr. and Mrs. Larsen had raised their children, until the bungalow became too small to breathe in. Gina grieved her sister but reconciled her heart to what was probable—that Amber would never be recovered, had probably already died—and she resented Christopher's obsession.

Mr. Larsen also found the tragedy unbearable. The loss of his daughter and of his wife as he knew her and of his son's future ended in the loss of a will to live. And after his suicide, Gina took her mother to a small community in the northern part of the state, where she had been pursuing a degree in nursing and could visit her mother every day at a home that specialized in the care of seniors with dementia.

The facility took every last dime of their father's savings, investments, and life insurance. Only the tiny Santa Monica house remained for Christopher.

After a year of searching for Amber via legal means, Christopher sat in the family living room, as dark and empty now as it might be forever, and decided it was time to break the law.

He started in the dungeons of the prostitution world, where he followed shadowy labyrinths into dark holes, showed his money, and was granted entrance to long halls that smelled of vomit.

The first time was the hardest.

"He wants Felicity," his guide said to the pimp at the door.

Christopher took hold of the woman's arm, meaning to intimidate, but she smiled at him. Lipstick had bled into the fine lines around her mouth. "You said I could pick," he argued.

"You look, you pay," his hosts said at the same time.

Most of the doors along the hall were closed, if exposure from holes that had been punched or kicked through the hollow cores didn't count. He expected the prostitutes to be hanging on doorjambs and felt embarrassed by his surprise at finding them nearly invisible here. Through the few open doors he saw quiet shapes curled on the beds, facing the walls, or sitting on the floor staring in a drugged stupor or, maybe, resignation. Lighting was almost nonexistent. Three gold bulbs giving off weak light seemed designed to hide rather than to reveal. Christopher was surprised by the cold sweat lining his palms.

At the end of the hall the madam unlocked the door with a key. She pushed it open into a space that he thought might be a closet converted to something more profitable than storing clothes.

She held her upturned hand out to him. He gave her all he'd brought with him. The woman counted his bills.

"Fifteen minutes," she said, walking away, though Christopher was sure he'd brought enough for an hour. "But take twenty. She needs the practice."

He was prepared to see someone other than his sister. He braced himself for an emotionally flattened female, strung out and detached. Or, at the other extreme, a seductive cat. In the middle: possibly tears. It could be anything. She, he mentally corrected, could be anyone.

He wasn't prepared for a child. A child who believed she was an adult.

The poor lighting and heavy eyeliner cloaked her true age, but the fragile lines of her bird-like legs gave her away. She wore only underwear and a loose top that slipped off one shoulder. Blond hair. Possibly brown eyes. Bloodshot. Full cheeks that still carried memories of baby fat. His sister, and not his sister. Relief and sadness jostled for the same seat in his heart.

She didn't look up when he came in, but he heard her sigh. The door closed behind him, and Christopher was caught off guard by the flash of a thought that he could do anything he wanted in the next fifteen minutes. No one would ever know. No one but him and this girl with brown eyes that silently asked, "What'll it be?" as if he'd come to order lunch.

He wondered if she had a brother, and the moment passed.

Her bed took up half of the available space. The carpet was covered in cigarette burns and steeped in the odor of tobacco. In one corner, a cardboard box appeared to hold a change of clothing. A desk lamp on an accordion arm was clamped to her headboard.

A paperback book handled until the pages curled open lay next to her pillow.

"I'm Christopher," he said, and she snorted.

"I'm Anastasia. And don't call me Ana."

"I thought they said your name was—"

"I was kidding." Derision animated her face, and Christopher understood.

"What's your name, then?"

"Do you need a lot of small talk?" she asked. "Because that usually doesn't work out for me."

Christopher sat down on the floor and consciously focused on her eyes, which was difficult in the light. The bride of Frankenstein's monster might have been envious of the girl's makeup.

"What do you mean?" he asked.

For a moment he thought her only answer would be the disbelieving stare. But then she said, "You talk instead of doing what you really came here to do. Then the clock runs out and you complain. They don't like it when you complain."

He sat forward so that he could withdraw a photo from his pocket. Amber's ninth-grade school picture.

"Well, I only came here to talk," he said.

She snorted again and tugged the sleeve of her shirt down over her elbow.

"No, no"—he held up a hand—"wait. I'm looking for someone." Christopher held the wallet-size picture out across the closet-size room. "Her name's Amber—"

"Mine's Crystal."

He sighed. "Okay."

That derision again, shooting from her eyes. But this time she didn't snort. She took the class picture from his fingers and lifted it close to her face.

"She's my sister," he said. "Have you seen her?"

The girl of many names examined the details of the image for so long that Christopher thought she might launch into a catalog of potential sightings.

"No," she finally said, handing the photograph back. "What else, before we get on with it? I think I could tolerate you for fifteen minutes if you'd stop talking."

No. The most expensive disappointment he'd ever paid for. The biggest brick wall ever slapped up in front of him. He had told himself it would be only the first of many. Telling himself and experiencing it weren't the same. He leaned back against the door, knees up in front of him, elbows balanced on knees, looking at the picture.

"You have any brothers or sisters?" he asked.

The girl sat like a statue on her bed. He thought the question had angered her far more than his desire to know her name. That glare. She made no further motion to undress.

The effect was to transform a prostitute into a pouting child jealous of privileges that could never be hers. Christopher studied her and she didn't flinch. Maybe she had a sibling; there wasn't one here now, was there?

"Is there someone I can call for you?" he asked, and he pulled his cell phone out of his back pocket, wondering if it would work in a dungeon.

She leaned forward, eyeing the phone the way a dog anticipates a reward. Her eyes darted to Christopher's, and then she pounced on it and bounced away again to the corner of the bed, tapping at the keypad and forgetting that a stranger sat in the room with her. He was too stunned to ask her anything more, but he watched the girl sit there, holding the tiny cell phone with both hands, curled up into a tense ball.

And then the real girl showed up in the room.

"Hi, Mom," she whispered, and she closed her eyes. "Yeah, I know. But I'm calling now." She hugged a pillow and turned to face the wall. "We're just real busy, you know. I can't help it."

For fifteen minutes Christopher watched this bizarre encounter between the fantasy of the girl's confident but fictional stories ("We got a great apartment with a view of the pool") and the reality of how desperately the child needed her mother.

There was a fist on the door and a firm shout straight through it: "Time!"

"Yeah," Christopher shouted back. And the person moved on.

He began to stand. The girl clutched the phone more tightly, but she knew better than he did that she had to get off the call. "Look, my ride is here . . . Yeah, maybe next week . . . Okay. Quit worrying . . . You too."

She looked at Christopher and said, "Oh no." Her eyes bore nothing but teenaged worry over the potential for getting busted.

He smiled and took the phone back. "I told you I only came to talk."

She glanced at the door.

"Quit worrying," he said in his best imitation, and he put his hand on the door, pulled it open. The crack-lipped woman stood outside.

"Best I've ever had," he said to her. She cackled.

"Honey, I'd say you haven't had much."

Christopher left them both. Halfway down the hall he heard a voice reach out for him. "Name's Libby," she said, and then her door closed again and a key turned in the lock.

Christopher rose to the upper levels of the earth once more, covered his head with his baby-blue and yellow Bruins hoodie, and headed straight for an Internet café. From there he typed an anonymous e-mail to the Las Vegas Police Department, tipping them off to an underaged prostitute at an illegal brothel within city limits. And then he gave them the phone number at the top of his call log, suggesting that the person who answered might know a thing or two about an elusive girl named Libby.

TWENTY-THREE

THE LIGHT COMING THROUGH THE FROSTED GLASS of the east-facing bathroom window had shifted and bounced off the mirror, casting a beam across Serena's hands.

Amber said, "He did that for a year, working in Santa Monica during the week, saving enough money to drive to Las Vegas on Friday nights. He'd stay until Sunday and see as many girls as he could, showing them my photograph and asking if they'd seen me. They were always more curious about what he was doing than they were about me—scared that if they didn't put out they'd be punished, but he always covered for them. They'd say, 'Why no sex?' and he'd say, 'Because you're my sister.'"

The cost must have been astronomical, even if his housing expenses were covered by the shattered family.

"He lost forty pounds, skimping on food and sleep. And somehow word about him spread. The girls in those situations, the illegal ones—they're kept out of the light, but some of them find their own ways to create community. We pass notes, we learn to recognize each other, we figure out each other's stories. Some of us form bonds."

"Did you know he was looking for you?"

Amber shook her head. She wore tiny glass studs in her ears that caught the sun. "Of course, the pimps got wind of him. It got harder for him to move around unnoticed. He experimented with tracking devices, the kind people use in their pets, to help lead police to the girls, but that had its problems. They were expensive. Not everyone was willing to let a first-time customer shoot a pellet into their arm."

Serena straightened at this news, thinking of the device she'd seen taped to the back of his poppy pin.

"I found one, at least I think that's what it was, with his things. Kaleo took it."

"He never fully abandoned the idea, but he didn't quite know how to make it practical either. When the raid rates began to spike, some places started photographing their customers. Pimps aren't exactly colleagues, but they started putting things together. He cut off his curls, dyed his hair, had to start asking for girls who didn't fit my description. It was frustrating work. He couldn't even fully confide in the police.

"He roped Kaleo and William into helping him, but they weren't as vested as he was, they had their own jobs—there were so many limitations. He wasn't even sure I was in Nevada, and he hadn't expected every girl he met to remind him of me. The emotional side of it took its toll. He started smoking to keep his nerves in place.

"I think he might have been involved in getting between fifty and seventy-five girls out during that year—but he'd never guess, and there wasn't any way to track what happened to them, how many went back in. Most of them didn't even know more than his first name. And the brothels are like weeds. Pull one and five more crop up in its place.

"He got the idea for Fire Followers that spring. His weekend drives took him through the pass between the San Bernardino and San Gabriel Mountains."

"Regions known for their forest fires," Serena said. Both

ranges were part of the Angeles National Forest—the Station Fire had happened in the San Gabriels.

"The Old Fire burned nearly a hundred thousand acres around Lake Arrowhead. The April after it happened, one week before Christopher found me, he went up to the lake on his way home to clear his head, to try to evaluate whether all his efforts were for nothing. And at a bend in the road the scenery opened up in front of him, and all he could see for miles and miles through this scorched earth were these amazing orange poppies."

"Fire poppies," Serena said.

Amber seemed surprised that she knew them.

"They're very rare—they bloom after a fire because the ash has the nitrogen in the soil that they need. They're called fire followers. Of course you know that."

"I forgot you teach biology."

"The fire poppies are unique to California, at least here in the States."

"He said he felt like he was looking at a field full of women who'd been held captive for years and years and were seeing sunlight for the first time. It was beautiful. What had happened to the place was awful and devastating, and yet it was the most appropriate symbol for what we do."

"How'd he find you?"

Amber took a long breath. "Roman kept me for a while, until he got bored. He prefers the ones who fight him. They resist, he beats them, they grow more fierce, he drugs them into compliance. He keeps up the cycle until they give out. After a few broken bones, once a rib, I just didn't have any more fight in me. So he passed me along to the brothel he supplied at the time. He hadn't been doing the work long, and he had a partner, a guy who ran the house while Roman would travel to different states collecting girls. He ran a small enterprise at the time, but he specialized in underage girls.

They fetch almost as much money as the professional escorts—even more in a way, since the pimps aren't running a legitimate business governed by the powers that be. The youngest girls are less likely to carry diseases, many are virgins, and the worst sex addicts have fetishes they just can't satisfy at the legal whorehouses with adults."

Serena didn't smoke herself, but she could see why Christopher would have taken it up. She looked at the floor as she listened.

"I'd been there eighteen months when Christopher showed up. He showed my picture to a girl named Clarice, and when he asked her if she knew me, she said, 'I think so.' It was the first time anyone had said anything to him but no.

"One of the problems in getting girls out of the business is that prostitutes are considered criminals. A lot of them go to jail while their pimps vanish. He didn't want that to happen to me, though he could prove I was underage, so I had a better chance. I was sixteen by then. He moved cautiously. He studied the house. He went back several times in one weekend and got Kaleo and William to do the same, separately. It took hardly any time for the women to figure out that something was up, but the three of them were just as quick.

"William was the one who was actually brought to my room. It was his second time at the house—he was the most reluctant, the least recognizable in spite of his crazy red hair. But William doesn't even come close to fitting Christopher's description, as you saw. He called Christopher. Christopher called the police, then called Kaleo, who was already in the house. Kaleo knocked out the pimp and William carried me out, and the three of us walked away before the police even showed up on the street."

"What did you say? What did you think?"

Amber shrugged. "It's a blank. I don't remember any of it, I'm sorry to say. I go back and forth between wishing I did and being glad I don't. There's enough that would be nice to block out.

I was so strung out on whatever they used to keep me cooperative. I remember the detox after, that was the first thing. Well, I remember something about being carried out. I think I weighed all of ninety pounds, and William . . ." A half smile reached her eyes. She shrugged.

A heavy fist hit the door three times. "Amber?" Kaleo called.

"Another minute," she said, then lowered her voice again. "They're good men, Serena. Christopher was a brother to everyone, and those three are inseparable. Were."

"I'm so sorry. I wish I understood how he got tangled up in my mess."

"I think you're the one who's entangled. See, when Christopher brought that house down, it devastated Roman's business. He was out of state then, and he stayed away when he heard what had happened. His partner tried to give him up, but Roman just vanished and he's never resurfaced except in the form of people like Phil Lancet. We've been able to connect him to Roman in second- and third-hand sorts of ways. He never did business the same way again. He developed small cells of prostitutes in different states headed by different people, ridiculously small operations that are easy to move quickly, or that don't amount to any great loss if they're shut down. His layers of groomers and traffickers and pimps are more involved than a pyramid scheme. We think *he* might not even know all the people who work for him. But he knows us. He's kept a close eye on Christopher."

"How did he know Christopher was the one who turned in the house?"

"Like I said, word of him was already starting to spread. The pimp had seen him, and the police had received enough calls from him over the years to pick up clues to his identity. They came knocking right here"—Amber pointed toward the front door of the house—"within a week and confirmed everything."

"But no one filed charges."

Amber shook her head. "The rescued girls uniformly denied ever having seen him at the house. He had applied for status as my legal guardian by then. The officer in charge turned a blind eye in exchange for the promise that Christopher wouldn't return to any Las Vegas brothel."

"But Roman figured out who he was."

"It wouldn't be that hard, I guess. Someone here broke a human interest story and published our names, about a year after I came back. Roman might have seen it or just put other records together. He has people working for him in the strangest places, which is why it's not hard to think you could be one of them."

Serena leaned forward. "So you think Christopher was onto Roman somehow, and I was the one who was in the wrong place at the wrong time."

Amber's frown warned her not to shuck the blame for his death too quickly.

"I'm not drawing any conclusions," she said. "But Christopher hasn't been able to enter a brothel in the Southwest since then without finding a gun between his eyes and an unwelcome mat at his feet. They know about him, and Roman would be the one to have spread the word. Especially since we think he owns about a third of the places operating in Southern California and Arizona right now."

Fatigue and hunger drummed Serena's head. Amber's story raised troubling questions, chief among them the possibility that Lance, who had been a perfect gentleman and pleasant companion for the past six weeks, might not be who he said he was.

But why not?

"You asked why Christopher helped you," Amber said.

"If I were him, I would have run away."

"Christopher helped you because he believed you're his sister.

Nothing in his world is"—her voice caught in her throat—"*was* more important than saving a life."

"But he didn't even know me."

Amber's laugh was so light, so beautiful, a shocking contrast to her rumpled clothes and grief-stricken face. "That was the last reason he ever needed for helping someone."

She touched Serena's hand. Her fingertips were cold compared to the sunlight but also soft, and Serena almost told her about the bizarre things she had seen in Christopher's presence. She almost asked if Amber really did have rippling scars across her back. But she didn't know how.

"I wish I could have done something for him," Serena said.

"You can."

For a moment she believed Amber was going to press her to spill all the details of who'd moved her brother and why.

"What could I possibly do?"

"I want you to plead guilty to that boy's charges against you. For Christopher, I want you to take the fall."

TWENTY-FOUR

SERENA DROVE THROUGH THE SIDE STREETS OF Santa Monica wondering if she should drive straight to Mexico. Do not go home for supplies. Do not stop for anything but cash from the ATM. Of course, this kind of behavior would look exactly like a guilty plea.

Amber's rationale had made no sense to Serena, though she nodded as if every word were brilliance. Her goal: to get out of there as quickly as possible. The key to this was to avoid asking any questions. But she couldn't stop herself from objecting.

"Why on earth would I plead guilty?"

"Because Phil won't expect it. Tell him you have an appetite for minors. See what he does. If he learns you're not the good teacher he thinks you are, he'll tip his hand to you."

"What does that mean? Any boyfriend would flip over that kind of news."

"Not this boyfriend. He finds out you and he have similar passions . . . he might want to make you a business partner."

"I might have to make you a partner," Lance had said once. Serena hated how the mind made random, meaningless associations.

"Or he might throw me to the wolves."

"I'm betting your confession won't ever fall on anyone's ears but his. He'll take you underground and lead you straight to Roman."

"It's the dumbest idea I've ever heard."

"What is Christopher's death worth to you?"

"My life. Don't twist this."

"Twist it? Do you know how many children in the United States are sold for sex? One, two, three hundred thousand. If the number were only *ten*, it would be too many. I'm not asking you to throw your life away. I'm asking you to save a few of theirs. What do you have to lose?"

"My career. My reputation. My freedom. For starters."

"Not exactly an even trade from Christopher's point of view, is it?"

Serena shut down then.

"Okay. I'll do it." It was the only way Amber was going to let her go.

Afterward, the redheaded man Will returned her car and her keys silently while Kaleo and Amber argued about this strategy. She watched them while Will dug through his jacket pocket, thinking the argument had a strange ring to it, like a B-movie squabble between two criminals who were equally guilty but not equally bright.

What were these two guilty of?

Kidnapping. And insanity. Because that's what Amber's plan amounted to.

When Serena put her key in the ignition, Kaleo called Amber a fool. Serena agreed. What kind of person could believe that a complete stranger would throw herself in front of a train for an uncertain result?

Perhaps the kind related to a man like Christopher Larsen.

The kind saved by him.

Guilt tweaked Serena's heart. She tried to ignore it.

Will leaned down through the window and pressed a poppy-stamped disk into her hand. It was identical to the one she had given to her father, and to the one Amber had shown her in the bathroom.

"I choose Amber even when she's wrong," he said. "So if you're telling the truth, don't forget this one: you were Christopher's last success story. Make it count."

They were all crazy.

Serena drove away without saying good-bye, without reiterating any promises about what she would or wouldn't do, without making arrangements to contact them in the future. She marveled at her freedom and at their gullibility. Did they actually believe she would tell Lance she was guilty of unlawful sexual intercourse with a minor?

Their behavior made no sense at all. Kidnapping, interrogating, failing to hide the details of their work, their location, their disputes—what was going on?

She had to bring order to this chaos of nonsense. This task was no different from creating a lesson plan or applying the scientific method. Develop a theory. Design an experiment. Compile the data.

This was the theory that first emerged in Serena's mind: Kaleo, Will, and Amber were part of their own human trafficking ring, and Lance Liebowitz was on a case to take them down. They had to stop him. They would use her to do it.

How? Lance had said the police wouldn't arrest her until the DA had a convincing amount of evidence firmly under wraps. She didn't know if the same principle applied to trafficking cases, but it seemed reasonable. She also suspected that there were other agencies, legal agencies like Lance's, that were involved in bringing down this kind of operation. If they could consume Lance with a public sex abuse case that involved an intimate partner . . . if they could turn her against him by feeding her the most amazing sob stories in which they were the heroes rather than the villains . . .

maybe they could buy time to make their getaway. Or maybe they had a vendetta against Lance and just wanted a little revenge.

Casting them on this strange stage as criminals made sense of their strange house, with all those creepy photographs. Not rescuees, but abductees. She wished she might have snagged one of them for the police to compare to their missing-persons reports.

It would explain Christopher's presence at the ruined house yesterday, as well as Kaleo's and Will's today.

But why would his own people kill Christopher?

Serena gasped: because they *didn't*. Because the entire thing was staged: the shooting, the high-school setup. Connecting Christopher to Brock wasn't a warning to Brock but to *her*. Brock was one of theirs, somehow. They'd put Brock up to this insanity.

She couldn't very well go to the police right now, could she, as the prime suspect in a high-profile case? Her information would be considered unreliable.

Serena's angry heart raced. Was her attachment to Lance Liebowitz just her own rotten luck? Good girl in a bad place at a bad time?

Another question cast a deeper shadow over her dilemma: Why hadn't Lance come up with this theory the moment she was accused?

Santa Monica and Pacific Palisades were neighbors, but in this part of California she could jump on any number of freeways and point her future in a dozen different directions as easily as she could head next door. She could go to Mexico, Oregon, Canada, Arizona, Nevada.

Las Vegas.

"We can always go to Vegas. Easy place to get lost."

"I didn't figure out where I was for two years."

Serena shuddered and her mind filled with teenage girls she knew from school, children really, kids like Becca, crammed into a windowless pit under a seedy dive and forced by inhuman beasts to do things no human should ever have to do. Those women she had dreamed of with scars all over their bodies. Their plight made her furious and powerless. Had Lance seen such a place? Was he motivated by human decency or something else?

Lance had this kind of nobility in him. He'd demonstrated it in his kind treatment of her, in his professionalism, in his savvy. The reason he wouldn't have talked about such a case with her was because legally he couldn't.

Serena turned off of the Pacific Coast Highway and headed up the hill that led toward Lance's home. She felt betrayed by her own senses. Until Amber made her demand, Serena had believed the tales. She believed them because Amber and Christopher had the same eyes. Serena was the gullible one.

But on the chance that the part about Christopher experimenting with tracking devices was true, Serena heaved the stone Will had given her out the window.

By the time she pulled into the driveway, Serena's head was spinning with facts that didn't fit together. She forced herself back to the strategy. Observe. Test. Collect the data. This approach calmed her. She set her mind to determining what she would test first.

Lance opened the door for her before she laid a hand on it, looking as immaculate and cheerful as always.

"You're not my prisoner, you know, but please don't ever run off without your phone again. I've worn a hole in my carpets waiting for you to show up."

He was wearing his green silk tie with the navy blue spades. The tie he referred to as his victory tie. She didn't recall he had any court appearances to make today.

"I'm sorry," she said. "I had to drive. Think."

He took her by the hand and led her inside. "There's big bad wolves out there in your forest now, Red. Isn't there enough space here for you to think?"

Something about the remark derailed her, and it took her a moment to pinpoint what the disruption was. Something about Red Riding Hood. Kaleo had made a similar allusion, only in his scenario she was the wolf.

Who was the wolf in Lance's scenario? Easy: reporters, teachers, parents, school boards, the entire public. Ruthless human traffickers who were building empires. And identities could shift as quickly as one could lift a finger and make an accusation.

The identities of everyone she'd encountered in the past twenty-four hours were morphing with lightning speed.

Serena held on to Lance's strong hand and let him pull her into the house. As she followed him, a sickening dread struck Serena in the stomach. A fact so plain that it was law and needed no testing at all: Lance was a defense attorney, not a prosecutor. Why would Amber's crew need to take him down? They might need someone like him one of these days.

All her theories collapsed into piles of mental rubble, and all the lies she thought Amber had fed to her were resurrected on dusty particles of truth.

One theory remained standing, the one Serena had tried to ignore: Amber was telling the truth and Lance was not who he claimed to be. And as he poured cold coffee from a paper cup into a mug and slipped it into the microwave to warm it for her, she quickly decided on her first test: whichever one would prove this theory wrong.

Amber stood on her parents' front lawn long after Kaleo stormed off. She couldn't believe she'd asked Serena to plead guilty to the accusations brought against her. Not even the truly guilty would do that!

The front lawn, where she had run through sprinklers as a child, was smaller than her apartment living room. Since returning from Las Vegas she thought it was also greener and softer. Christopher used to say this was because he kept up the appearance with green Silly String. "Grass in a can." It was the first time Amber had laughed after he brought her back from hell.

It wasn't Silly String that gave the grass its fine qualities, though. It was Christopher's dedication. The fertilizing, the mowing, the weeding, the seeding, the watering—he did these things religiously as part of his weekly routines, even when the demands of Fire Followers were at their peak. When she asked him about it, he said it was therapeutic. His best ideas came when working on the lawn.

She believed his best ideas actually came from the fish taco vendor down the street, and that working on the lawn was how he paid tribute to their father, who used to say that a trim lawn covered a multitude of sins.

Amber hoped it was true because Christopher seemed to forget that there were other living, overgrown, jungle-type things on the property that needed tending.

Dried palm fronds rustled as William came up behind her. She knew it was William because he was the only one who ever stooped to pick them up and put them in the trash. But not before he collected the gigantic fans and followed her around, bowing and fanning and murmuring "Your Highness" until she cracked a smile.

Today they drooped from their brown papery stalks as he held them at his side like a broom.

Together they stared down the street in the direction Kaleo's car had peeled away. A police cruiser approached from the same direction, moving slowly but purposefully.

"I'm an idiot," she said. "I might have just alienated the only witness who can help us catch Christopher's killer."

"Nah. Kaleo alienated her before you ever showed up."

"Do you think we'll ever see her again?"

It was typical of William not to reply to questions that didn't have answers. Instead he offered, "I'm sorry I couldn't get to you in time this morning," which was all she really needed to hear.

"Let's blame Kaleo for that too," she said.

They stood together silently, easily—though she hoped he'd dump those fronds in the trash can before the police pulled into their driveway.

She also wished he'd step between her and anyone else who had questions about Christopher because her breaking point was on the horizon. She wished he would take her hand the way he said he had when he'd pulled her up off that flea-riddled mattress in a drugged stupor. She didn't remember much about that moment except for strength coming up under her like a lifeboat.

William would never take her hand, of course. No man who knew her story would. Touch was risky. It was impossible to say exactly why or when or how a touch would become an electric jolt that sent her mind back to its basest survival instinct. The last time it happened, a clerk from the Home Depot had been helping her load cut lumber for a street fair booth into the back of her pickup truck and accidentally bumped her shoulder. He knocked her off balance and took hold of her arm, trying to prevent her from falling onto the corner of the tailgate. Amber had given him a black eye and then lost three hours of her day to hysteria.

She glanced at William out of the corner of her eye. He was wearing the blue knit cap with tassels though the sun was shining. His wiry red hair exploded out the bottom around his neck.

"More questions," she said, eying the detective at the wheel. She'd met this one at the high school. A frown permanently lined his brow, and he seemed not to observe human beings with as much care as he observed their surroundings.

"Want me to do the talking?" William offered.

Amber nodded because already her throat was too thick with thoughts of Christopher to tell a cold lawman of the things that mattered most about him.

"I asked them to give us twenty-four hours before they release his name."

"Gina." William said the name of Amber and Christopher's sister like a heavy sigh.

"She's going to blame me for this too, you know."

"I could tackle that for you too if you want."

"I do want, but that's one I'll have to handle myself."

"Bring it on," William said. He held the fronds up like shields.

Amber lifted her hand toward him. It was a stiff and silly gesture that immediately embarrassed her. What was he supposed to do? Ignore her vulnerability? Take her fingers and risk getting punched? Besides, his hands were full. She dropped hers, hoping he hadn't noticed.

"Here we go," he said. He tossed the fronds to the side of the driveway, leaned over and took her hand, then turned to face the detective, shielding her from that concentrated frown.

TWENTY-FIVE

KIERA DREAMED OF HER MOTHER BERATING HER for letting her little brother get into the peanut butter jar, screaming at her, insulting her; she couldn't figure out why the dream filled her with warmth and hope. She woke in a fog where her senses contradicted her. She was freezing, but sweaty and wrapped in a blanket. She lay on a soft surface, but it cut into her like a bed of nails. Nausea washed over her in waves, but she laughed at it. Her throat was raw. Her body ached. She could feel the bruises inside her legs, on her ribs, at her neck, and they made her feel real, alive. A survivor.

What exactly had she survived? The answer to this lurked behind the ominous fog. She floated through it in a watery boat that was sinking, and she didn't want to be bothered with bailing it out.

Someone else's fingers touched the back of her hand and she shrieked, exploded from the blanket and went after the person like an eagle, talons clawing at the face and wings beating the body. But for all the power she felt rise through her, it was easy enough for the other person to pin her arms and push her back down onto the unbearable bed.

"It's Becca," the person said. "I'm not going to hurt you."

The name meant nothing to her, but the voice was familiar. The kind voice that had said, "Fight hard." A crush of hurt pressed down on her. She didn't remember fighting, but her body told her she'd been in a boxing ring.

"It's the only advantage of fighting," Becca said. "They'll drug you. It helps. And the fighters stay here longer."

"I don't want to stay."

"Here, it's just the one monster. Out there, millions."

Kiera could hear her own breath driving in and out of her nose. Had Becca seen what that monster had forced her to watch? She doubted it. Her ears throbbed.

"Roman'll keep you longer. He might hurt you more—for some reason, fighting turns on lights in the dark corners of his mind. But his drugs are good. You'll remember less."

Kiera wanted to cry. Couldn't remember how to do it. Couldn't remember much of anything. Except what she had seen. It was an infected tattoo on her memory.

"It'll wear off," Becca said.

The fog? The pain? The shock? She didn't really want it to.

"Relax," Becca ordered. But not the way her mother might have ordered it.

"You tell everyone to fight?" Kiera's hoarse words were barely a whisper.

"Doesn't matter who I tell. You'll either do it or you won't. Nothing to do with me. Relax," Becca said again. She worked gently to pry open Kiera's fisted fingers, and the warmth of her skin unfroze the joints. Concentrating on her hands made Kiera think of her art class, the only class at school that she loved. Fingers gave her some trouble. They were the hardest to draw. They were proportionally longer than most people thought they were, as long as the palm, which made them seem spidery at first sketch, but then just right. She wished for a piece of paper. A stub of pencil. She would draw her closed fist. Then she would draw Becca's warm hand opening hers like a flower.

Her frantic breathing eased up.

Becca pressed something hard into Kiera's palm. She set her mind on this unknown thing that filled the center of her hand. Was it a rock?

"I'm going to tell you a story."

"I'm so tired."

"The best time for a story." Becca sat on the floor without seeming to fear the creepy crawlies. The edge of her wool blanket drooped over Kiera's wrist. "I was here awhile before someone told it to me, and I wish I'd heard it on my first day."

"How long have you been here?"

Becca didn't answer and Kiera accepted that. No answer would have given her hope.

Dark creatures pressed in from the fog of Kiera's mind. She held them off by lifting the stone up toward the light from the vent, which had shifted from moonlight to rising daylight in the time she'd been gone. It must have been hours.

"Is it a true story?" she asked.

"I like to think it is."

The rock was the size of a quarter. In its center was a simple image of a flower with four petals. Someone had drawn on it with some kind of lead pencil or black cinder. The edges were smudged from handling but the shape was clear enough. Concentrating on it pushed the terror back into the margins of her mind.

"Did you make this?" Kiera asked of the drawing on the rock. She ran her fingers around the smooth edges. Perfect, round, warm. She worried about messing up the picture.

"The girls who know the story make their own. You can have mine. I'll make another one."

"Tell me."

It seemed to take no time at all for Becca to tell the fairy tale of a girl caught up into this life and rescued from it by her brother, a

bursting out of Christopher's
s if she'd just robbed a bank.
e'd killed him?

the backpack when Kaleo took
racker clutched in her palm. It
equipment, which was still here
any information programmed

traight to a transfer house and
ome take her, after putting up a
e was working for Phil Lancet,
sed him that way.

r him after all? It was a hinky
ave too many women in this
he girls with promises of love
couldn't play the part as well.
Europe where they could pose
s, because the targeted victims
more than the security of affec-
ure—?

rough the site.
rouble, this website would fail
n. At the top of the page was a
banner stating that they were

man who had not even paid attention to her until she went missing. Then he devoted his life to finding her, even though he'd been told it was impossible. She was a flower hidden in a field of weeds, nearly choked out of existence. But he vowed to tear up the field until he found it, and then after years and years of searching he finally did. Now he was on a quest to save them all. And he would come for them, given enough time. Some girls had already been rescued, snatched out of harm's way without any prelude. Some had met the mysterious hero, who paid to talk with them but not to violate them.

Kiera liked the story, though she doubted it was true. All they had to do was believe and be patient. He wouldn't stop until every last one of them was home.

"I never thought I'd want to be home," Kiera whispered.

"Things look different in here."

"You should keep it." Kiera tried to press the stone back into Becca's palm. Her fingers refused it. The stone dropped to the hard ground and rolled away.

The noise awoke Kiera's memory and she rolled off of the mattress onto the filthy floor.

"Don't worry about it," Becca said.

Kiera smacked the cold and unspeakable grime with her bare hands, searching.

"I found it," Becca said. "Here."

"Not that," Kiera said. Her palm came down on the stone disk she had lost moments before being dragged away. "This."

She held it up to the weak light and looked at it for the first time.

It was a machine-made stone slightly smaller than Becca's, stamped with orange ink and red words. *Fire Followers* formed a protective ring around a lacy flower with only four petals.

The fog cleared out of Kiera's mind before she could brace herself for clarity.

"Where'd you get this?" Becca asked.

Kiera couldn't speak; she could only gasp for breath. *From the man in the truck*, she wanted to say. *From the hero shot in the back. From the one who came looking for us.*

Becca picked her up off the floor and set her back down on the mattress. "Kiera?"

Tears clogged the girl's throat. The man would never give flowers to another person, ever. He would never rescue another sister. He couldn't even save himself.

He would forever lie on the bloody floor of Kiera's memory, where no drug could mop him up and take him away, where no happy story could rewrite his ending: that he should survive his first injury and be taken by the second, a gunshot straight to the heart. The monster, Roman, had made the man look at her while she cried on her knees, hands wrenched behind her back by plastic ties, so confused.

"I'm sorry," he whispered to her before the gun cracked and the smoke rose from the barrel and he toppled over sideways.

"Now we're even," the monster said before turning to face Kiera. "And I've selected you to spread the word."

A memory plagued him: Seren[...] car, hauling off with his backpack [...] Why hadn't she just taken it when s[...]

Nothing.

Stanford & Barker.

There was nothing of interest i[...] it from her. Nothing but that little [...] was worthless without all the other[...] in the bungalow. It didn't even hav[...] into it.

Nothing.

Hendricks, Kopp & Owens.

And why would she lead him [...] just stand there, waiting for him to [...] pretty darn respectable chase? If s[...] he wouldn't like to know she'd ex[...]

Nothing.

Strauss & Liebowitz.

What if she wasn't working [...] theory. The United States didn'[...] business. In the US, men wooed[...] and protection, and women just [...] They did more damage in Easter[...] as employers with well-paying jo[...] there needed the security of mone[...] tion. How exactly would a teache[...]

Wait. Liebowitz.

Kaleo went back and clicked [...]

If he were a person in legal[...] to inspire his confidence in the f[...] capitalized announcement on a [...] not presently accepting new clie[...]

Kaleo resisted the answer. "Phil. Or Roman."

"So if Phil or Roman did the killing, why write Brock's name on Christopher's chest?"

Kaleo had no answer.

"Maybe Brock is the man to lead us where we really want to go."

"He's a kid, not a man," Kaleo said, to get the credit for assessing *something* correctly today. "Makes me sick, but they're all just kids."

There was a buzz at the front gate, but Lance couldn't answer it. He was in his home office on the phone, making arrangements with his partner to spend the rest of the day by Serena's side. Or so he told her.

Serena went to the intercom and security cameras in an alcove by the front door. On the black-and-white screen, a deliveryman on the other side of the wrought-iron portal held a small flower arrangement.

Her anxiety kicked into gear, even though she could see a legitimate-looking floral delivery truck behind him.

She pushed the response button. "Yes?"

"Delivery for, uh"—he looked at the card on a fork among the blooms—"Mija Liebowitz." He mangled the pronunciation: My-juh Lyb-ow-ites.

My-juh?

Serena smiled. *"Mija,"* she said aloud. An endearment both common and special. *My daughter.* The flowers were from her parents, who would be the first people to suggest she not return to her apartment for a while, nor use her real name to tip off anyone to her true whereabouts.

She pushed the button again. "Please leave them at the gate," she said. "Thank you."

Serena watched the man do as instructed and drive away.

She thought she would wait until Lance could retrieve them, but when she went to the office his door was closed and his voice on the other side was a steady flow of conversation that she wouldn't interrupt. Back in the alcove she checked all the security cameras for the entire property and once again saw nothing out of the ordinary.

She fetched the flowers, then laughed at herself when she was safely back inside the house, because the tiny adventure had given her heart a neat little cardiovascular workout.

"You need to relax," she chided herself. She set the bouquet on the kitchen counter. It was a small arrangement of green and gold mums, as understated and comforting as one of her dad's hugs. She pulled the card out of the plastic fork, then opened the minute envelope.

Mija, you are at the front of our minds and the center of our hearts.

Serena knew it was true. She sat at the counter and called her father, stroking the mums' bushy soft petals with her thumb.

"The flowers were just what I needed," she said when he answered.

"Ah, I doubt they will solve all your problems," he said kindly.

"They remind me of all that is still right."

"Yes. An important memory to carry with you through dark times."

"*Papá*, I was hoping you can help me with something."

"Then I hope I can too."

"It's about the man who died, and the place where it happened."

She told him everything, confessing to a mystery rather than to a crime, from the flowers to the doll to the visions to the conversation with a man who no longer lived. She left the kitchen, which caused her voice to seem louder and more overwhelmed than she wanted it to be, and moved out to the patio. The Pacific Ocean had the capacity to swallow her confusion without judging it.

So did her father.

"I have no answers for you," he announced when she finished. "But maybe I have an insight."

She smiled and sat down on a padded lounge chair. "Then that will have to do."

"Do you remember what the Safe Place was before your *mamá* and I came by it?" he asked.

"It was a hotel, I thought."

"Ah, well, a hotel for the sick. It was an old hospital steeped in old ways that did more harm than good. There was a lot of death here and not a lot of healing. It was abandoned for many years, well before your *mamá* and I married. The city grew too fast, the smog got thick. White people didn't like us or our black neighbors buying up their old houses, and businesses moved east. And then there were the ghost stories."

"People thought the city was haunted?"

"The hospital. It was a magnificent building for urban legends, if you think of it."

"You never told us this," Serena said, referring to her two siblings.

"By the time you were of an age to hear them, they had faded away. But this is not what I mean to tell you now."

Through the screen door at her back, Serena heard Lance's footsteps in the kitchen.

"The old building stood on the route your mother and I used to walk to Mass each week. It was very early in our life together, before you kids came along. Each time we would go by it, *Mamá* would stop and face the doors. They were held closed by a heavy chain and a lock the size of my fist. And I would say, 'What is it, Enid?' and she would say, 'I thought I smelled something.' And I would say, 'Probably rats,' and she would shake her head and stand there for many more seconds, as if she might like it better to go spend time with these rats than with our priest."

"She did this every week?" Serena asked.

"Eh, I think for about a month. But when I began to tease her, she stopped speaking of it, and I felt I had done the wrong thing. I said I was sorry for that, but she stayed silent. Then one day as we walked by, it was I who stopped by the front doors and could not be torn away."

"And what stopped you this time, *Papá*?"

"Music. There was music coming from behind those doors; you could not convince me otherwise. It was not from a neighbor or a boom box or a passing lowrider. It was from inside the boarded-up hospital."

"What music?"

"An old Celia Cruz song. You are too young. But her music moved. It could make even sadness dance. Her voice had such energy, such strength. I started dancing right there on the sidewalk. Grabbed Enid's hand and did a little salsa."

"And she let you?"

"Well, no."

"You embarrassed her."

"No, that wasn't it either. The problem was she couldn't hear the music."

For a moment Serena believed she could hear that expansive ocean over the sound of the Pacific Coast Highway's constant traffic, and the sound was a music of its own.

"The song was only in your head?"

"To this day I believe it was no more in my head than those scents your *mamá* smelled that I could not."

"I don't understand."

"There is nothing to understand, *mija*. There are places in the world where you will encounter things so real that you will be surprised others don't have the identical experience. But then you will realize that the clarity given to you is a gift from God. Perhaps this gift is just for you, maybe it will also touch the lives of others—like the light that struck down Saul on the road to Damascus. It happened in a particular place, but the gift was for the person."

"So, music for you and aromatherapy for *Mamá*."

Her father laughed. "No, no, no. It was for us to give to the women we would meet: a new song for life, good food for the road. When we understood this, we understood how we were supposed to spend our lives."

"Dance and eat good food?" Serena teased.

Her father laughed, a generous sound.

"It was pozole your *mamá* smelled that day, *mija*. Pozole that day and every day since."

WEDNESDAY

TWENTY-SEVEN

AT TWO IN THE MORNING, SERENA WOKE COLD TO the realization that Lance had never cooked a hot aromatic meal in his kitchen, had never filled his house with music, though he had the best sound system money could buy. The emptiness of his home was unbearable.

She realized Lance wasn't in the bed. She rose and left the plush bedroom to look for him, feeling the magnitude of being alone in a ten-thousand-square-foot house. The mansion felt like a morgue. The tiled hall was frigid like the slab that probably held Christopher Larsen's body, preserved for the coroner's investigation.

With the halls constructed on a rectangle around a spacious courtyard, walking through Lance's house was a little bit like doing rounds on the YMCA's indoor track. The chill in the floor eased the pain of her blisters, which still ballooned on her big toes. She'd had no time to tend them and almost turned toward the bathroom, where Lance kept a first-aid kit.

But that particular bathroom was on the opposite side of the house, and she was already in front of the double doors that swung open into Lance's home office. She stood outside with one hand flat on the panel, which had been finished with layer upon layer of gloss to show off the natural grain of the wood. It wasn't right that she go in alone, though he'd invited her in with him on plenty of occasions. It wasn't right that she questioned Lance's integrity.

Earlier he had shielded her from a particularly excruciating interview with the LAPD, in which the goal had been to connect her to Christopher Larsen through Brock Anderson, who had apparently denied knowing the man. With a legal sleight of hand that continually drew the detective's attention away from her, Lance had protected her secret and prevented her from having to say very much at all.

"How did you do that?" she asked when the detective left Lance's house.

"Mind control," Lance said. "That and the fact that the coroner's estimated time of death doesn't correlate with the time that you were there."

Serena didn't ask any questions about this. The possibility that Christopher had survived and suffered for much longer than she realized was almost unbearable. It seemed like a bitterly unfair end for a man who'd already sacrificed so much for his sister, who'd suffered so much. Were some families just cursed?

But at two in the morning Serena realized that in order to believe this line of thinking, she must also believe that Amber had told her the truth. And try as she might to convince herself that the woman's story was fabricated for her benefit, she couldn't. She couldn't shake the sense that Amber was entirely authentic.

So authentic that Serena didn't tell Lance about her visit with the Fire Followers. Which felt a little like cheating on him.

She pushed the door open and went into the office. Lance wasn't there, but on the other side of the spacious room a sliding glass door exited to a garden path that ran around the perimeter of the house. The curtains hadn't been drawn, and moonlight on the white carpet filled the space with soft blue light. The door stood open, wide enough for a person to slip through. A light breeze lifted the curtain. Outside, a low stucco wall bordered an arched wood gate that led to the driveway.

The space looked different without him in it. Serena looked around, keeping an eye on the sliding door, hoping he'd gone out to the wraparound patio. Better that than an intruder having come in.

A house this big called for a home office, even if its owner almost never used it. Lance Liebowitz wasn't a freelancer; he belonged to an established firm. She had looked him up online, though she had never been to his Hollywood office. When she pointed out to him that the firm's website wasn't exactly inspiring, Lance laughed and said that after the Philippines, he was in no rush to hurl himself back into a full-time caseload. He had plenty of work without Internet referrals anyway. The home office was a spare and simple space, the room of a man who'd hired someone who didn't know him to decorate with the most expensive, trending pieces. The dark woods and Southwestern motifs fit the home's style but didn't reveal anything of Lance's personality—his relaxed manner, his easy smile, his stress-free demeanor, his interest in the Philippines. It made sense, though, that he would take souvenirs from his trip to his Hollywood office, where everyone would be chatting about his adventures, rather than set them up here where no one ever visited.

She briefly wondered why he had so few friends. The demands of his work, he had said. His need for solitude after spending long days with idiots and criminals. He didn't need a lot in the socialization department, he claimed. He was easily contented. With her.

The plaques on the walls certified his membership in various legal associations, and she wondered why these were here rather than in the main office. The desk was neither cluttered nor orderly, but blank, as if posing for a magazine spread. The bookshelves held pieces that he might have picked up in the course of his travels or while surfing online. They were pretty (a painted clay pot, a sculpture fashioned of a saguaro skeleton, a Native American headdress in a shadow box) but somehow common, invisible, and she'd never thought to ask about them.

For a moment she wondered if the room *was* an accurate reflection of Lance Liebowitz, and her perspective was the thing that was skewed.

But this doubt passed, because if Kaleo Iona and Amber Larsen hadn't brainwashed her with an alternate reality, she'd never have thought such a thing.

Serena drew a law book off the shelf and let it fall open. The translucent pages, dense with tiny type, stuck together like a new book that has never been read. There was no dust. It smelled like fresh ink rather than musty paper. She put it back, justifying this as well. The books were purely decorative, like everything else. Lawyers had paralegals to look up whatever had to be looked up in such volumes these days, and they probably had their own books. Their own computer databases. Did lawyers even rely on libraries anymore? She had no idea.

She opened a desk drawer. It was empty. All of them were empty. Her justifications ran short at this point. The last time they were in here together was to make the video she had posted online. She looked up, her back to the sliding glass door now. In the other corner of the room, not far from where she'd entered, the video equipment was still set up. A chair in front of gauzy curtains. A window for natural light. A camera on a tripod. The laptop where Lance had edited the film before posting it. The entire process had taken a matter of minutes.

How much did he know about video editing?

This was silly. There was an answer for everything, of course, and she was making mountains out of molehills. If she couldn't trust Lance, whom could she trust?

But she shivered and went to the sliding glass door to close it. She stood there and crossed her arms, wishing for things she couldn't have, like facts and certainty.

The office sat on the southeast corner of the house and looked up into foothills rather than out across the ocean. From here she could see the approach of the wide driveway and the dark green, woody oleander that lined the concrete and the opposite hillside covered in eucalyptus and cypress. An embankment that sloped downhill into a narrow ravine was covered in various types of ivy and squatty shrubs. She could see the topmost portion of this ravine just over the low stuccoed wall.

A narrow concrete stair about four feet wide bordered by old pipe railing hugged the hill and pointed downward. She had never noticed the stair before, which might or might not be part of Lance's property and might or might not lead anywhere. But tonight the moon brought out the white of the steps in contrast to the darker green foliage that had hidden it before.

Such stairways were common in Pacific Palisades. Decades ago, before the freeway was laid, these steep staircases used to provide agile residents with beach access and shortcuts between the zigzagging hillside streets. Today some of them dead-ended in new structures and overgrown lots. Others were more often used by adventurous walking tourists than by residents.

Compared to the recovering burn area in Angeles National Forest, these hillsides were lush and green. Even when the forest's hillsides were fully recovered, that chaparral landscape wouldn't look like this one, which was fed by moderate temperatures, mild rains, and comfortable sunshine year-round.

There, a man with a gunshot wound would leave a trail if he was dragged across the ground. Here, not so much. The tight ground cover, the wide leaves, would close behind anyone who passed, leaving little evidence.

Lance slipped his arms around her from behind and she gasped.

He laid his lips against her neck and murmured, "Didn't mean to scare you."

Serena found a light laugh in the bottom of her lungs. "You're stealthy." She put her hands atop his on her waist.

"Trouble sleeping?"

"My mind just won't stop. And my feet hurt. Where were you?"

"Your hands are shaking."

"Because they're trying to find their way back into my skin." *And*, she thought, *because I have been lying to you, and because I am afraid that you might be lying to me.* But she tried to sound accusing. He chuckled.

"This isn't the best view in the house," he said.

"But the moon is here, and the Pacific is black."

"The oil derricks are all lit up tonight. A clear view. I thought you liked those."

Dozens of derricks lit up the black-water horizon at night like beacons of calm in the middle of the vast unknown. The eyesores by day were transformed into a twinkling peace by night.

"I do," she admitted. "But you know me and plants." On the hillside, the ivy leaves glistened as if pointing the way to the Emerald City. Judy Garland just might skip right down Lance's driveway in her red shoes and blue gingham dress. "What's going to happen to me?" she whispered.

Lance gave her a squeeze. "Do you trust me?"

She snugged her robe across her body. "Yes." She didn't know if that was a lie or not.

"These investigations take time. I'll do the work. But you can help me make sure you are absolutely clean when it comes to that dead man."

Christopher. "Do they have a name yet?" she asked. Perhaps he could verify that much of Amber's story.

"If they do, they haven't released it. Are you sure you've never, ever had any connection with him before?"

Serena stepped out of his arms and looked at him. "I have never seen him before in my life."

"You said he was carrying pictures of you in his pocket."

"Mr. Walter told me. I haven't seen them. For all I know they're fake as Brock's video of me."

"Brock does seem to be the common denominator here. I need to dig up as much as I can on that kid and discredit him."

"How?" she asked.

"We find everything that makes him look like a seventeen-year-old boy with no respect for authority. A history of lying, criminal behavior, any kind of deviance—"

"Maybe we should just tell someone what happened up there," Serena said. "Truth all the way. It'll hold up."

"Not until we know how Brock and this other man are connected."

Serena sighed and turned back toward the view of moonlit greenery.

"Let me come into the office with you today," she asked.

"Won't be in the office. Court all day, except when I can get away to see you. Why?"

There were several reasons. She didn't want to be alone. She wanted to know that he actually went to a real office each day when he left her. She wanted to know who Lance Liebowitz really was.

"Do you know anyone named Phil Lancet?" she asked. A good detective should have watched his face for a reaction, but she couldn't. She was incapable of acting, of keeping up a deception for any length of time. He responded immediately, with the same tone he used when asking her where she wanted to go for dinner.

"No. Where'd you hear that name?"

"Before he was shot—the man wanted to know if I was working for Phil Lancet." Already, lying to him was getting easier.

Lance stared at her until she looked away, sure he knew everything.

"I'll look into him," he said. He didn't write the name down, she noted. Perhaps because he had no paper and pens in the desk. Or because it was a name impossible for him to forget. "Maybe he's a connection to Brock."

She shook her head, her mind going back to all the evidence that a huge house like Lance's might conceal, and all that might be exposed up at the abandoned property.

Like boot prints in sawdust. Serena caught her breath. She'd been upstairs twice, trekking around the place as if it were her own.

"I told you I went into the house," she said quietly. One time, two times—did it matter?

His voice held caution now. "Yes."

"There was sawdust. My boots . . ."

Lance didn't respond.

"Right out in the open. Fresh. Any police officer might find them."

Lance moved close again, looking out the window, standing inches away without touching her. He was mad, she thought, because he thought she was stupid. Or too smart for her own good.

"It's okay," he said, and he sounded sincere. "It's okay. Are you the only woman in the world who wears your particular size boot, in your particular style?"

His words lacked comfort.

"When you called the police to report the man's injury—"

"It was an anonymous tip."

"Did you call from here?"

"Of course not."

His offense stung. "I didn't mean—"

"What exactly did you mean, Serena?" In the slim space of a second she caught a glimpse of a Lance she'd never seen before, a burst of impatience, of condescension.

"Nothing. Nothing. I'm just trying to think of everything."

Such as the fact that when she'd returned to the house yesterday, there was no sign of a police investigation anywhere in the area. No CSIs carrying kits, no barricades of yellow tape, no restrictions on people running over bloodstained driveways. No impressions of official boot prints come and gone in the dry sooty dirt.

Lance hadn't called the police. But why? To protect her? Or to cover up his own role in whatever had happened up there?

He reached out and encircled her shoulders. An apology. Or a magician's blanket thrown over the things he didn't want her to notice.

"What's that staircase out there?" she asked, pointing. Anything to silence all the unspoken thoughts between them.

Lance took a second to focus. Then he shrugged. "It's an old thing that doesn't go anywhere anymore. Seventy-three steps down to a cinder-block retaining wall."

"I've never noticed it before."

"Not worth noticing," he said.

Lance squeezed Serena's hand tightly and it felt just a little bit like a warning.

TWENTY-EIGHT

THE MEDIA WAS ON LANCE'S DOORSTEP WHEN HE left to go to court that morning, and she wondered what had finally helped them discover where she was staying. From the inside of the house she watched Lance exit the secure garage and drive by them in his Porsche, tinted windows rolled up and doors locked. There were five or six photographers and one camera crew that she could see. She stayed away from windows and watched two of them examine a wall as if they thought it could be scaled.

Eventually they decided that the wall was secure or that the price of trespassing on a lawyer's property was too high. But they lingered like unwanted guests. She felt angry at Lance's refusal to take her with him to court, though his argument for sheltering her here was strong enough. She could have bent low in the front seat as he drove out and they never would have noticed.

Serena's phone rang. She didn't recognize the number but answered anyway.

"Yes?"

"Serena, we need to see you." It was Amber Larsen.

"So you can hold a gun to my head and make me confess to something I didn't do?" She moved up the stairs into the turret that overlooked the courtyard, where she could see the entire property in case the paparazzi decided to enter uninvited. She'd have to take care around the windows up there, as they were a little more exposed and a couple of those cameras had intimidating telephoto lenses. The spiral staircase led to a carpeted round room with three-sixty views.

"I'm sorry about that. It wasn't the best idea. But you can still help us—Kaleo and William learned a few things about Brock Anderson yesterday that you ought to know."

"So tell me."

"It would be clearer if we showed you."

"Why does that sound like a line?"

Amber sputtered, "A line?"

"Basically the same thing as a lie."

"I know what it— Maybe because you're so used to hearing them from Phil. I mean Lance."

Amber said it the way Serena had often tried to speak to her students, speaking frankly but with respect, because they would never listen otherwise. *You've got the mind for this work, but you've locked it away in a closet. Why?*

"Tell me anyway."

"We've found a connection between Brock and Phil."

Not Brock and Christopher, but Brock and Phil. Brock and Lance. What on earth was she supposed to believe?

"Come see the photographs."

From up here the camera-wielding loiterers looked like guards at a prison camp. Against her will Serena thought maybe Lance had summoned them, a ploy to keep her from leaving again. It would work, because her car was parked out there where they paced and waited. Already they'd given it the attention reserved for special exhibits at the Getty Museum.

Serena's eyes drifted to the roof tiles over the office where she'd stood in her bare feet just a few hours ago, holding Lance's hand and fearing his intentions.

Beyond the roofline her eye caught sight of the white stairs nearly buried in ivy.

"So are you saying that Lance and Brock know each other?" she asked.

"Not exactly."

"That they've met each other?"

"All I said was that there's a connection."

"I'm connected to the governor of California because we live in the same state."

"Please come."

She had shifted to the windows that faced the opposite direction, straining for another glimpse of those stairs, some hint of where they might lead except into an impenetrable tangle of ivy. Lance had said something about the stairs ending at a retaining wall, but she couldn't see one from here. Too many trees. Too many folds and rolls in the hillside.

"It's kind of hard for me to get away right now," she said, and as soon as the words left her mouth she saw a set of steps running away from the property, rushing downhill at an angle that would be perpendicular to the stairs she'd seen last night. From here it was impossible to tell if they belonged to the same staircase or to an independent one. Their point of connection, if it existed, was well below her line of sight.

Serena glanced back at the high driveway where the photographers milled about, smoking their cigarettes and keeping a competitive distance from each other. She judged the height of the wall that separated the property from the overgrown concrete. And although she knew far less about mathematics than she did about the growth patterns of ivy, she judged the top of those stairs to be beneath the photographers' view.

"Amber, I need to call you back."

"But when—"

Serena ended the call and exited the turret door and rushed down the stairs. In the bedroom she forced her tender feet into the most comfortable pair of shoes available. She collected her purse and borrowed the pocket cash that Lance had left on his dresser, about ten dollars held down by a paperweight of blown glass. The heavy sphere looked like an artistic blue and green rendering of the earth. A brass plate on the bottom declared the piece to be presented to Lance Liebowitz in gratitude for his service to the American Bar Association's Justice Defenders Program. She stuffed the bills into the back pocket of her jeans.

She tossed an olive green wrap around her shoulders, because it was the closest thing she had to ivy camouflage, and at the last minute she picked up one of his baseball caps, should she need it out in public. Then she hurried to Lance's home office. With daylight pouring in through the windows, she second-guessed her need to find out where those stairs led.

But the insecurity passed and she left the office through the sliding glass doors, stooping low so as not to be seen moving behind the stucco wall. Then, instead of exiting the property via the gate, she hopped the wall there and winced when she landed on a rocky bed of ground cover that seemed to spear her shoes.

The rapid clicks of a camera lens startled her until she realized they weren't aimed at her. She was technically in the open now, outside the property boundaries but cloaked by the thick stand of oleander that lined the road. The shrubs had been grown here for privacy and as a windbreak, and they were as good as a wall for cover so long as she didn't make a ruckus on her descent to the stairs.

She went down without catching anyone's attention.

At the top landing she could see that ivy wasn't the only growth obstructing the stairs. A haphazard shelter of feather palms also kept them hidden, and the overgrowth disheartened her hopes of finding a way out of Lance's house unnoticed. If this flight were still functional, the city would have done a better job of maintaining it. As it was, the encroachment left hardly enough room for one foot on each stair.

She descended quickly, breaking stems and squashing a few snails and slugs on the way. The fragrance of chlorophyll, fresh and alive, filled her head and emboldened her. She leaped steps, felt her purse bounce against her hip.

The retaining wall that Lance had said she'd find at the bottom seemed to be made of leaves rather than cinder block, though bits of gray peeked through in spots. She put her hand on it and found it to be solid, as impenetrable as the paparazzi at the top of the hill. The impasse rose some ten to twelve feet over her head and gave her the sensation of standing at the bottom of a waterfall. It ran to her left a mere eight to ten feet, then appeared to end abruptly at the top of the ravine. From here she couldn't see any sign of Lance's Spanish mansion, just a pale blue sky and an ocean of fluttering green leaves like sequins.

And a blazing orange that was no color found in nature. The assaulting neon shade peeked out at her from behind the greenery and she lifted the leaves aside. Behind the living curtain was a bright piece of fresh graffiti.

She touched the paint and it lightly stained her fingertips. Some of the orange color had transferred to the ivy leaves, which had marred some of the paint after being released to cover the design.

The work was signed by a smaller group of three distinct letters, falling backward into the wall like a person into a pool. BAD. She recognized it. Not just a simple word, but a signature, a double entendre. Brock AnDerson. It wasn't especially clever but it was easy to remember. How many times had she seen it doodled in the margins of worksheets, marked across the face of binders, and in one case, emblazoned across a Dumpster at the back of the gym?

Never the same place, the same colors, or the same design. But always the same three letters, the same font, the same stylistic complexity. The same brazen arrogance.

Brock's tag was an expletive so common that in some circles it had ceased to be offensive. It was small as tags went, maybe three feet high and four or five feet long. Sweeping the ivy aside with one arm, she could see the entire piece. She noted two shades of orange and three varieties of blue, outlined in black and accented with white airbrush effects. The colors were arranged to create depth, and the popping effect reminded her of the trompe l'oeils she'd seen sidewalk artists create with their rich chalks. This work appeared to fall into the wall, as if the spray paint had knocked the cinder blocks out.

Brock Anderson was here, leaving a mark slightly more creative than a scratching on a bathroom stall. Was this where Lance had gone on his midnight prowl last night? To meet the artist? So the two of them could plot more trouble for her?

Now she really wanted to know what Amber had discovered.

First, Serena withdrew her cell phone to snap some photographs of the work. She took a step back, attempting to capture the whole image, and felt her foot slip off a small ledge, crushing the undergrowth.

The ivy came loose from her fingers as she lost her balance and fell to one knee.

Her shoe had found another step, leading away from this landing at a steep angle along the face of the retaining wall. It was covered in years of overgrowth and the fallen fronds of ferns and palms, a natural mat that looked hazardous but not impassable.

She couldn't find a rail to grip as she cautiously tested the existence of more concrete stairs underneath all the plants. Serena stayed close to the wall and, when she reached the end of it, found that the flight made another sharp turn, this time to the right, and continued downhill. There was poison oak here too, as common as the snails. She could see it now as she stepped out of shade into sunlight. The slightly reddish and rounded leaves stood out from the rest, scattered evenly all across the ground.

About twenty steps down, the plants seemed to recede. The rail appeared again, popping up from the mess of growth, and gray steps emerged as if crawling out of a swamp. This, she believed, was the flight she had seen from above.

She pulled out her phone and called Amber back. And then she followed the steps down.

Posing as a nosy neighbor, Phil had told the media where Serena could be found: at Lance Liebowitz's home, he said, though the mortgage to the Pacific Palisades address in fact belonged to his real self, Phil Lancet. And when he left the house, parting the crowd with his black fenders and tinted windows, he drove Phil Lancet's favorite Porsche, just to see if even one of them might look into the registered tags.

This recklessness was part of the thrill, the delivery from the boredom that set in when taking a risk led to no terrible effect. It all seemed too easy, once done—the fabricated website, the staged home office, the trinkets that were easy to make for any occasion, like paperweights with brass plaques. The consummation disappointed, the way it had after wooing Serena into his bed for the first time and then waking the morning after, realizing that taking her was hardly different from conquering all those sorry discarded girls. Would anything ever be enough? He was starting to doubt it, and the doubt was like a splinter in his brain that he couldn't remove.

Escalation was the only salve, and summoning the media to

Lance Liebowitz's home did the job of raising Phil's heart rate to a level that made him feel alive again.

So alive that he stepped on the brake and rolled down his window three inches, mainly to hear the music of clicking cameras and loudmouthed journalists and perhaps have the opportunity to say, "No comment."

One voice shouted louder than the rest. "How does your client know Christopher Larsen?"

The name was like acid on his ears. Christopher Larsen. Of all the self-righteous activists in the ever-loving world, how had *that* one come into play here?

"The victim found dead at Mission Acres High School. The name written across his chest is your client's accuser—is this true?"

Phil flashed a condescending smile at them. "You're on private property. You have one minute to leave before I call the police."

Phil rolled up his window and continued to the bottom of the steep driveway, trying to stay focused. His destination that morning was not the nonexistent law offices of Lance Liebowitz, nor court, but a cul-de-sac where he could sit and see, with a decent set of binoculars, whether Serena would take an interest in that unremarkable staircase she had noticed the night before. Brock had come to that flight last night, scared out of his mind, to demand more money in exchange for holding his silence. No one was supposed to be killed in this mess, he'd shouted, as if he hadn't already murdered his own moral conscience.

Deal with it, Phil had advised.

The teacher took her time this morning. The tick of every second was a hammer on Phil's brain. Christopher Larsen.

He watched through his binoculars and commanded his cell phone to place a call to John Roman.

Phil skipped greetings and small talk, went directly to: "What would you say if I killed her and then set her up in your front yard with your name scrawled in blood down her arm?"

"You do that. At least then I could cover it up and keep your antics quiet."

"Right. Killing Christopher Larsen and plastering my nephew's name across his chest—that's my idea of staying out of the public eye."

"You think I did that?"

"Who else in the world wants that man dead more than you do? He's your oldest grudge. Not to mention a pretty good choice for screwing up my fun with Diaz."

"True, but *you're* the one who'd kill him, Phil. I'm not like you. I've been quite content to just keep an eye on him for the last decade. He hasn't done me any more harm than a mosquito."

"You can't open your mouth without lies falling out. Tell me the truth."

Roman chuckled. "Are you being funny? Sometimes I just can't tell. All of us here know you did it, Phil. Either you or your nephew himself."

The announcement surprised him; Phil almost didn't notice that Serena had finally emerged and come down the stairs. It took her seconds to uncover a bright painting on the retaining wall. Brock. Stupid, stupid kid.

I'm at the mercy of idiots.

The anxiety that characterized their previous conversations was gone from Roman's voice today. In fact, he seemed almost bored with Phil's diversions.

Roman continued, "So around here we think you've concocted some evidence tying your girl toy to the murder. I'm curious. When are you going to tip off authorities to the crime scene, Phil? When you find a new game to play with another sweet thing?"

Phil wished he'd thought of it himself. He watched Serena take a snapshot of Brock's artwork.

"Of course," Roman murmured, "I guess it's possible that she really did kill him. Did you talk to your man about what happened up there?"

"What? Yes. No." Phil was flustered. After Serena's frantic call, Phil had given the trafficker instructions to move the injured intruder with the girls. He told them not to worry about Serena. But he didn't ask for a blow-by-blow account of what happened. He'd assumed his man had taken the shot—but had he actually said that? "He told me he was taking the guy to you."

"Maybe that explains why the body never showed up here." Roman paused. "And why your man is dead too. The girls came with only one driver."

In an instant all of Phil's assumptions changed. He hardly noticed that Serena had bobbed out of view. But he knew where the stairs ended. He pulled out onto the street.

He turned a corner. Why had Serena gone up to the house that day instead of coming straight to him? Had Brock tipped his hand in making his allegations? After the phone call from his man, Serena had gone back to the site. Or maybe she'd never left it. Why? To fetch the body and kill the witness?

"You don't think she's about to turn the tables on your game, do you?" Roman was full of false concern.

"I have it under control."

"I'm sure you do."

In a different situation it would have been the type of karma Phil could appreciate: teacher takes student on field trip, student tells criminal uncle about remote location, criminal uncle uses location for dark deeds, teacher shows up at inopportune time and foils uncle's work. Today, though, it just wasn't funny.

"But if you've called me for advice—"

"I didn't."

"I'd say you should get rid of her before she takes you down."

"Is that wisdom or a warning?" A new light shone on the events of the last six weeks, events Phil thought he had orchestrated: Brock's request for money. His complaint about his teacher. All the right words to pique Phil's interest in the sexy young woman. What if it was Roman's doing?

"Are you trying to cut me out?" Phil asked when Roman didn't respond.

"You are the bones of this operation, Phil. I need you fully present. Get rid of her."

"What if I get rid of you instead?" Phil said.

"If you take any longer, you won't have the chance."

Phil threw the phone onto the passenger seat. Humiliation bit hard. He should have anticipated that Roman would undermine him. The time had come to part ways.

Ahead, Phil spotted Serena standing on the residential street corner, a ball cap pulled low over her eyes. As much as he hated to admit it, the only way to wriggle out of Roman's grip this time would be to dump the house, the identity, the woman. He'd have to do it all swiftly. Then he could plot a more thoughtful revenge.

He might have settled for a hit-and-run, but an old Toyota pulled to the curb and Serena slipped inside before he had thought through all the pros and cons of that option.

Besides, he kind of liked the idea of putting her dead body in Roman's front yard.

TWENTY-NINE

AMBER DROVE. WILL SAT IN THE FRONT SEAT AND Kaleo in the back, and Serena sat as far away from him as possible.

"She made me promise not to cuff you this time," Kaleo said under his breath.

There was a shine of sweat on Serena's temple and at the nape of her neck where her hair was swept up into her hat.

"What did you want to show me?" she asked Amber.

"I wanted to show you that you can trust us," Amber said. "But the truth is that we don't know if we can trust you. We can't keep wasting time begging you to help us if you don't want to do it."

Kaleo could see his friend caution Amber with his eyes and then put his hand on her leg. And rather than put them all into a rollover accident, the touch seemed to settle her down. This so surprised Kaleo that he forgot what he was going to add to Amber's challenge. If something had happened between those two, Will hadn't said anything to him. Maybe the tightness that characterized their group had been to Christopher's credit alone. The possibility of this irked Kaleo, because he didn't want to think that he might have lost even more than a best friend when Christopher was murdered.

Serena didn't flinch at Amber's tone. Kaleo waited for a catfight that didn't come.

"I do want to help. But I've got my own skin to save. If I were you I wouldn't trust me either."

Amber pulled out of Pacific Palisades onto Highway 1, a narrow ribbon with ocean to one side and foothills to the other. The mudslide-prone land was held in place by retaining walls and nets. To the southwest, whitecaps warned of a storm to follow the wind, though the horizon didn't look too ominous.

Kaleo picked up his camera off the floor by his feet and turned it on, switching the display to the picture view.

"Where's Phil?" he asked.

"Lance is in court."

"You know that for sure?" Kaleo asked.

Serena gave him her attention, and he was caught by her eyes. He didn't know what he'd expected there—an angry spark, the fear that darkened them the last time he'd seen her. Instead he saw something like curiosity, as if she had noticed him for the first time and he had teriyaki sauce on his nose.

"I guess he might be somewhere else," she said.

Kaleo had the irrational urge to take her out to dinner for his birthday. He rubbed his nose clean of the sauce that didn't exist.

Serena continued, "But if he's playing a part, he has to keep up appearances, don't you think?"

"As long as he needs you to believe him," Kaleo said.

"He wouldn't let me go to work with him today." Serena offered this fact to them as if she'd made a Herculean effort on their behalf.

"You asked to go? You might as well have asked him to take you to meet John Roman."

"Well, he didn't cuff me to a table before he left."

Kaleo suppressed a smile.

They passed a curved line of homes built on sand and stilts.

"Where are we going?" Serena asked.

"As far as it takes to get your help," Amber said.

Kaleo leaned toward Serena to show her the pictures he and Will had snapped yesterday afternoon.

"That's Brock," she said.

In the photos he was hanging out with another young man about his age. The pair drank beers in a sand-dusted parking lot. They leaned back against a retaining wall lined with aloe vera plants, the prehistoric-looking succulents with spiky leaves that oozed a gel that soothed sunburns. Brock's head was tipped back in a hearty laugh. Behind them, the digital kiosk of a local bank flashed the date and time. The photo was taken Sunday, three days ago, at 2:26 p.m.

"They look so young," she said softly.

Kaleo pointed. "That's Jett Anderson, Brock's cousin."

"Cousins hang out together," Serena said.

"Drinking beer," Amber said ironically.

"Even smart kids do dumb things," Serena said.

"Like mixing alcohol with antidepressants," Will added.

Serena's eyebrows went up as she caught his meaning.

Kaleo said, "Brock looks really good for a kid who's supposedly at a mental hospital fending off suicidal thoughts, don't you think?"

Serena took another look at the image. "Are you saying he faked the suicide story?"

"That's unclear. He was admitted to the behavioral health center in Burbank," Kaleo said. "But he discharged himself against doctors' advice early Sunday morning."

He opened a manila folder. It contained a photocopy of a newspaper clipping from the *Los Angeles Times* Entertainment page, a wedding photo of a young couple with their barefoot wedding party on the Malibu shoreline.

"Brock Anderson's mother is Tory Anderson," Kaleo said.

"I met her a couple of times when Brock was disputing his grade."

"She's a reality-show producer," said Will. "Third generation."

"But the first of her clan to have a subpar career," added Kaleo. "Her last show was a huge flop. *Incognito*."

"Never heard of it," said Serena.

Will said, "They would take a plain Jane or John off the street and make them up into some celebrity look-alike, then see how many people would fall for the twin. The decoy got cash prizes based on how many people recognized them, asked them for an autograph, whatever. Bonuses for luring paparazzi into a tabloid picture, stuff like that. The real star was on a panel that judged the performance, gave points for acting skills, for daring, and so on. It just got awkward for the real celebrities."

"Bizarre," Serena said.

"Like anyone who watched it," Kaleo said, directing the comment at Will.

"And beside the point." Amber sounded impatient.

Kaleo handed the photocopy to Serena and pointed to the photo caption.

Warner princess Tory Lancet weds financier Barry Anderson.

Standing with the bride's family, a young Phil Lancet, who looked identical to Serena's Lance Liebowitz, was named in the copy as Tory's brother.

"Do you believe he's Phil Lancet now?" Kaleo asked.

Serena frowned. "You're telling me that Brock is his nephew? They're related?"

"Strange he'd never mention that about the kid he's going to discredit in court, don't you think?"

Will handed a printed photo back over the seat. Kaleo took it as Amber took a curve and Serena swayed into Kaleo's arm. He thought she looked pale, but it might have been the road. They righted themselves.

"And look here," Kaleo said. "Jett Anderson is Barry's nephew. Cousins Jett and Brock both work for Uncle Phil."

Serena took the photograph and handed the camera back to Kaleo. She stared at the picture for a long time. Jett and Phil stood in the mouth of a concrete drain exchanging a stack of bills. Bright graffiti decorated the drain behind the men.

"We haven't actually documented Brock and Phil's professional connection yet," Kaleo admitted. "But if it quacks like a duck—"

"I think they met at the house," Serena said. On her phone, she pulled up the graffiti photo she'd taken minutes earlier. "This is Brock's work, and it's adjacent to Lance's house, on an abandoned stairway."

Kaleo compared it to the painted drain in the photograph. "Could belong to the same artist."

Serena shrugged. "Even with all this, I still don't get the connection to me. Or to Christopher."

No one offered her an answer.

"What does your gut say?" Amber asked.

She shook her head. "That people are lying to me, and I have no idea how deep and wide the lies go."

"What other lies has Phil told you, besides his name?" Kaleo pressed. "Oh, and his career, and how much he loves you, and how he's going to save you?" This question made Serena's eyes tear up, and Kaleo almost felt bad for causing it. He said, "We've never lied to you, Serena."

He thought she tried to test this by waiting for him to look away first, which of course would prove nothing. She dropped her eyes sooner than he expected. Sooner than he wanted.

Will spoke to her without turning around in his seat.

"Did Phil advise you to make that video that you posted?" he asked.

"Yes. We thought we could get out ahead of the lies with the truth."

"Have you spoken with detectives?"

"Of course."

"Why?"

"Uh, because I have to."

"No, you don't. How many times?"

"Twice now. Why? What's the big deal? When I talked to Brock, he—"

"You talked to Brock?" both men said at the same time.

Serena's seat wasn't plush enough to swallow her up, though she seemed to press into it wishfully. "Lance thought it might help if I could find out why Brock's doing all this. You know, kids want attention until it gets to be too much, and then they start to push back . . . What?"

Will had twisted in his seat. "I'm not even an attorney and I know that's the stupidest, most self-incriminating idea any half-brained person ever had."

Serena looked stricken.

"He was talking about Phil, not you." Not even Kaleo had the heart to tell Serena she'd been an idiot.

"You ever hear of clandestine pretest calls?" Will asked.

"No."

"Detectives use them in the early stages of investigation, usually before a perpetrator knows they're being investigated. The victim calls the accused, says things to put the guilty party in the position of saying something incriminating right there in front of witnesses and the public record."

"That's not what I did—"

"Doesn't matter. Rule number one of the innocent's defense,

Serena: Shut up. Don't try to explain things, don't try to defend yourself, don't talk to police, and definitely don't talk to a minor who's surrounded by an army of protective adults. Let the evidence speak for itself. Otherwise you'll hang yourself on good intentions. Next time you talk to Phil you might want to ask him about that, see what he says."

"Will's a PI," Kaleo said. "He knows what he's talking about." Then he waited for Serena to crumple. Instead, she set her jaw and sealed her lips. "He didn't mean for you to shut up with us."

"I just don't know what to believe. All of this"—Serena indicated the pictures, the clipping—"how do I know you haven't made it up?"

Amber responded by yanking the car into the nearest parking lot. It belonged to the old Malibu Inn, which had been around since the Roaring Twenties and, after being on the brink of extinction for a couple of years, had reopened with sparkly new bells and whistles and a celebrity chef to go with the place's celebrity-studded history.

She threw her arm over Will's headrest and twisted toward Serena.

"You called us, so stop wasting our time. If you don't want to help us find out who killed Christopher and why Brock's targeting you and what Phil has to do with it, then don't. I don't really care about what happens to you right now. You're the reason my brother's dead—keep that in mind."

Serena turned her head away from them all and stared out the window, and Kaleo saw defeat rather than defiance in her posture. He had seen this kind of withdrawal before, in the stooped shoulders of women who had come out of prostitution only to be welcomed by the world as wasted, worthless creatures. And in that moment he believed she had never been Phil Lancet's coconspirator.

"Usually I get to be the angry one," Kaleo said. He reached

out and touched her arm, and she flinched like he'd shocked her. "We all want the same thing. And trust me, it's not the same thing Phil wants."

Still she had no words.

"What do you want, Serena? That's the only test that really matters."

It took her a long time to answer, and for a full minute Kaleo thought she wouldn't respond at all.

"What do you want?"

She grabbed the handle on her door and yanked it back.

"I want to get out."

THIRTY

PHIL LANCET—FOR NOW SERENA BELIEVED THAT this was his real name, or at least closer to his real name than Lance Liebowitz ever was—had pulled into the parking lot while Serena's companions were waiting for her to answer Kaleo's question. She was avoiding their scrutiny by staring at the blue-gray waters licking the piles of the little Malibu Pier when Phil cut across her stare. She saw the glistening black Porsche, the tinted windows, the matching sunglasses that were unnecessary in this timid sunshine. And she knew, as he pulled into the lot and passed so close to Amber's car that he might have kissed it, that Phil was looking directly at her.

The man who would not allow her to come to his place of work had followed her.

Phil Lancet. She tried out the name in the safety of her mind and thought she might be sick. Her attraction to Lance had been nothing more than an infatuation with a fictional character. But the physical reality of her delusion was still all over her skin.

"What do you want?" Kaleo repeated.

"I want to get out," she said. Kaleo fell back into his seat with a disgusted kind of sigh. Will and Amber didn't say anything at all.

Explaining herself was not a part of Serena's plan any longer. But she hoped that Kaleo, if he thought it through rather than got mad about it, would see what she was doing and figure things out. After all, he was the one who had given her the idea, though he might not remember it right away.

Serena threw open the door and exited the car, leaving the photographs behind, and Amber peeled out before she had the chance to close it. The top corner of the door frame nicked her arm.

Phil had parked in the farthest empty space on the opposite side of the small lot. He exited, closed the door, and leaned back against it. He crossed his arms.

Serena started walking. And as she placed one foot in front of the other, the ocean breeze catching her pant legs and slapping them against each other, she thought of her first day as a teacher, walking down the halls to her classroom, where she would be faced throughout the day by more than 150 students who would, she feared, see right through her. They would know she had never been in charge of her own classroom before. They would know she was barely five years older than some of them, unable to exert her authority in spite of the many strategies she'd learned. They'd test her and find her as fragile as their outdated textbooks.

"They're just as scared of you," her father had said. "Don't show the fear. Show the respect. They'll give you what you give them."

Phil waited, hiding behind those sunglasses, striking a pose that might mean anything from casual indifference to cold-blooded opposition. Seagulls coasted on the air around the parking lot, making the restaurant their own. The wind caught her hair and sent it sideways across her face. She reached him, finally, and spoke through the strands.

"You and I seem to have secrets."

"I like a little mystery in a woman," he said easily.

"Then you should love me." She removed his sunglasses with a light touch. He let her take them. Her fingers tingled with nerves, and he moved his to his pockets. She wondered if he carried a gun, if it would be run-of-the-mill for him to shoot a woman in public, in the middle of the day. It was hard to meet his eyes, but she would have to. It was necessary to expose herself in order to hide the fear.

"I find you more fascinating every day," he said.

"And yet it turns out I hardly know you."

His smile was coy. Pleased, she thought. Happy to peel back the curtain.

She continued, "Or maybe I know you better than we think, being cut from the same cloth."

"What cloth would that be?"

"I don't know if I should say. Are you still my attorney? It seems you're more vested in other business ventures."

"Such as?"

"Let's stop pretending that you and I are anything other than what we really are, Lance." She would have to be careful, life-in-the-balance careful, not to call him Phil. "You know what I mean. Can I trust you with my secrets? Or will you throw me in the trunk of your car and bury me with all the other girls who die in your care?"

That smile again. He didn't seem at all upset that he'd been found out. There was a broken seashell next to Phil's shiny shoe. He picked it up and chucked it at a seagull.

"Rodents with wings," Phil muttered of the bird.

"I need a good attorney," she said. "I think you could represent me with a unique kind of sympathy. Can you?"

"Oh, I can do better than that, Serena. Consider me like . . . your priest."

"Of some ancient religion where they feed virgins to volcanoes?"

He shook his head. "You have it all wrong. We feed them to the highest bidders."

Serena nodded. If she didn't get this right, this might be her last view of the expansive Pacific. The waves crossed over each other at angles, disoriented, suggesting an undertow at work beneath the surface.

"Then maybe you can take my confession after all."

Inside the Malibu Inn, Serena chose the counter at the front windows, where they could sit with the ocean before them and the entire restaurant at their backs. She took the tall swiveling stool in the corner. After they ordered, Phil pulled his stool next to her and draped an arm over the back of her chair, leaned over her shoulder so that their mouths and ears were only inches away from each other's. It was as close to a private world within a public place that she could hope to get.

Serena had come to the Malibu Inn as a child, in its post-heyday years when the signed black-and-white photos of Hollywood glitteratzi who once frequented the restaurant yellowed in greasy frames and covered every inch of the walls. In the fifties, back before trendy coffeehouses and upscale bars, the restaurant was owned by rock legend Neil Young, who gave his stage to talent like Eric Clapton and Tom Petty. As the landmark aged into the eighties and nineties, the wood tables grew sticky with layer upon layer of dark lacquer and the sloshed drinks of happy people devouring good food and live entertainment.

Now the place was as transformed as Serena's life—only the restaurant had fared better. The new decor was California-stylized surf and turf, the dining rooms spacious under an open-beamed ceiling, surrounded by colorful murals and bright wood siding and mirrors to enlarge the appearance of the space. It was slick and appealing but not yet restored to its former status. That would take time and luck.

Phil waited for her to speak, falling easily into his role of contented boyfriend. They watched the winged rodents waddling through the Malibu Pier parking lot across the highway, unafraid of people who might leave trash for them to scavenge.

It would be too risky for Serena to say she was guilty of raping Brock Anderson, which was what Amber wanted her to do. In light of what she'd learned that morning, Phil probably knew the truth. Of course, he might also know she was lying now. It would come clear soon enough.

"What Brock says I did," she said. "It's not true. He's just a boy with dirty fantasies. Though they might improve if he knew what I'm really capable of."

She could feel Phil's breath on the side of her cheek and she thought it quickened. But he didn't speak. It felt dangerous to say too much. She recalled Will's words. Don't try to explain yourself. Let the evidence speak for itself. Well, she was a little short on evidence, but if she cast the right light on events, they might look like something fresh, new, surprising.

"The school is a perfect cover for people like us, Lance. Thousands of students to pick from. I'm like a lifeguard at a pool, with a prime view of the ones who are drowning."

"People like us." Phil said the words like he was tasting them. Liking them. "How did you find out?"

"The people in the car when you pulled in," she said. "They work for me, and I think it pays to know the competition."

Phil played with his spoon. Stirred the ice water she'd requested.

"What is it that you think I do?" he asked.

Serena smirked and left it at that. "Why do you think we hooked up, Lance? Not because you wanted to date a biology teacher. Not because I couldn't resist your smooth tongue."

A burst of mirth escaped Phil's mouth.

"I never say no to a challenge. Though you turned out to be much easier than I expected."

The backhanded remark brought a flush to her face. And self-doubt to her throat. She was a fool to think he might believe her story.

"Brock doesn't seem like the drowning type," he said.

"I don't know. Maybe I think you put him up to it."

"Why would I do that?"

She looked at him and saw something like admiration in his eyes. It gave her an idea.

"Because you're a greedy man. Isn't that what our work is all about? Greed? Thousands upon thousands of fish in this sea and you want to put me out of business. How better to do that than to strip me of my right to be a teacher? You're greedy for what you can't have," Serena said.

Phil answered by kissing the nape of her neck, just behind her ear. Serena's skin crawled with goose bumps, but she didn't push him away.

"I can have anything I want," he said, and she knew he didn't quite believe her yet. She had to give him something more substantive.

Serena sighed and tried to sound bored, though her pulse was knocking against her ears. "Brock has done some grooming work for me. He has a cousin who does the same, works for some guy named Phil who has ties to Nevada. If I'd known about it ahead of time, I wouldn't have picked Brock for the work. It's not like our people can sign noncompete clauses, is it?"

Phil chuckled.

"So this Phil, as it turns out, has deeper pockets than I do. Brock wanted more than I had to give. He's mad about it."

"And what did you tell him?"

"That he should go work for Phil, if the life is so sweet with him."

Phil's concentration deepened. He picked invisible lint off his pants.

Serena shrugged. "I guess it wasn't an option."

"Groomers can be territorial."

The server brought their food and silenced them. A mixed-greens salad loaded with oranges and avocados and tomatoes for Serena. Grilled fish for Phil. She had no appetite. He squeezed a lime over the pico de gallo that topped his fish, then forked the food, still keeping Serena ensconced in his other arm, as if she might bolt while he ate.

"I get the feeling you're no respecter of territories," Serena said, thinking of Roman. "You want the power your boss has. That's your real challenge, isn't it? The thing out of reach?"

Phil looked at her, chewing, amused. She was stabbing in the dark without a good enough sense of her target. She should have paid better attention to everything Amber and the guys had told her. She had to think on her feet.

"I have what you want," she claimed.

"You have power over my boss?" He was teasing her.

"I have a channel bigger than any he ever dreamed of."

"Is that so? We have twelve hundred women—give or take. They wear out, they die, we take new recruits as demand requires. It's not worth keeping tabs. One hundred seventy locations—give or take. We open new ones, we close others, we move the girls before goody-goodies have a chance to pinpoint the brothels. An online network of groomers and traffickers and pimps so complex that no one knows where the threads start or end. We're invisible."

His low voice would never reach beyond their tight circle, but she wished someone would overhear, swoop in, tear him off of her and throw him in a cell. Imprison him for life to be subjected to the same abuses he'd inflicted on other human beings. The scent of the citrus vinaigrette on her salad, of the lime-drizzled fish on his lips, made Serena feel nauseated. She had some difficulty continuing the conversation and was saved only by the fact that whispering was required. Her words came out more like a gasp.

"Twelve hundred." She tried to mock. "Do you know how many kids go through LA Unified? It's the second-largest school district in the nation. I have the means to compete. You and I could triple your man's number."

"But I have a noncompete clause," Phil said sarcastically.

"Keep me in the schools, Lance. Get me off this hook called Brock. Defend me well, and I will pay you back with more than you ever thought you could have."

Phil swallowed. "This naughty schoolgirl side of you really turns me on. Can you put your hair in pigtails for me tonight?"

Serena didn't have to pretend being offended. But she measured her words.

"Yes. And then I'll shoot you through the heart the way I did Christopher Larsen."

Finally, she had Phil's attention.

"You know the name. The high and mighty activist. He followed me. He'd expose us all. I don't let people like that just walk away."

"How long have you been doing this?" he asked. His voice took on the tone of an executive granting an interview to a prospective employee.

"Long enough to be valuable to you," she said. "But I'm not greedy. I'm patient. And I'll defend my territory to the death."

Phil wiped his mouth with a napkin.

"You killed Christopher Larsen."

She thought he was trying to decide whether to believe her. It was a fool's claim, a potentially deadly one, since she had no idea who actually dealt the fatal blow. It might have been this man sitting right beside her. But she had jumped off the cliff and there was no getting back on the ledge.

"And then I had his body put up at the high school as a warning to Brock. It's time he stop messing with me."

Phil removed his arm from the back of her chair and straightened the collar of his coat, then faced Serena and put an elbow on the counter.

"You're lying," he accused.

Her stomach plummeted. "About which part?" She turned her attention to her salad. She forked an avocado and studied it. "We all lie when it suits us. But if you think it's time to tell the world the truth, Lance, well, I'll be happy to tell them who you really are. What exactly was it that you spent the last year in the Philippines doing? Not serving the cause of justice, I'll bet."

There was that grin again, that lopsided thing that she'd seen in her students' faces when they shared YouTube videos of extreme daring: part disbelief, part fascination, part admiration, part longing that they, someday, might star in such a role in spite of the risk.

Serena popped the avocado bite into her mouth, wondering if her terror was visible. His certainly was, masquerading as eagerness. She could see his pulse in the side of his neck. It took all of her concentration to swallow and hold the food down.

"If I'm going to help you," he said, "you'll have to sort out your lies from the truth for me."

Sweat on the tips of her fingers threatened to make her lose hold of the fork.

"Now if I did that, where would be the challenge for you?"

THIRTY-ONE

AT HER BROTHER'S HOUSE, AMBER THREW HERSELF out of the car while it was still rocking on its wheels, trying to recover from being thrown into park before it had come to a complete stop. She left her door open and blazed a trail to the back porch, the porch overlooking the pool Christopher swam in every day, where there was a swing she could rock on until her mind came to rest. The passenger side of the car was pinned against the garage wall, so carelessly had she pulled into the narrow space. Kaleo and William couldn't open their doors. Amber didn't care. Let them take it as a sign they should stay put and leave her alone.

On the porch she remembered that the swing's eye hooks had fallen out of the rotting beam weeks ago, and Christopher had never got around to putting it back up. She stood there, staring at the stupid little rusty patio set standing in its place, and felt herself coming undone from the inside out.

She heard William climbing out of the compact car, all height and limbs. The backrest of the driver's seat creaked under his weight. His boot snagged the emergency brake. He hit his head on the door frame. But then he was there, standing as close as he could get to her without touching. He looked at the patio set, and his silence seemed to find just as much fault with it as Amber could have.

She kicked one of the chairs and it toppled over.

"Who put these here?"

Kaleo had. She remembered the day he'd brought them over. She remembered being indifferent about them. She couldn't use the swing and the weather was warm and they wanted to sit outside and Christopher was so busy. Now she wished she had insisted on the swing. She was mad at everyone—at Christopher for not foreseeing she would need it; at Kaleo for so easily replacing it; at Serena for creating her need for it. Amber glanced back at the garage. Kaleo stayed in the car as if sensing his future might be at stake.

"She said he saved her life," Amber muttered. "My brother died saving *her* life. And this is how she repays him?"

William shoved both of his hands into the loose pockets of his old cargo pants. He kicked over a second chair as if that was the best way to agree with her. And it was.

"What a waste!" she said. "Serena Diaz is the most worthless piece of . . ." She couldn't think of a euphemism that captured the true, miserable essence of her worthlessness. "Aargh! She might as well have killed Christopher with her own hands. She *did*. She's responsible. I hold her responsible." Her *s*'s sprayed the air.

She stomped her foot, and the metal table with the round perforated top rocked on the old porch, unable to find its resting balance.

"She's someone's sister," William said quietly.

Amber sputtered. "Don't make me mad at you too," she ordered.

He put out the toe of his boot and stopped the table's metronome rocking.

"When Christopher was looking for you, he always believed he'd find you eventually. He never gave up on that. But what almost killed him were all the girls he found that he couldn't get out."

If Amber hadn't been so angry with Serena, she might have resented William's bringing it up.

"And not just the girls he couldn't get out, but the ones who didn't have anyone looking for them."

"I know." Already she felt less furious.

"We'd leave these places at all hours and he wouldn't even be able to talk to me, sometimes for days. He'd go through a carton of cigarettes. And then out of the blue he'd say, 'If everybody just had one person who cared, everyone would be okay. Just *one* person.'"

"Serena has a decent family. Why couldn't they be enough for her?"

"Maybe because they weren't there exactly when she needed them."

"And Christopher was. He shouldn't have been. She wasn't worth it."

"She's someone's sister," William said again.

"I should have let Kaleo rip her apart." Amber couldn't keep the bitterness out of her voice.

"Christopher would have died for you," William said. She felt his eyes on her.

"But he didn't have to," she said.

"No one would do it if they didn't have to."

"But *her*." Amber put her hands on top of her head, grasping for some kind of unavailable reason that would satisfy her grief. "So many other girls needed him more."

"Can you say that for sure?"

Amber closed her eyes. Insisting on it seemed like a betrayal of Christopher's judgment.

William started, "He used to always say—"

"'On the road to rescue, you can't speed by the people who are broken down on the shoulder.'"

"Yeah, that."

"Isn't that why we're still such a small-time operation, after ten years of this?"

"Now you sound like you're mad at him."

"He left me."

"Not before you were completely safe," William said. And she knew he spoke the truth. "We don't know what happened, Amber, but we know Christopher. We've got to trust that he knew what he was doing."

"He left us with so much work to do." Her anger finally gave way to the real despair behind it. "I can't do it without him."

"But *we* can."

"Without Serena's help?"

"When did she become our only option?" William asked.

Amber wasn't sure. She had just put so much hope in finally being close to Phil and Roman after so many years of distant sightings. It had lightened the weight of losing Christopher by a fraction.

"Forget Serena," he said.

She looked at William and saw the kind of compassion Christopher used to shower on her. Patience, confidence that she'd be okay. And also something else. Strength. Hope. She needed both, and he seemed to be holding them out for her to take.

"The work's never done," she said.

"Let's do it anyway."

She reached out to let him help her. His body was warm and solid, alive. She slipped her arms around his waist, between his shirt and his light jacket, and let him fold her up in arms far stronger than her own. She laid her ear on his heart and let the sound bring her back down to earth.

Serena Diaz would be easy to forget.

"I wish you'd started talking to me about these things years ago," she said.

"Christopher was better at it."

"It's a different kind of better. Coming from you."

He rested his chin on the top of her head.

THIRTY-TWO

PHIL DROVE, WHICH MEANT THAT WHEN HE DECIDED to bypass the turnoff to Pacific Palisades, he could just do it without consulting anyone. He aimed for the 10, but Serena didn't ask any questions until he merged with the light midday, midweek traffic headed north on the 405.

"Where are we going?" Serena asked.

"To the place where Christopher was killed."

"Why?"

"Because I want to see it for myself. I want to see you in your environment."

Phil hadn't believed Serena's story until she mentioned Brock's cousin Jett. The explanation made some murky things clear—such as why Brock had seemed ripe for the picking when he came to Phil, and why Serena had been so trusting, and why Roman was so perturbed in the beginning.

"If you want me to defend you to the best of my ability, I'm going to have to gather a few firsthand facts about what happened, how, and where. Since I can't exactly get them from the police."

"Because you didn't call them, did you?" Serena asked. "When I told you Christopher had been shot, you said you'd call, but you didn't. Why not?"

Phil smiled at her. "Does it matter? That might be what saves you now. You should be more appreciative."

"I don't need to be defended against a murder charge. It's the sex crime that will tank my career. Our future."

"One thing at a time. The only reason you haven't been charged with murder is because they haven't found the real crime scene yet."

She studied his profile, processing this silently.

"You don't want them to find it, Serena."

"No, I don't."

"So before we deal with the Brock problem, what do you say we go contaminate a crime scene?"

"So long as you don't do it with my blood," she said. She was rock solid, unflinching.

Serena Diaz was the most thrilling variety of woman, a sexy wolf cloaked in a wool wrap and not a stitch of anything else. Whether she preyed on young people or was preying on him remained to be seen, and the game was exhilarating. She was as innocent of Brock's charges as she was of knowledge that Phil had engineered that drama. He was fascinated by the real possibility that she had indeed killed Christopher Larsen.

Phil was still poised to win this game, albeit on a different field. Serena wanted into his world. Well, he would invite her in, welcome her, feed her milk and cookies. And then tell the world what she had done. Mission accomplished. Not quite as satisfying as having run innocence through the heart on a glistening silver blade, but still satisfying, to have conquered a worthy opponent.

The site was not as Phil remembered it, which was helpful in pretending to Serena that he'd never been here. Of course, he'd never been here during daylight hours.

"Why did you pick this spot for dealing with Brock's surprise?" he asked. "It would have been wiser to pick someplace like . . . a church." He took the car over the dirt road gently. It was not the place for a precious Porsche. "If an advocate of Brock's had followed you—"

"I get it, Lance. I was stupid. I took care of it."

Phil grinned.

Serena directed him to turn into an overgrown driveway that would do a number on his paint job, but that wasn't what caused Phil's smug pride over the nicely placed insult to melt away. A tickle started at the base of his skull, and when the drive curved and the plants seemed to close in on the rear fender, foreboding took a free-fall into his belly. He second-guessed the wisdom of coming.

Phil Lancet had never in his life second-guessed anything that Phil Lancet ever decided to do.

The route, barely one car wide, was uneven and rutted. Pebbles pinged the undercarriage.

A figure dashed straight across the plane of his rearview mirror. Straight across the road behind the car. A wispy form with flowing skirts and flowing hair.

He twisted in his seat.

"What?" Serena asked.

It might have been a person, except for the scurrying-rabbit speed.

"Thought I saw someone."

She looked for herself.

"Probably a deer," he said. "Just surprised me."

She studied him until he grew annoyed. He probably should have picked a word other than *surprised*.

The driveway was long, perhaps a mile, but it took Phil and Serena up to the large stone-faced house sitting in a gray-green clearing. The skeletons of burnt scrub oak mingled with the leafy survivors and stood in a ragtag vigil around the structure—also burnt, also showing signs of stubborn survival.

"There it is."

"How did you ever find this place?" he said.

"Just lucky, I guess."

"For both of us," Phil said. But at the moment he was getting stronger internal signals that luck had nothing for him here. He looked at his palms. They were sweaty and left ghostly marks on the steering wheel.

This kind of nervousness was completely foreign to Phil. He had come here of his own will. It had been his idea. There was no threat here, in this place that only he and a handful of allies could find. And John Roman, who had become an unknown quantity. He tried to ignore his unease, but his mind turned to new possibilities. When Serena had learned of his involvement in sex trafficking, why hadn't she also figured out his true name? The extent of her cleverness, sitting next to him looking like ignorance, was impressive. This might be a trap.

A burst of darting shadow drew his eyes to the hillside. The same shapeless figure he had seen behind the car minutes earlier was nowhere to be seen. But it was there, no debating it. If Serena had noticed, she seemed unafraid.

He understood then that he could never trust her again. Not because she was a liar, but because he was no longer in control of her knowledge. People who lived in the dark were a threat to no one. But here she stood, like the moon, with a large portion of her mind reflecting light that he hadn't shined.

Phil parked alongside the smaller of two entrances at the back of the house.

"Where did it happen?" he asked.

"Around the front. But you can see where we brought him."

She pointed. A maroon stain covered a bit of the gravel in front of the stoop. They should shovel it up.

He kept his eyes on her, noting the nuances of her behavior. Her hands in the pockets of her jacket made fists. Her eyes refused to make contact with him. They exited the car and she strode purposefully past the bloodstain and around the front corner of the house. She didn't wait for him, and he was unwilling to let her out of his sight.

"How'd you get him out of here?" he asked, thinking of his traffickers guarding the house. "Did you kill one of my men?"

She didn't answer.

Two darting shapes snagged the corners of his eyes, both approaching without taking care to hide themselves. But when Phil tried to focus on where they'd gone, all he got was . . . nothing.

He quickened his steps to follow Serena, and the forms popped into his peripheral vision again, three of them now, then vanished when he tried to see their trick. He mentally reviewed their meal at the Malibu Inn. At no time could Serena have slipped any mind benders into his drink or his food. He was always attentive to that, as it was his own preferred method of getting someone to see his point of view.

Still, his heart rate had jumped when the three shadows popped up like spirits from a Dickens novel, so much closer this time. They gained on him, then vanished. It was only a tiny adrenaline-induced increase, just a few beats per minute. Just enough for him to notice.

"Who helped you move the body?" he repeated, rounding the corner of the house. Here the ground sloped away into a small amphitheater-like clearing, with the house at the top of the rise like a tower of box seats. Serena was walking briskly downhill, toward stage left, but Phil hardly noticed her. His attention was commanded by something far more important than where she was headed and whether his men could be killed or bought off.

A crowd had gathered in the bottom of the bowl, a cast of women assembled for a curtain call. Two dozen or so stood shoulder to shoulder and holding hands behind each other's backs, so that they embraced and supported each other and formed a solid wall of bodies.

They faced away from him, though he knew they knew he was present, come on scene like the star performer amid the crush of extras. But there was no audience, and the girls mostly ignored him.

Then they began to multiply. There were at least a hundred now. They crowded and spread and overtook the corners of his mind.

"Serena!" She was out of sight and didn't answer. A dull pain flared up in the bicep of Phil's left arm.

At the sound of Serena's name, one of the young women turned her head in the direction that Serena had gone. She was the only one who responded to Phil's voice.

He knew her—the bridge of her nose had a peak dead center, where he had once broken it getting her to do as she was told. It was his first year in the business, and he hadn't yet learned the less forceful methods of eliciting cooperation. The lobe of her ear dripped blood where he had torn out a hoop earring as a punishment for failing to meet a quota. The memory of it hit hard, the details so vivid that they knocked the wind out of him.

He'd taken the earring ten years ago.

He'd taken the girl's life a week later.

She twisted her neck far enough to catch his eye. She winked.

The pain in his arm reached all the way up to his shoulder and immobilized him. It ran down his back like a snake and then, fanged, drove itself straight through his back and into his heart.

Phil fell to his knees as the women began to move. They walked backward in his direction, an army of fluttering shadows met by more that arrived every second.

He turned, thinking of running. These frail, ghostly girls would slaughter him with their faces averted and their hands clasped behind their backs, by winking at him. The pain in his chest deepened as his heart rattled the cage, shrieking at his mind. It was impossible to breathe.

It was impossible to *believe*.

Phil could no longer estimate the number present. Those closest to the house looked upward, watching the top-story windows, or farther, up over the hillside. Others kept eyes in Serena's direction. Steadily, they closed in.

Phil could feel the death of his heart coming on like this crowd. They tightened their noose without any interest at all in the victim at the center. They squeezed with the aim to crush, cinching the circle. The air thickened enough to smother and to deafen.

He thought he heard Serena talking to him, making unreasonable demands, such as, that he speak. Kneeling there in the green-gray grime of the old Station Fire burn, he believed he'd never be able to speak again.

THIRTY-THREE

THE ROAD BACK TO CIVILIZATION HAD NEVER SEEMED as long as when Phil sat in the passenger seat clutching his shirt at his chest. He was conscious but not speaking, though his mouth stayed open most of the time, seeking air. Whatever the cause, Serena feared it was lethal. It was hard to think of anything but the fallout that would happen if this man died in a car she was driving.

When they returned to the main road, Serena lifted her phone to her ear, announcing her intentions to have an ambulance meet them down in Tujunga. Better than at the abandoned house, which would raise more questions than either of them dared answer. Still clutching his shirt with his right hand, Phil's left hand shot out and knocked the phone away from her. It tumbled backward, over the driver's seat into the back. His knuckles grazed her cheek.

"You need a hospital," she said when she recovered from the surprise.

"Doctor," he gasped. "No hospital."

"Where?" she asked.

He gestured on down the road. *Just keep going.*

"And if you die before we get there?"

She didn't expect an answer. She didn't get one.

She hurried as fast as she could without risking the attention of police or highway patrol.

What had that place done to him?

Serena had seen Christopher's abandoned flip-flops the moment she came around the corner of the house. They waved at her from their conspicuous spot on the ground. She aimed for the shoes, figuring that the reason for her movements would be immediately obvious to Phil, behind her. It helped to have a purposeful aim. She thought it might make her lies more convincing.

She saw a dark stain where the earth had swallowed up most of the blood Christopher had lost as he lay here.

"I'm sorry," she whispered, and she tried to pick up the flip-flops without disturbing anything nearby.

"He was wearing these," she had said, turning around and holding them up.

Phil wasn't looking at her. He was standing near the crumbling ruins of the porch, staring at something on the other edge of the clearing.

"Phil!" she shouted, and then she thought she would have to make the second run of her life from this very spot because he would hear her mistake.

He didn't react to her voice.

"Lance, hey!"

He fell to his knees and held his hands up in front of him, fending off an invisible enemy. His entire body pleaded but he didn't speak. Then he doubled over with his face in the dirt and threw his hands over his head.

The idea of leaving him there passed quickly. Right now, every move seemed like the wrong move. She thought of calling Amber but feared Phil would hear the conversation.

When she reached him she stooped to touch his back. He exploded like a jack-in-the-box, and his swinging arms connected with her shoulder. She fell backward. Christopher's flip-flops cushioned her wrists when she hit the ground. Phil was on his feet then, silently flailing against something she couldn't see or hear, something like bats attacking his head. This went on for long seconds before he dropped again and rolled onto his back, grabbing at his heart. The thrashing stilled into a sort of flinching.

Serena went to him, keeping a distance. This time he seemed to see her. His eyes locked onto her face and his body seemed to relax. He extended his arm toward her and she hesitated to take it. He stretched until his back arched, a plea for help. She offered it.

It took several terrifying minutes to get him to his feet and into the car. He was cooperative but disoriented and pained.

Now he kept gesturing to her, waving at the windshield or out his window. *Just keep going*.

They drove for a long time, Phil directing her along a new route, down toward North Hollywood, then Studio City, and eventually Beverly Hills. As she followed his instructions, his distress seemed to fade a little, enough for him to add a few words to his gestures.

"You're that scared of hospitals," she mocked.

He offered her a half smile.

But she wondered.

They exchanged the ugly freeways for the streets where new money mixed with a century's worth of faded glory, like an aging woman with a noticeable face-lift. There was something both attractive and repellent about Beverly Hills, and the best Serena had ever come up with was that it didn't feel like home, though she'd spent her entire life in Southern California.

They drove into a neighborhood of high walls and decorative gates and lush foliage designed as much for privacy as for beauty. As the streets headed up hills the properties became larger and less visible, the gates more staggered.

The driveway Phil led her to was different from the others, which were wide and seemed to boast of the possessions beyond, treasures the average passerby could only dream of and certainly would never be admitted to see. This one was modest, wide enough for one vehicle and monitored by a single security camera. There was no number on the adjacent adobe wall or on the street. There was no mail receptacle that she could see. She wondered if it was a service entrance.

They sat in the driveway for interminable seconds. Phil leaned his head back against the seat.

"What now?" Serena asked.

Phil pointed to the security camera. Then he waved at it, held up his middle finger for whoever was watching on the other side, and waited.

Eventually the gate swung open and Serena drove into a world within a world. The driveway wasn't a service entrance after all. It approached the front of the mansion, a rambling ranch style of understated size and design. The road was laid out at the side of the property as if the occupants didn't want to be bothered with the view of anyone approaching. Instead, a perfectly thick lawn, dense gardens that still bloomed at this late date, and towering shade trees twice the height of the house boasted their own version of heaven.

Or hell in disguise.

Was this one of Phil's private residences? Perhaps he'd heard her slip of the tongue after all. She wondered if she might ever be allowed to leave.

Or maybe he really did have a private physician ensconced here. To help patch up trafficked girls until they were suitable for service.

Phil's face was pasty pale and his eyes had closed.

The driveway was paved and they approached silently, wrapping around the back of the house and coming face-to-face with a three-car garage. Two of the doors stood open, revealing gleaming cars and two mechanics in greasy coveralls. They turned to see who the visitors were.

She stopped in the center of the turnaround and waited for Phil's instructions.

A third broad-shouldered man emerged from a rear door and stood on the stoop under the covered porch, where he waited for them. Phil reached out for the door handle but seemed to lack the strength to pull the latch. Their host made no move to help, and so Serena leaned across his body and pushed the door open herself before getting out and going around the car.

The other man was tall, massive actually, and could have lifted Phil out of the car with just one hand. He put his huge hands on his hips and scrutinized her. There was something about his look that made her skin ripple. She avoided his gaze because now was the time to pour all her mental effort into staying focused on her act.

"Lance is sick," she said, offering Phil her hand.

"Then he should go to the hospital."

Phil pulled himself out of the car without taking Serena's fingers. When he could stand, one hand on the door frame and the other on the roof of the car, he took several slow, pained breaths before turning to the man on the covered porch.

"He needs a doctor," Serena tried again, slipping her shoulder under his arm.

"Let him die."

Phil grunted at that and the man smirked. Serena didn't know what to do.

"Funny," Phil pushed past his lips.

"Maybe after I lose everything, I can try my hand at being a comedian." *After I lose everything?* Serena couldn't guess what he meant. From the waistband at his back, the man withdrew a large pistol with a silencer affixed to the end and lifted it toward them. He moved the barrel around as if indecisive over who or what to shoot. The barrel eventually pointed at her head. She ducked behind the open door. Her lungs worked double time.

"She's jumpy," the man observed.

Phil was stooping again, taxed by the effort to stand, but he shook his head as if this kind of welcome was routine and tiresome.

"Serena Diaz," he said by way of introduction, flopping a hand in her direction. "She's here to double our business."

"All by herself?" the man asked, and this time he laughed.

Serena forced herself to stand. She cursed her weak stomach and her hot face. Phil looked at her and raised an eyebrow. She thought he might pass out. She feared what the other man might do to her if he did.

She supported Phil once more, hoping her blushing looked like fury instead of fear. She turned to Phil's inhospitable partner and spoke the way she spoke to a class of thirty teenagers gone crazy. Boldly enough, fearlessly enough to cover up all her doubts.

"If you don't want what I'm offering I can take it somewhere else," she said.

The man fired a quiet shot into the front passenger tire. Serena's knees buckled, but she had a firm grip on the door frame.

"Next time call first," he said to Phil.

He tucked the gun back into his waistband and finally came off the porch. He took long strides and closed the distance quickly, but his eyes were on Serena the whole time. She matched his bold stare and hoped the lightness in her head wouldn't turn into a dead faint.

He let his eyes slip over her body. She had a physical sensation of hatred for this oak tree of a man, who had dark features and a flat nose and wide eyes that pinned her against the car, then used her as if she existed only in some alternate reality of sick fantasies.

When his eyes returned to hers he extended a hand.

"Welcome," he said. Like a lamb to be roasted for dinner, perhaps.

The bones of her hand felt brittle as she placed her palm in his. She hoped he wouldn't feel the trembling, the loud rattling of her pulse.

She managed to smile. "You must be John Roman."

"I prefer Lance leave introductions to me," Roman said.

"I can figure out some things all by myself," she said. What she hadn't figured out was whether he'd find her intimidating or stupid, using his real name without seeming to know Lance's. She wished then that she'd waited for him to reveal himself.

His powerful palm slipped over the heel of her hand and then around her wrist. His overlapping fingers pinched her skin.

Then he kissed the back of her hand.

"If we're going to do business together, we should also do a little socializing," he said. He began to walk away from the car and her resistance was involuntary. She shot a pleading look at Phil. He wasn't looking at her. He was doubled over again, tugging at the pain in his chest. If he was acting, it was a good show. She'd believed everything.

"Lance," she said.

Roman yanked her arm. "I'll send someone out for him."

THIRTY-FOUR

SERENA AND ROMAN DID NO SOCIALIZING AFTER leaving Phil behind in the driveway. He hauled her into the house and down a long and windowless hall. Track lights gazed adoringly at expensive artwork staggered along both walls. It was the only light here.

"You won't mind if I stash you someplace comfortable until I get him straightened out," he said. It wasn't a question.

So she didn't answer.

The house didn't look so large from the outside. But the broad-shouldered man took turn after turn through an odd configuration of dim passageways until Serena thought it was a trick and he was taking her in circles. They passed a painting she thought she'd seen before. But then, she suddenly realized, they were all nudes. Not of the classic type.

She thought she saw others. The figure of a woman stepped out of the hall and into the cover of a shadow so quickly that she might have been a trick of the light. As they passed a partially open door, the silhouette of a man smoking in an easy chair caught her eye and then was gone. The stench of tobacco lingered.

Roman finally paused in front of an unusually wide door. He opened it as a footman would onto an extravagant wine cellar. Serena knew upon seeing it that if she were more of an aficionado she would have been deeply impressed. The room was beautiful even to her untrained eye.

"Make yourself comfortable," he ordered. "I'll send someone to open a bottle for you."

"That won't be—"

The door closed on her words.

Ambient gold light spilled out of the cellar's numerous recessed alcoves, casting shadows at the bottom of the wide crescent stairs, which seemed better suited for the entryway of a grand house. The warm glow was at odds with the controlled chilly temperature. The alcoves were lined with brick and stacked with rack upon rack of horizontal wine bottles. In one of the spaces a long table flanked by upholstered chairs suggested the occasional wine-tasting party. At the head of the table was a rolling cart stocked with bottle openers, corkscrews, a variety of wineglasses, decanters, and bar towels.

Half an hour passed, during which time Serena looked at most of the labels on most of the wine bottles. Their art was more tasteful than what Roman kept on display in his halls.

This diversion exhausted, Serena returned to the top of the steps. She reached out for the door handle and knew before she touched its decorative lever that Roman had locked it. True enough: it rattled in her grip.

So this was what it felt like to be overpowered by a brute. To be afraid of what a man who made a living violating human rights might do to you, because letting you go certainly wouldn't be on his list of options. To sense that the end of your life might be only minutes away.

Roman must know she was not like him. Anyone could see it—probably Phil as well, though she thought she'd convinced him of a few things. The two men were probably having a little meeting right now—Phil completely and miraculously recovered—over what to do with her.

Serena closed her eyes and took deep breaths and put her mind to the memory of every woman she had ever seen at her parents' shelter: the women who got away. Some courageous, some terrified, all scarred. But all alive.

She would get away.

In her mind's eye she saw Christopher standing in the courtyard garden of the Safe Place, smiling at her. She stood at the security gate that welcomed women who needed help and locked their abusers outside. Christopher was waving her in, saving her life again—but this time by opening his arms to her rather than pushing her off, telling her to run.

C'mon, he seemed to say. *Get a move on. We've got work to do.*

Her panic evaporated. She went to him, feeling the uneven bricks of the path under the soles of her shoes. As she approached he held something out to her between his thumb and finger, a small cylinder about two inches long. She turned her hand over so he could drop it into her palm, but when he released it, the thing rolled right off her hand. It was soft and weightless, and she didn't hear it hit the ground.

Serena opened her eyes, looking for the imaginary object at her feet.

Of course, there was nothing but her wishful thinking in the room.

Was it possible to fall in love with a dead man or was this only what it felt like to know death was coming quickly?

She turned around to sit down on the steps and her foot kicked something off the ledge. It bounced and rolled all the way to the concrete floor.

It was an old cork, cast off from a wine bottle, stained red on one end. A vineyard's logo had been stamped on the side. There was more than one cork littering the wide steps here, she realized—not passed through the imagination but dropped off trays or tossed aside by those not in the habit, as teachers were, of saving potential project supplies.

The cork was brittle and split in two easily when she applied her thumbnail to it.

The sound of a key in the door caused her to step down to the next stair. She thought of hefting a wine bottle as a weapon, but she would need the advantage of surprise to use it, and that moment had passed.

Maybe because she was prepared for Roman, the sight of a woman caught her off guard. It might have been the one who moved aside like smoke as Roman dragged Serena through the house. She was tall and slender with café au lait skin, a stunning runway model except for her slightly hunched shoulders, curved forward as if to protect her heart. Elegance lifted her head. Her ink-black hair formed a loose and classy knot at the nape of her neck.

She carried a small tray of cheese, crackers, sliced apples, a cluster of grapes, and a bulbous wineglass that contained a few ounces of red wine. The entire presentation looked deadly.

"Mr. Roman would like you to please make yourself at home," the woman said. She overemphasized the required politeness by dipping her head. "If that's possible in a place like this."

The ironic welcome only reinforced Serena's decision not to touch any of the food. The wine sloshed gently in the cup and caught the light. At the open door, the brass plate that held the lock also glinted. Serena toyed with the brittle cork. It could easily be jammed into that plate's small hole. If she could prevent the lock from engaging, she could get out.

The woman descended to the bottom step and carried the tray to the table. In her hands it seemed designed for a gathering of twenty people. Their eyes met for the first time.

Serena didn't catch the true nature of the emotion that crossed the woman's face at that moment. It was there and gone in a blink. And then the woman set the tray down in the air, where there was no table underneath it, and the cavernous space exaggerated the noise of her mistake. It seemed five silver platters and ten crystal wineglasses had hit the floor simultaneously. Wine splashed Serena's blouse. Wafer-thin shards spilled like diamonds all the way to the wall.

Serena felt responsible for the accident, though she had no idea why.

"I'm so sorry!" she said, but she made no move to help. Her feet were rooted to the ground, as if taking a step might slice open her feet. Her hands were raised in the air, clean and dry, while red wine glued her shirt to her belly. There was a broken piece of cork in each hand.

The woman stared at the mess just long enough for Serena to see that fear of punishment had frozen her. Her adult guard had come down with the tray, and childlike dread was in every line of her brow. What kind of spilled milk was this? And what kind of terrorizing parent might John Roman be?

But Serena knew. Her instinct was to give this stranger a reassuring touch, but she hesitated. Would kindness raise the woman's suspicions? Would she confide in the man she feared? There might be reward in it for someone in her position.

The woman's mask of composure snapped back into place before Serena had answers.

"It's nothing," Serena said, trying to sound neutral.

"Wait here."

She bounded up the steps and left the room like a jaguar, swift and graceful and able to avoid the broken glass without looking at it.

Serena did not try to copy her movements. The woman would return just as quickly as she had gone, with brooms and towels and a fresh shirt, no doubt. Glass broke under Serena's shoes as she crushed it in her rush to the door, which the woman had left open.

She stuck her head out into the hall and looked to the left, then craned her neck around the door to check the right, thinking that she and Roman had arrived from that direction. But in truth, the tunnel-like passage looked the same either way: dark, spotted by lighted art, empty of humans. Serena dropped the cork halves on the top stair. Then she darted to the right, looking for daylight. Within thirty seconds she began to doubt she'd ever see it again.

THIRTY-FIVE

DENISE WILCOX TOOK A SEAT AT HER TINY DESK AND worried about Roman's rage, though it might not come down on her for several more hours. She knew who the woman in the wine cellar was. The very sight of her was responsible for the catastrophe of the spilled tray. Serena Diaz, the headline maker. And not only that, the news anchor had claimed, but Serena had connections to the Safe Place, now tainted by the daughter's crimes. In Denise's memory, it had always been tainted, nothing more than a house that had tried to save her mother but couldn't. Clearly Serena was the same spoiled brat now that she had been then, when they were children. This was a woman who would make her life more difficult than it already was. And she was the one Phil wanted to bring in as a partner.

But at the moment Denise had a bigger problem: her brainless stupidity had made it possible for the woman to escape, and she couldn't think of any explanation that Roman would forgive.

So she waited, as she had become quite good at doing, for events to take their course. Silently, because silence and obedience were Roman's highest expectations of her, she sat in her assigned alcove across the hall from his study to receive whatever demands he felt like making.

At the time, Roman was not in the study. Perhaps he was at the cellar, discovering Denise's incompetence. Through the open door she could see his partner, Phil Lancet, waiting for him.

Phil rested in a chair near the window curtain, which he had pulled back without Roman's permission. Denise envied him that freedom. But not too much. He sat with the rigid muscles of someone who dreaded what was coming. Just like she did.

Still, he was recovering with remarkable speed for a man who had appeared to be at death's door such a short time ago. Phil was upright now, his posture and his color restored by the influence of some powerful medications. The physician had returned to his own vices in another part of the house.

Roman appeared at Denise's desk like a magician's trick and placed a packet of papers directly in front of her. She recognized it. This envelope with a Pacific Palisades address had been sitting on Roman's own desk for about a week now, growing thicker by the day.

"These are for Lourdes," Roman said. "He knows what to do with them."

"Yes," she said, pulling it toward her. She stood to take the package to Roman's courier.

"And I have something else I need you to do. Wait here."

"Yes," she repeated.

He went into the study.

A key was taped to the outside of the envelope. Denise touched it. The duplicate was still warm from the lasers of Roman's key-cutting machine. She had seen him take it from Phil's pocket while the man was unconscious.

"Panic attack, was it?" Roman was saying to Phil. He passed by the window and yanked the draperies closed again, then went to his own desk, a dark walnut monstrosity that had looked less intimidating with light from Phil's window spilling over one side of it.

"Felt like a heart attack." Phil scowled. "Where's Serena? Did you lock her in one of your dungeons?"

"Where's the proof that she's our friend?" Roman said.

Phil reached behind him for the jacket draped over the back of the chair and started fishing in the breast pockets.

"I haven't had time to verify her claims," Phil said, "but take this." He put a small device into Roman's outstretched hand.

"What is it?" He held it up to the light, and Denise saw that it was a digital recorder.

"Her plan to take over the world." Phil smirked. "Or at least make sluts of every child who goes through LA Unified. Even if it's a lie, it's enough to protect our interests."

"She didn't know you taped her?"

"No."

"I'll just safeguard it, then."

"You do that."

Roman's computer slept. He jiggled the mouse to wake it. Phil came around to the other side of the desk and sat, his body made heavy and graceless by exhaustion.

"She calls you Lance," Roman said.

"She hasn't figured that part out yet."

"A street-smart woman can't see what's right in front of her face?"

"A testimony to my expert deception, not her lack of savvy," Phil answered.

"You're a moonstruck idiot."

"It takes a lot for a woman to capture my attention."

"And how did she do it?"

"She killed Christopher Larsen."

Roman looked up at Phil, his hands suspended over the keyboard. "So I was right about that," he finally said.

"You were. You should put it in writing. And then Serena had the body put up as a warning to Brock Anderson. Let me tell you, it worked. Kid's scared out of his mind."

Out in the hall, Denise fiddled with the brad that held Lourdes's envelope closed.

"I like her because she dreams big," Phil said. "But she isn't big yet."

"You like her because she's got you under her thumb, and that's a new challenge for you."

"It is more interesting," Phil said.

Roman's printer kicked out a fresh page.

"Denise," he called.

She rose quickly and went. He handed her the page off the printer.

"Send this off," he ordered.

"Yes."

"And upload this to the server." He handed her Phil's digital recorder.

"Don't you want to listen first?" Phil asked.

"Never listen to women before your second drink of the night."

The paper Denise held contained a message for Timothy Rollins, a freelance writer who sometimes paid for Roman's offerings by giving him anonymous connections to the *LA Times*. The message said simply,

Lance Liebowitz to file guilty plea on behalf of Serena Diaz tomorrow morning.

Denise waited for Roman to clarify which of the three tasks he wanted her to complete first. Already she was invisible to the men.

"I don't like your nose for risk," Roman said. "Tell me why I shouldn't shoot you both here?"

"Too messy," Phil replied without opening his eyes.

"Right. So I'm going to send the two of you home now, with a clear understanding."

Anticipating that Roman would send her to fetch Serena, Denise darted from the room. She was already at her alcove desk when Phil said agreeably, "If Serena exposes us, you'll kill me. Probably her too. And you'll do it in a way that never traces to you. Nothing ever sticks to the mighty John Roman."

"I'm glad we understand each other."

"C'mon, Roman. Even you should be able to appreciate how well I picked my target."

"Apparently she picked you," he replied as he left the study. He turned in the direction of the cellar without looking in Denise's direction.

It would be best if she was gone when he returned from the wine cellar. Denise grabbed up Lourdes's envelope by the bottom end. As she lifted it the brad caught the cord of her lamp and, instead of toppling the lamp, the brad snapped off. The sheaf of papers inside dropped like a guillotine onto the surface of the desk. In a lucky save she prevented the stack from scattering. Quickly she forced the pages back into the packet.

But not before she saw the top page. A note written in a woman's neat hand on cute notepaper bordered with cheerful red apples.

My friends have become my enemies.

She didn't even have to read the whole thing to make sense of the key words that jumped off the page. This was a suicide note.

And it was penned by Serena Diaz.

THIRTY-SIX

THE HOUSE COULDN'T POSSIBLY BE AS BIG AS THE maze of halls caused it to seem. Serena tried to piece together her location from her memory of the house's appearance from the outside, but that didn't do her any good. She blamed her disorientation on the relative darkness of the halls and rooms. Though it was probably early afternoon, Roman's place was dusky through and through. A blue-black pall draped the furniture, the flooring, the decor, so that everything looked the same: vaguely defined, obscure, deceptive. She walked into the same empty bedroom twice. Or two different bedrooms outfitted with identically arranged furniture.

The second time she went in, Serena slipped behind the heavy draperies in search of a window but found only a cinder-block wall. A bedroom with no windows. It sent a shudder through her. The unnecessary curtains made it difficult to breathe. With her palms pressed flat against the cold, rough surface, Serena began to despair.

She left the room again and strained her eyes for a new direction.

When she reached the head of a narrow set of descending stairs, she took them because they were the only element that looked as if she had never seen it before. She stepped carefully down each black stair, hoping that the basement level might have its own exit. It was an improbable hope.

At the bottom she could see two doors lit by emergency lighting set low along the walls. Rooms? Exits? There was one on each side of the short passage and a dead end ahead.

Footsteps sounded in the hall overhead. She'd been out of the wine cellar nearly five minutes now and had no way of knowing if her escape had been discovered. Serena placed her ear lightly on the door closest to her and listened for any sound of human movement. There was nothing to hear but the sound of her own pulse. She placed her hand on the doorknob and turned it about an inch before it stopped. Locked. Or merely stuck? She jiggled the hardware, but the lock held fast and the door rattled loudly.

She turned to the second door and had the same experience: silence behind the barricade, knob locked, door rattling. Serena rested her forehead against the wood panel. She had to keep moving.

Three light knocks sounded against the door. They came from the other side.

The startling noise was so soft Serena doubted at first that she'd heard it. Still, she stepped back and studied the door as if staring might cause the sound to repeat itself.

It did. Three more light knocks, almost inaudible but definitely real. She returned to the door and spoke just as softly into the joint where the door met the jamb.

"Hello?" she whispered.

There was a light scurrying like mice, what might have been bare feet gliding along a concrete floor or excited whispers among several people. Then silence that stretched out for several seconds.

"Who's there?" someone finally said. A woman, Serena thought, cautious but strong. The sound of her voice struck a terrible note in Serena's heart. For all that Amber, Kaleo, and William had told her about the nature of Phil's and Roman's work, she had never foreseen the possibility that they might keep prisoners in their own houses.

For what else could this woman be?

"I'm Serena," she whispered into the door.

The scurrying mice consulted each other and then the spokesperson returned. "Are you out?" she asked.

At first Serena wasn't sure what the question really meant, but then she thought the girl was asking if she was also held hostage here against her will. She opened her mouth to say no, then thought twice. It might be only a matter of hours before she was locked in a room in a basement like this. Exactly like this.

"Where's your key?" the voice demanded.

"I don't have a key," Serena said. "Are you locked in?"

No scurrying this time, just silence that seemed to last forever, until it was ended by an odd sound at the base of the door, the scraping sound of something being forced through a space slightly too small for it. Serena glanced down at her feet just as a disk popped out from the narrowest of gaps. She stooped to pick it up. It was a stone the diameter of a quarter but the thickness of three stacked together. It felt smooth under the pads of Serena's fingertips, worn soft by anxious wishes. She knew what it was even before she lifted it toward the light.

The fire poppy seemed to take flight from the rock. Serena held it to the weak wall lighting, her mind whirling with amazement and questions. *How'd you get this?* was at the top of the list. *Who are you? Where are you from? How many of you are there? How can I get you out?*

She didn't have the opportunity to ask any of these. On turning away from the light with the stone in her hand, she saw a movement in the deep shadows of the stairwell, an almost imperceptible shift of an elbow, or the tilt of a head, or the rise of a chest. She couldn't be sure what it was that had caught her eye. All that mattered was what the movement meant: Roman had found her.

There was only one way out for Serena, and maybe also for the girls behind that door. It pained her to take it.

Serena smacked the door with the flat of her hand.

"Shut up," she ordered, "or I'll send Roman."

And she left them, silencing the sounds like cracking icebergs coming from her own heart. She spoke to Roman before she reached the bottom of the stairs, before he might think he had surprised her.

"I'm sure Lance has told you that keeping those girls in your house is a step above idiotic. Just from a legal point of view."

"Some need a little more training than others before I'll turn them loose on a man," he said.

"Turn them loose," Serena mimicked. "You have such a sense of humor."

She moved by him without stopping, fearful that he'd reach out and grab her as he had before, unlock the doors below, and throw her in with the victimized girls—or worse, into the room that was empty.

When he didn't, she paused on the stair above him, just high enough to allow her to look down on his head.

"What's there to train?" she said. "There are more efficient ways to get them to do what you want."

"Those ways aren't as fun," he said.

"Now you sound like Lance. Really, why do you keep them here?"

Roman grinned. "Because they're fighters. I like them scrappy. Like you."

Serena returned his obscene pleasure with a sneer and held out the Fire Followers disk. He glanced at it but refused to take it as she said, "This is why I took out Christopher Larsen, see? He was on to you. How far did they get? I'm starting to have second thoughts about working with you."

"For me," he said, as she slipped the stone back into her pocket. "You'll be working *for* me."

She resumed her walk up the stairs, because although she managed to hold back her tears, she couldn't prevent them from turning her eyes glassy.

"What good are you to me if I know more than you do?" she asked.

"Oh, I doubt that very much," he said. "I know all about you, Serena Diaz. And I know even more about Lance Liebowitz. So I'll tell you this one secret." He did take her arm then and wrenched it hard enough to make her turn around. "You might be able to fool him, but you don't scare me one bit."

She tried to stare him down with silent defiance but succeeded in doing little more than raising the temperature of her face. She wrenched her arm out of his grip.

"Know where you're going?" he asked.

"Back to the wine cellar." She shot an angry look back at him.

"Good guess," he said.

"And I'll come and go as I like."

"I can see that."

He let her lead the way around the dark maze of his house, mocking her with a Cheshire-cat grin until she was so flustered that she finally stood aside. He seemed miles ahead of her at every turn. With a polite nod he took her straight to the wine cellar, but instead of locking her in, he made his own way in, stepping carefully around the mess of broken glass and scattered cheese, which had started to curl up at the edges.

"Prone to the occasional tantrum?" he asked.

Serena bristled and stared down the hall in the opposite direction, the way she should have taken when she first came out. She tried to sound condescending.

"Your girl's a klutz." She had uncrossed her arms and was making mental preparations to run when Phil came around the corner, looking much more like his usual cocky self than he had earlier, headed straight for her. His presence unbalanced her. Where did they stand now, after this brief and bizarre separation? She had no way of knowing.

The wine cellar took on a new and more terrifying kind of darkness.

But Roman stood at the bottom of the steps and she at the top, out in the hall with Phil. Roman was in the far alcove on the left, which appeared to have the fewest bottles. He withdrew one from the topmost rack and turned it over to read the label. Phil reached the door but didn't descend. He glanced at Serena and gestured at the mess and mouthed, *You?*

"You've improved," she said, to avoid explanation. The shadows of the hall accentuated the dark circles under his eyes.

"Nothing wrong with me after all," Phil said to her. "Turns out it was all about the location." But he dragged a hand over his face and his shoulders stooped.

"That doesn't bode well for our future transactions there," Serena observed.

"We'll put it under your jurisdiction right away," he said. "Problem solved."

"Screaming Eagle Cab Sav," Roman said, holding up the bottle. "Two thousand and seven."

His elevated voice was magnified by the cavernous space.

"I'm sick of Napa," Phil objected. "If we're going to celebrate our new partnership, let's do it with something French."

Serena couldn't guess what the French had to do with these obscenities.

Roman turned the label to face Serena and said to her, "This is a twenty-five-hundred-dollar bottle. Six twenty-five a glass. But that's not enough for him anymore. Your boyfriend's tongue eventually loses its taste for everything. Don't say I didn't warn you."

"Let's have something from Côte de Nuits," Phil said.

"It's a celebration, not a bribery," Roman said, slipping the pricey-enough Cabernet Sauvignon back into its slot.

"I'm thinking a Grand Cru would be perfect."

"As in four grand?" Roman chortled.

Serena questioned what she was hearing. A four-thousand-dollar bottle of wine?

"Yes," Phil said. "If you have the Musigny." He seemed to notice and enjoy her ignorance. "French," he said. "From Burgundy. Only produced in one tiny corner of one tiny field."

In the nook, Roman was waving his fingers over the other bottlenecks as if doing a magic trick. They finally landed on a bottle at the end of the row, high in the corner.

"For you, Lance. My last one. Lance Liebowitz." He sounded out each syllable slowly. "I believe your name is written all over it."

Roman walked the bottle up the half-circle stairs, admiring the label and wiping the whole thing down with one of the bar towels, though Serena couldn't see a smudge or speck of dust anywhere on it. He polished it until the opaque glass sent the muted light to all corners of the room. She had the disturbing impression that he was caressing it, not in the way a man parts with a prized possession, but in the way a hunter admires his best knife.

She took a step backward into the hallway, ready to run out of harm's way should Roman bring that bottle down on Phil's head.

Instead, he extended it to her. "Don't take this personally,

Ms. Diaz. We could celebrate our new partnership together, but I'd rather you not linger in my house. A woman of your notoriety shouldn't go missing too long."

She took the bottle and received a sudden and distinct impression that holding it was a grave mistake. She hugged it to her body.

Phil snatched it out of her hands as if she'd crush it. "Don't do that. You'll overheat it." He carried it away down the hall, leaving her with Roman.

"I'll toast our partnership to your empty seat," Serena said. "We'll drink to success."

"To rubies and diamonds," Phil shouted.

Roman's smile stayed on Serena, though it contained no warmth. "To bottomless appetites."

THIRTY-SEVEN

ALL PHIL WANTED TO DO WAS LEAVE THE HOUSE
with that precious wine, because something was wrong and it had
nothing to do with him. He moved swiftly down the dark halls,
mentally urging Serena to hurry, wishing for the sunlight and
ocean views of his own home, which cast enough light for him to
see what his enemies were up to. He had to go, and he had to go
now, because if he waited even three more seconds he knew that
Roman would announce that everything was a joke, including
their freedom to leave with their lives.

His boss dallied with Serena, drooling over her. They saun-
tered. Strolled out of Roman's cave.

Silently—because speaking hurt his head—Phil cursed his
need to wait for her at the front door. He cursed the ancient old
doctor who worked for Roman, who didn't speak English and
probably wasn't licensed to practice medicine in the United States.
Probably had tried to kill him. He cursed the medications that
muddied his thinking. He cursed the hallucinations that had put
him in this position, requiring him to come here to Roman's home
before he had the upper hand in the situation. He was unprepared.
He'd been forced to present his partnership proposal too early. The
plan was only hours old.

Phil stopped in his mental tracks. That's what was wrong: the fact that Roman was so ready to sign up. Why?

It was too big a question for the moment.

At the front door there was fresh air. Phil breathed deeply and fabricated an expression of contentment. It was so foreign to him.

Roman's secretary appeared outside on the porch. She wore the plunging neckline and short slit skirt that Roman preferred. It wasn't a bad look, really, though Phil found it predictable and therefore uninteresting. The blouse would be nicer if it were sheer. He stared, imagining, and refused to step aside for her. She hesitated. *Oh, pity your dilemma*, Phil thought. *Which is worse—that I'll manhandle you as you squeeze by, or that Roman will be mad you lingered outside?*

Serena appeared at his side, worsening the logjam.

And then Roman was there, and what happened next caused Phil to realize that he was no longer in the game at all, that at some point in the last few miserable hours all his strategies had been trounced, and he was the last to know.

At first the encounter seemed awkwardly innocent: three people wanting to pass through the same space at the same time without wanting to be the first. Emboldened by the fact that she was leaving the house alive and feeling the success of her role-playing like a warm glow, Serena made the first move.

"Excuse me," she said to Phil. The man was distracted, still mentally fogged by his breakdown at the house. He stood as if alone, holding the wine bottle like a football in the V of his elbow. Serena continued to play her part, putting a firm hand on his arm to indicate he should move or at least wake up. When he didn't, she squeezed past him. Out on the porch, the attractive woman who had dropped Serena's food tray stepped aside to let her pass, eyes averted.

"Don't be embarrassed," Serena murmured to her, judging the remark to be both sincere and sly. The moment she uttered the words, the woman glanced up at her briefly and all embarrassment fell hard on Serena's own shoulders. No—what hit her was worse than embarrassment; it was shame. Because the eyes that looked at her held only reproach and anger.

The woman blinked and looked away, and Serena realized that someone would be punished for her opportunistic escape from the wine cellar.

"Your girl's a klutz," Serena had so carelessly claimed, and she wished for the chance to take it back.

There was nothing she could do about it. Even now, under the hard eyes of John Roman, any behavior that might alter his beliefs about her could jeopardize everything. Including her intentions to find a way back to the women in the locked room.

This truth did nothing to unknot the dread in her stomach for what this woman was about to face.

"Denise," Roman said from inside the house. The sound of his voice stirred the players in the scene like vegetables in a soup pot. Phil came to himself and stepped through the doorway. Serena made room for him. Roman filled his vacancy. Denise crossed the threshold and passed like a ghost into the house, so slim and wispy that she easily avoided touching Roman's broad and blockish shoulders.

Roman reached out and grabbed her hand, toppling her graceful entry. She fell into his side before righting herself again. Reluctantly, she turned herself around to face Serena and Phil, her arm twisting behind her back.

Her eyes locked on Serena's, fearful instead of judgmental now.

"Your tire's been repaired," Roman said to Phil, giving a nod to the Porsche that had been outfitted with new tires and returned to the driveway. "Until next time." Then he closed his front door on Serena's dread.

Phil released a heavy, resigned sigh and plodded on down the porch. He fished for keys in his left pocket and seemed surprised to discover them in his right. They clinked against the glass bottle as he fingered the ring to find his car key.

Inside the house, Denise screamed.

Phil stepped off the porch and kept moving toward his car.

Serena's mind emptied of all logical thought. Her will had nothing to obey but her heart, whatever the cost. She leaped for the door and threw all her weight into opening it.

Roman was leading Denise out of the spacious entryway and into the black mouth of a hall on the other side of the room. He was leading her by her hair. The classy knot had come undone, converted by force into a leash.

The sensation of her hair in a killer's grip rushed over Serena's memory. So did the terror of feeling alone in an inhospitable place, where dead bodies were easy to hide.

"Hey!" Serena shouted. She crossed the room in long strides. "Hey, hey, hey!"

Roman ignored her mama-goose cries. Denise stumbled backward, both hands on the back of her head where he pulled. Serena could hear her breathing. Gasping. She reached out a hand to Denise, though too far away to help.

"Roman, let her go."

All three flowed straight back into the bowels of the house, Serena objecting, Denise flailing, Roman ignoring. Even when Serena caught up and tried to get between Roman's grip and Denise's hyperextended neck, Roman didn't acknowledge her presence until he punched through the door of a small bedroom and hurled Denise onto the bed against the far wall. Only then did he turn on Serena. He opened his mouth to tear her down, but she was, to her own surprise, already ahead of him.

"Is this what I can expect from you?" She screamed it at the top of her lungs, a declaration rather than a real question. "Is this how you treat the women who agree to work *for* you rather than *with* you?"

He frowned but didn't speak. Straightened the cuffs of his shirt. She thought she had caught him off guard.

"Because if this is what you have in mind for me, I will tell you right now we do *not* have a deal. There is. No. Deal."

Denise had curled into a tight fetal ball between her pillow and the corner of the room. Serena's intellect began to reengage her brain at that point, and it painted a high-definition picture of just how reckless she'd been. Here she stood, deep in the guts of a house invisible even to the nearest neighbors, with a man who had no conscience.

But her emotions were hot as blazing coal and her mouth was a runaway train.

"What you do to this woman will make or break my ties with you, do you hear me? Whatever you do to her is no different from doing it to me. Because she and I are sisters."

Roman's eyes went from Serena's olive complexion to Denise's milk chocolate arms. Sisters? Where had she come up with that word?

On the bed, Denise was still, watching the events from behind the curtain of hair that had flopped over her eyes. Compared to the opulence of the house, this room was spartan: four-drawer dresser, twin bed, writing table and chair, lamp. Personal possessions feminized the space: a book of poetry on the nightstand, a doll on the pillow, a pair of sequined shoes posing under the shelter of the chair.

The idiocy of what Serena had just done settled over her like a shroud. What kind of person who dealt in the sale of human beings had the capacity to express moral outrage over the mistreatment of one woman?

Behind her, Phil started to laugh. He had followed without her noticing; whether his presence would work for or against her remained to be seen. His cackle was strained, though. Nervous.

Roman's was not, however. It was as full-bodied and hearty as a laugh could get.

Serena sensed death around the corner.

She turned to Denise. "Come home with me tonight. Work for me. He won't need you here anymore."

Roman snorted.

Denise cleared her throat and then gave Serena a surprise of her own. "My place is here." The two exchanged a look that Serena couldn't decipher. "Thank you, Serena."

What? *Thank you, Serena, but I'll stay here and die anyway, if you don't mind.*

Serena's body still quaked with the still-strong surge of adrenaline. She was completely confused about Denise's choice to stay in Roman's prison. He'd kill her.

Wouldn't he?

"Fine," Serena said. She turned to Roman. "We'll talk tomorrow." She turned her back on him and went to the door. She wondered what a gunshot wound to her spine would feel like. She wished Christopher could have told her. And she wondered if she would be able to ensure Denise's survival even as she died, as Christopher had hers.

Apparently not.

Hot tears rose behind her eyes.

She pushed Phil aside as she passed through. Surreptitiously she cast a final troubled glance back at Denise, whose eyes were still glued to her figurative sister. The woman sank to her bed and perched on the edge, then reached for the doll on her pillow.

A black-haired doll in a frilly pink dress worn threadbare by eighteen years of affection.

THURSDAY

THIRTY-EIGHT

SERENA DREAMED OF FOUR WOMEN IN A COZY house. Four women she hardly knew, but who somehow weren't strangers at all. Four scarred women laughing, one of them holding a doll. Somehow she was still alive.

Serena realized something was wrong when Phil woke her, not in his usual way of turning on the lights while she slept, as if he'd forgotten she was there, but by nudging her foot with his. It was a weak shove that caused her heel to slip off the glass table where it was propped and hit the floor with a jarring stab of pain.

Burgundy wine was sprayed across the floor and fine furniture like a violent crime. Her glass lay tipped on its side. The sight startled her. Pink and purple hues of sunrise mingled with the liquid dripping off the leather sofa and sent her mind an important message: *You've overslept.*

There was so much wine because she hadn't swallowed a drop of it. Instead, she risked a drunken dispute with Phil in exchange for waiting him out.

"Drink some."

"I'm not in the mood."

"It's a celebration, woman. The least you could do is join in."

"When I'm good and ready."

"That's a thousand-dollar glass!"

"Don't waste it on me."

"I won't then. Trust me, I won't."

Frankly, she was surprised he hadn't chased his own glasses with hers. And his ability to hold his alcohol was infuriating, nerve-wracking. She nodded off before Phil had, missing her earliest chance to call Amber and Will and Kaleo. Hours to act, gone.

She needed to tell them she'd found Roman's lair.

Brock Anderson worked for Phil Lancet, who worked for Roman, who locked frightened women in the basement of a Beverly Hills home for unspeakable reasons. Was it enough to bring this nightmare to an end? That would depend on what other information Fire Followers and their contacts with the FBI or LAPD had. She still wasn't sure who'd killed Christopher, or why they'd put his body on display, or why he had saved her life, or why Phil Lancet wanted to destroy it.

Too many disconnected links.

She turned toward Phil, expecting the sedative effects of the alcohol to have worn off already. If they had, even the shortest phone call to Amber would be too risky.

He was staring at her, lips slack, with something worse than a groggy sleep behind his eyes. Death. Her eyes darted to the empty wine bottle, to the bloody spill.

This was why Roman had let them leave. He had plans to silence them indirectly.

And what had become of Denise? Serena couldn't believe she had stayed.

"You knew," Phil grunted. He gasped a shallow breath.

"No. No, I didn't."

But he had seen her untouched glass. It certainly looked as if she'd known.

He raised his arm toward her hair as if to stroke it—or to grab hold of it. She scrambled away, not sure what strength he had left in him. Not much. He couldn't even sit up straight. Neither one of them had much time.

"Why did you hire Brock to lie about me?" she demanded.

One corner of Phil's mouth formed a sardonic smile. "For fun. And it was fun."

"What's Brock's connection to Christopher Larsen?"

"You."

"I don't understand."

Phil's eyes had closed.

"Why me, Phil?" She'd used his real name. But it didn't matter anymore, did it?

"There, see? You knew me better after all. You win."

Serena dashed for her purse, which she'd dropped in the entryway. It contained her phone.

His thin voice followed her. "Are you good, Serena?"

The question didn't make any sense. She rifled the bag for her phone and finally found it.

"How do you define good?" she muttered.

"Better than me." His voice was weakening and pointed away from her, toward the sunrise across the windows. She stared at her phone, forgetting which buttons to push, seeing only the smiling face and brown curls of Christopher Larsen smiling back at her. A good man. A far better man. The kind who cared less for his own life than for the lives of others.

She cleared her head and returned to Phil, starting to dial.

"I'm calling an ambulance." She sat, facing him, on the arm of the sofa.

"No." He pushed at her arm with limp fingers, having no real strength. She stopped the call before it went through.

Phil's breathing was quick and shallow.

"Go fast," he said. "Sweep the office."

"Sweep?"

"Finish him."

"Who? Roman?"

She thought Phil nodded.

"Get him."

She would get Roman, but not for the reasons Phil would see him brought to justice.

"Be good," he whispered. "Be quick."

Serena had never faced violent death firsthand, but for the second time in days she watched a man's life leave him. Though Phil had used her for his own entertainment, the sight neutralized her anger. He had ruined her career and her reputation, but that wasn't enough for her to wish any man dead. Death and justice weren't the same thing.

"Quick," he said. And he bumped her knee with the back of his hand.

The sound of several cars approaching on the driveway changed the meaning of Phil's word in the space of a second. Not *Get Roman quick* but *Go fast, be quick. Get out of here before they find you and believe what Roman wants them to believe about you, Serena Diaz.*

The good girl gone terribly, terribly bad.

Serena jumped up off the sofa and ran back for her purse. In the entryway, she paused only long enough to look at the security monitors and confirm that there were two LAPD squad cars and one unmarked sedan pulling into the driveway beyond the front gate. For a second, the sight paralyzed her. Why were they here?

Fire Followers might have called them, thinking Serena had turned or that Phil had harmed her. She quickly called up Amber's number in her phone and put the call through.

Amber answered on the third ring. "Serena."

"Did you send police to Lance's?" Serena said.

"What?"

"Why are there police here?"

"Uh, because you broke the law?"

"No, Amber. No."

"Well, I didn't have to call them."

Serena put herself in motion now as the only other explanation for their presence made itself clear. Roman must have tipped them off to a death at the house. But on what basis? And how could he tip them off without implicating himself? Who else would know about a murder but the murderer?

"There's an audio file online," Amber continued. "You, bragging about what you've done to kids like Brock and Jett."

What? How? Phil must have recorded her. "How do you think I got them to let me in?" Serena demanded.

She slipped into her shoes and bolted down the hall and down the stairs to Phil's office, planning to exit there to the hidden stairs, just as she had yesterday.

"Amber, pick me up where you did yesterday."

"And why would I do that?"

"I have Roman. If you don't believe me, take me to the police. But if you don't get to me before Roman does, he's going to eat me for breakfast." Serena took a deep breath. "He thinks I'm dead."

There was silence on the other end, and Serena had no time to wait for Amber to decide what she was going to do. She crammed the phone into the pocket of her jeans and burst into the office, more unprepared for the sight of it than she had been for Phil's death.

Upstairs, she heard men's voices announcing themselves at the front gate.

The immaculate office had been ransacked, torn apart as if searched—but for what? Books had been pulled off the shelves. The credenza drawers were open. Files that hadn't existed before were strewn across every flat surface. Olive green hanging files and yellow manila folders were a drunken chaos of upchucked white papers. The only semblance of order sat square in the center of Lance Liebowitz's glossy cherry desk, a stack of documents about an inch high topped with a sheet of stationery. She could see the sheet from the door. A familiar piece of notepaper. A white half sheet with a bushel of apples in the bottom left corner. And the name across the top styled like chalk on a blackboard: *Ms. Diaz*.

Serena approached the desk and picked up the note, which appeared to be written by her own hand.

> My friends have become my enemies. Lance Liebowitz is no attorney. He is guilty of worse lies than I am accused of telling. Where is justice? It seems I must make my own by stooping to the reputation that has been created for me. I hope my family will forgive me.
>
> Serena Diaz

The pounding on the upstairs gate intensified. If they had authorization to crack the security code or leap the walls, they'd be into the courtyard and then the house in a matter of seconds.

Serena didn't have time to read the papers under her note, though she could imagine what they contained. She could conceive of the elaborate lie Roman had concocted to blame her for Phil Lancet's death—a murder-suicide that would muddy all the other lies told about her over the past few months and contain the damage to Phil Lancet's troubled world.

She grabbed the whole stack and crammed it into her purse. Fear chased her out the sliding glass door this time and pushed her into a low, running crouch toward the ivy-covered stairs that would carry her off the property. Fear that the liars would win. Fear that Christopher's death would be nothing more than a tragedy. Fear that in the end, she'd be the only one to know the truth.

A sickening realization caused Serena to stumble on the top step. She had left the most important piece of evidence in the house, and it was far too late to retrieve it. She caught her balance and cast a regretful look back at the house, then resolved to stay her course. She hoped Amber would come for her. Because if she didn't, the only voice still speaking for Serena would be the one coming from that poisoned wine bottle sitting in front of Phil Lancet's body. The wine bottle Roman had wiped down and then pressed her to take, bare-handed, now thick with her own fingerprints.

THIRTY-NINE

AMBER REFUSED TO GO.

"I'm sick of her lies," she said, following Kaleo out the door of the Larsens' bungalow. They were halfway across the small lawn to the one-car gravel driveway before the screen smacked the jamb. "She's bragging about worse crimes than anyone first believed."

"She hasn't admitted anything yet," Kaleo shot back. "If she really does have Roman, he'd be the one lying. He has the means."

"Ten years we've been trying to get to him, and you think she can just find him in twenty-four hours? The only way she could do that is if she's working with him. It's a trap, Kaleo. Don't let her pretty eyes fool you. She's not one of the girls we're trying to rescue."

He opened the car door and dropped onto the threadbare bucket seat. "You're the one who told her to lie," he said.

"To *Phil*."

"Maybe it actually worked."

Kaleo peeled out of the driveway, equally angry that Amber disbelieved her and that he did think Serena had pretty eyes. It was possible that Amber was right, considering the way Serena had abandoned them all without explanation yesterday. Kaleo had watched her walk straight into Phil Lancet's arms.

When he approached the corner in Pacific Palisades where they'd picked up Serena the day before, he didn't see her until she emerged from behind an oleander bush and rushed the car, with nothing to cover her eye-catching mane of curly black hair today. She jumped into the front seat without waiting for him to come to a complete stop.

"What took you so long?"

The retort on his lips fell away when he saw the tears streaking her cheeks. She hugged her purse as if it were a life preserver.

"Where's Roman?" he asked.

"In Beverly Hills. I don't know the address. I'll take you there."

"We need the police."

"No police. They're at Lance's house. They think I killed him."

"Phil's dead?"

Serena didn't say anything.

"How?" Kaleo asked.

"Roman."

Roman killed Phil but not Serena. Kaleo was instantly wary.

"So . . . ," Kaleo began. "If you take me to Roman's house, he'll just let us in?"

Serena was shaking her head.

"He won't let us in?" Kaleo prompted.

"I don't know what to do," Serena whispered. "I'm supposed to be dead."

"Roman tried to kill you too?"

"Phil took me to his house. I know where he is. He has girls there." Serena dug her fist into her pocket and withdrew the fire poppy stone. "They gave me this."

"This is Christopher's. How did they get it?"

"Christopher must have been with those girls at some point."

"At Roman's house?"

"Or at the Station Fire house. I saw a girl there the day Christopher was shot. Kaleo." He glanced at her as they pulled out onto the PCH and headed south, back to Santa Monica. "He's going to kill me. When Roman finds out I'm not dead, he'll do everything he can to kill me."

"Then we need a plan."

"I need a safe house."

"I'll take you home."

"No, take me to Pasadena. Is Amber at Christopher's house?"

"Yes."

"Get her out, Kaleo. Get her out now."

In the quiet of her room, Denise rose from the edge of her bed to start her day, still dressed in the expensive clothes that Roman insisted she wear, the ones that showcased her outward beauty and completely obscured her damaged spirit.

She let them slip to the floor and left them in a silky pile, then changed into his favorite red dress, to apologize for Serena's behavior and to assure Roman of her loyalty. *Yes*, the dress said. Roman's favorite word. And maybe Denise did it for herself too, the way she'd once read in a magazine that women who wanted to be admired should dress as if they believed they were admirable. Because this morning, Denise's heart did not feel loyal. And her own capacity for betrayal frightened her.

Denise stayed with Roman as a matter of survival, because as long as she stayed with him, death wouldn't come by his hands. He'd keep her alive—bruised and battered from time to time, yes, but alive. He, unlike that dog Phil Lancet, understood restraint.

But she had never wanted to leave Roman as badly as she did

last night, when Serena rushed him like a lioness. Denise had never experienced that kind of protection from any other human being on this earth. Not from her mother. Not from her employer. Not from some person who wouldn't know her from Eve. And never, ever, from a female who had looked at her with such resentment the last time they met.

What had changed her?

"She's not what she says she is," Roman had said to Denise before leaving her last night. "You know that, don't you?"

"Yes," Denise had replied, though she felt she didn't know anything.

"It's good to see that at least one person in the room can see what's good for her."

Roman's reward for her loyalty was to leave her untouched.

Denise's night had been filled with regret, the kind that barred sleep from the mind and filled the heart with self-hatred. Because Serena had taken a terrible risk to defend her, just five minutes after Denise had put Serena's fabricated suicide note in the hands of Lourdes.

Was Serena dead yet?

Though Denise had at her disposal the most expensive and complete set of cosmetics that Roman's money could buy, none of it could hide the circles under her eyes.

Denise reached Roman's office an hour earlier than usual and was surprised to find him already awake, pacing in front of the closed curtains that covered the window. A cell phone was pressed to his ear. She waited in the entry for him to notice her, and when he didn't she went to sit in the shadowy alcove that held her desk.

"What do you mean only one body?" Roman was saying. "Where's the woman? Where's the suicide note?"

Clearly not where Roman had expected them to be. Denise wished she could hear both sides of the conversation.

"Is the wine bottle there? . . . Good . . . Her prints will be all over it."

Serena's prints? But not Serena. Anticipation wiped out Denise's exhaustion. She didn't understand her body's reaction to this possibility.

"Then all you have to do is report a murder rather than a murder-suicide," Roman said.

Yes. Denise could imagine the person on the other end of the conversation saying it.

"That Diaz woman is your prime suspect. I'll provide you with a copy of the note. Make up some theory that she didn't have the guts to go through with it. And don't forget the videos."

From the dark hallway, Denise looked into the office through the open door. It framed Roman as he set the phone down and then leaned his knuckles against the desktop, looking like a world leader bearing the weight of the universe on his shoulders.

Denise had never noticed the hypocrisy of that notion before now.

"Denise," he said without looking up.

"Yes," she said without moving.

"It's time to empty the house."

"Yes," she intoned. There were procedures for such an event, and though it would be the first time she'd ever have to put them into motion, she felt no anxiety at all.

"I have to go. You have two hours. But first get me Brock Anderson's address."

"Yes," Denise said. And she turned on the light above her desk and booted up her computer and went to work.

Even then, she knew that today would be her last day.

FORTY

SERENA SPLASHED COLD WATER ON HER FACE AND took deep breaths that failed to calm. She could think of no place safer for women in her position than the Safe Place, designed by her father and a top-rated security company to hold evil at bay. But even in here, with Amber and Kaleo and Will and her parents surrounding her, she was afraid.

On the other side of the wall, in her father's office, Will and Kaleo argued about what to do. She could hear their voices, Kaleo's mostly rising while Will's stayed loud but level, punctuated by a silence that she interpreted as her father's calming influence. Amber was subdued, thoughtful.

Kaleo wanted to act through their contacts at the LAPD and the FBI immediately. Will believed that, as in the past, they wouldn't be taken seriously. It would be a waste of time, he said, to take them a lead based solely on the word of an accused sex offender and murder suspect. They'd be ignored. They didn't have any real evidence. Serena hadn't even laid eyes on the women she claimed were held captive at Roman's house. First they needed to get the evidence.

Kaleo argued that they had to move quickly, and Fire Followers didn't have enough manpower to storm Roman's residence before he vacated it with all the evidence Will wanted. They had to get the authorities to suppress the story of Phil's death, he said. They had to move before word of Serena's survival reached Roman and gave him reason to flee.

Serena dried her face, wondering how Christopher would have gotten her out of this one. She left the bathroom, stepping out into the hallway with the uneven carpeting and old electric wall sconces.

Her phone started to ring. She opened the door of her father's office and pulled her phone out of her pocket at the same time. The caller ID flashed blue on the black screen.

Brock Anderson.

Should she answer it? Yes—she needed no input on that question.

She opened the phone and turned on the speaker without saying a word.

As one all the mouths in the room closed and the heads turned toward her. The tiny office was crowded with anxious thoughts generated by worried people: Esteban and Enid Diaz, Serena and Amber, Will and Kaleo. And now Brock Anderson, the last in the form of a shrill whine that came across Serena's speakerphone.

It started with a long string of expletives before settling into a furious accusation.

"What are you doing? What are you thinking? Murder? You're just going to start killing everyone you don't like?"

"Is he talking about Phil?" Will whispered. He pulled out his own phone and went to Serena's side to record the conversation.

"If he knows about Phil, we can bet Roman does too," Kaleo muttered under his breath. He leaned back against Esteban's desk, arms crossed.

Brock's crazed panic had the odd effect of making her feel calm. It had happened in the classroom before, this sense that she could be the calm in the center of the storm. Her own falling apart would come later.

"I haven't killed anyone," Serena said.

"You *said* you did. It's all over the media. You killed that guy and set him up at the school to get back at me. And now my uncle? You're a freak, you know that?"

"Brock, I know, and you know, that I didn't do any of the things you accuse me of."

"No, you just murder everyone who crosses your path."

"That wasn't me," Serena said to Brock. "I didn't kill Christopher, and I didn't kill Phil."

"Then who did?"

"A man named John Roman killed Phil. He and Phil worked together and had a falling out. Brock, you and I are just bystanders. They used us."

"Oh ho ho, I don't let anyone use me."

"Phil used you. He used you to get to me. I don't know what he promised you—money, to pay your way to Cornell after you lost your scholarship?"

"*You* cost me that scholarship."

"Phil paid you to destroy my career," she said.

"Paid me? No, see, that's the problem here, Diaz. He never got around to paying me everything he promised, and now he never will, will he? You know what else he'll never get around to doing? Acquitting you of all the charges I filed. Nice move, killing the one man who could bail the two of us out."

"You went to see Phil at his house Tuesday night."

"A lot of good that did."

Will leaned into Serena's ear. "He must be alone. He wouldn't be saying all this if he wasn't."

Brock's hysteria had made him breathless. "You can sit there and say you didn't kill those guys, but no one's going to believe you, not any more than they're going to believe it's not you in my videos."

"Where did those come from?"

"How should I know? He had me pose for some pictures, but the rest? Phil's personal library? Apparently he didn't have to edit them too much. Or so he likes to brag."

Serena couldn't look at anyone in the room, but she found the voice to say, "Phil fed you the personal details—about my tattoo, my birthmark, what the inside of my apartment looks like."

Brock continued, "If I'm going to have to spend the next year in a courtroom, I'm going to come after you for every penny you and Phil owe me. I'm going to sue you until you bleed."

"Is this really the way kids think these days?" Enid wondered aloud.

Brock heard nothing through his rampage. "Do you think it was easy, humiliating myself in front of the entire world? You think it didn't cost me anything?"

"Phil humiliated you. Why'd you agree to it?" Serena asked. "No college is worth that."

"You don't know anything."

"I know that playing the victim has its perks," she dared.

"Shut up."

"I also know that Phil chewed up people and spit them out," Serena said. "He did it to hundreds of people. Maybe thousands. Me, your cousin Jett. And I'm sorry he did it to you."

Brock fell silent.

Serena leaned over the phone, braced her hands on either side of the table. "Brock, maybe if we worked together we could get our lives back on track."

"Not a chance."

"We're up against a bigger bully than Phil Lancet."

"Any bully's bigger than him, now that you've killed him."

"Roman killed him. And next he'll kill me, and then he'll come after you."

Brock's laugh was a snort. "Right. I've never even met the guy."

"You've never met me either," Kaleo said, "and that won't stop me from coming after you when we're done here—"

Brock swore. "You're not alone?"

"And she's got a mic on you too," Will said.

"Roman's house is falling down," Serena said, "because Phil Lancet pulled too many bricks off the bottom floor. Anyone who knew Phil will have to go. Including you."

Brock didn't respond.

"Work with us," Serena pleaded. "You might have evidence about Roman's network that you don't even know you have. The only way out from under this now is to amass as much evidence against Roman as we can."

Still nothing.

"Brock, please. The truth will come out whether you help me or not. We'll all have to own the consequences of what we've done. But I promise you I'm not interested in retaliation. I only want to stop Roman." The ensuing silence felt unreasonably long. "Brock," she repeated.

"He's happy to help," a new voice said, "even though he's never heard my name before this moment." Serena withdrew from the table as if it were charged with electricity. In the chair that faced Esteban's desk, Amber drew a sharp breath. Roman continued, "Why don't we get together and negotiate the practical aspects of that. What do you say, Teacher? Can you protect your student, or will you let me kill him first? Let's meet. Twenty minutes. Santa Monica State Beach."

"I can't get there that fast," Serena managed to say. "I'm in Pasadena."

"I'm sure Brock will be sorry to hear it."

Roman ended the call.

"I have to go," Serena said. She made a beeline for the door.

Kaleo reached out a hand to stop her.

Her father stood behind his desk. "No, Serena. This is for the authorities."

Serena turned around. "If a woman pounded on the gates out there while a man held a gun to her head, you'd try to stop him," she said. "You'd do it without regard for your own life. You always have, and until I became a teacher I never understood how that worked. Brock's one of my students. Not my favorite, granted, but he's mine."

"You don't owe him anything," Kaleo said.

"He's a kid," Serena argued. "He didn't have any idea what he was getting lured into. These men are professional liars." She glanced at Amber. "They can make the world's worst idea seem like the best option."

Amber nodded reluctantly.

"I have to do this."

"He'll kill you and the boy both," Amber said. "He'll try."

Serena closed her eyes, knowing Amber was right but seeing no way around it.

"This has nothing to do with you being a teacher," Enid protested. "You're not at school. There's no need for heroics. Others can take care of such things."

"Trained professionals," her father said.

"Dad, right now I'm the one who has something Brock needs. Don't make me keep that from him."

Her father fell silent, but her mother persisted. "I'm calling the police." She turned toward the phone.

"There's no time to convince them," Serena said. "They'll only want to arrest me." Her mother hesitated.

"I'll talk to them," Kaleo said, picking up the phone Will had used to record the conversation. "We have a confession."

Serena shook her head. "We have Brock's connection to Phil." She pointed to the documents she'd taken from Phil's office. "I have papers that Roman planted to document Lance Liebowitz's true identity, papers that can support evidence you've already collected, Will. Nothing more. Nothing on Roman."

"You have me," Amber said.

"For a positive ID, yes. But we need evidence of a crime," Will said.

Serena ran her hands through her hair. "I have nothing but an address. Girls in the basement."

"Long gone," Kaleo said.

"You have a four-thousand-dollar bottle of wine," Esteban said.

"With my prints all over it. Roman wiped the bottle clean before I touched it." But the light her father meant to shed lit up Serena's mind.

Enid was standing at the desk with the office phone's handset in her white grip. Her husband took it from her and returned it to the cradle.

"Where does a high school biology teacher get the funds to buy a four-thousand-dollar bottle of wine?" Serena asked.

"From criminal activity," Kaleo said. "This isn't getting us anywhere. We don't have much time."

Serena leveled her logic at Kaleo. "It isn't every day someone buys such a bottle produced in only one region of the world. It shouldn't be so hard for authorities to find out where each of those bottles has been sold."

"At least one to Roman," Will said. "Or to his Beverly Hills address."

"It's a long shot," Kaleo argued. "And once again, the clock is ticking."

Serena's gaze turned toward Amber, who had left the chair and now paced the tiny room as if a better answer might be hiding in one of the musty corners. Will followed her with his eyes, and Serena thought they held as much dread as her mother's. He reached out for Amber as she passed by. She stopped at his touch and looked at him. A wordless understanding passed between them, and Serena thought she knew what the look meant.

"Serena should go to the police," Amber finally said. "She's the only one who can take them to Roman's house."

"LAPD will arrest her," Will said.

"Safest place Serena can be right now," Amber said.

"Then I'll go with her," Kaleo offered. "Can we take some of that amazing food I smell with us? I'm starving."

"No," Amber said, turning to him. "You take Will's recording of Brock to Christopher's contact at the FBI. What's his name? Montague? You know him, right?"

"Will can do that," Kaleo said.

"I need William with me," Amber said.

Serena caught on. "No, Amber. You can't."

"I can," she said. "I have to be the one who meets Roman. It's the only thing that makes sense. Now let's go before we waste any more time."

FORTY-ONE

AMBER WALKED THE BEACH THAT SHE'D WALKED thousands of times in the years since she was born here. To the north, on the Santa Monica Pier, the Pacific Park amusements operated as if there was nothing unusual about this lazy fall weekday. For the roller coaster, the Ferris wheel, the aquarium, the carousel surrounded by the massive Hippodrome, everything was moving according to plan. To the south, airplanes from LAX took off over the tusk-shaped coastline.

Barefoot, Amber took high steps across the loose sand, which shifted under her weight and elevated her heart rate. The beach was cool under the breezy October sky and spare of sun worshipers. It was an open space, too open for an ambush, which was likely why Roman had chosen it.

John Roman, the man who hated daylight and preferred the women who could fight.

Today, she would give him the fight of her life—something she'd had no courage to do before Christopher had rescued her.

She could see Roman on the packed wet sand licked by the salt water. The young man she assumed to be Brock sat in the damp, facing the waves. Because Roman liked theatrics, Amber felt confident that Brock's head sat directly under the barrel of a gun, cloaked by a jacket draped over Roman's crossed arms.

If not for the fresh air stroking her face, she might have dropped to her knees in the sand. She hadn't expected the sight of Roman to resurrect her fourteen-year-old self. He was a groomer, trafficker, and pimp back then, not yet big enough to command an army of criminals. He had driven a knife into the heart of her childhood, and the pain of it felt fresh today.

Christopher wouldn't swoop in to save her from Roman this time. Either she would be able to entrap him, or she wouldn't.

Serena's clothes were too small for Amber, but the jacket fit and a Dodgers cap covered her hair, far too light and fine to pass as Serena's, even from a distance. It was all the disguise she needed, just enough to cast possibility over Roman's mind until she was within shooting distance. Then, she hoped, he would hesitate to kill the wrong woman, because he needed to kill the one who could expose him, not the one who feared him. One tiny hesitation was all the opportunity Amber needed.

William was in the parking lot monitoring the wire that would pick up their conversation. Kaleo had gone to the FBI with William's recording in hopes of getting them to come listen to the one he and Amber were about to make. Serena had gone to the police with the stack of Roman's planted evidence against her, and the true story, which could take them years to sort out.

Enid and Esteban Diaz remained in their tiny office. They lit a candle for their daughter and prayed.

Amber's aim was to speak without betraying her terror, and to get Roman to join the conversation. To admit that he had committed crimes against her and to boast that he was still doing the same to other young women. She would need to keep him talking long enough for Kaleo and Serena and William to arrive with people who could finally deal with Roman legally.

Simple but perhaps impossible.

Roman might have uttered his surprise to see her rather than

Serena. If he did, the breeze carried it away. But Brock, sitting on his knees in the sand, twisted his neck for a quick glimpse of her. The teen looked much younger than his hard voice had led Amber to expect. Too-long blond bangs poked his eyes, squinting to shut out sand and glare. His tousled hair and wind-kissed cheeks were boyish, rebelling against the image he probably worked so hard to create. But he was neither a child nor an adult, just a kid who mistakenly thought that his maturing body was proof of an equally mature brain. This was the lie he had probably been fed, as she once was, until the truth became a punishment.

But now she was twelve years wiser.

Roman was smirking when she reached him. "You're the last person I expected to see."

"Hi, Roman." She had some trouble meeting his eyes.

"What's your name again? I've forgotten," he mocked.

"I don't think you've forgotten the name of the family that ruined you once and will do it again."

He grunted. The wind pushed his hair up from the back. "Where's Ms. Diaz?"

"She's gone to the police."

"Good. I heard what she did."

"She's taken them the documents you planted at Phil's house, and your address in Beverly Hills."

Roman shrugged. "I didn't plant any documents, and I don't live in Beverly Hills. How long do you think it will take them to figure that out?"

"Longer than it will take them to figure out that you've kidnapped Brock Anderson and are holding him against his will. We recorded you threatening him. The FBI is on their way. Brock's parents. The LAPD."

Or would be, just as soon as Serena and Kaleo could convince them.

"That will be an embarrassing misunderstanding. Brock is here voluntarily, aren't you?" Roman nudged Brock's back with the toe of his shoe.

"Yeah," Brock snuffled. He'd been crying. He kept his eyes on the ocean.

"Why?" asked Amber. She shoved her hands into the pockets of Serena's jacket to keep them contained and still.

"We're both victims of Ms. Diaz's crimes. Just doing a little commiserating."

"Then you won't mind if Brock leaves."

In the distance, a roller coaster car rumbled through its first drop. Roman's eyes darted to the pier, to the bike trail and beyond, to the parking lots, perhaps searching for authorities. He could kill Brock and still have Serena to deal with, which might become a more complicated venture if he pulled the trigger now.

Amber neither confirmed nor denied the presence of others. She had no idea if they were there yet, or if they would even arrive, or if Brock's parents would believe Kaleo's claim about their son. Would she, if she learned Serena Diaz was at the root of yet another problem? Brock was old enough to keep his own hours, and he'd been with Roman for less than one.

The possibilities were enough of a risk for Roman. "Of course not," he said. "Thank you for your insights, Brock."

Brock jumped up with athletic agility and aimed for the pier, sprinting along the packed sand where he had the best traction. Amber kept her eyes on Roman. It was easier to watch him when he wasn't looking at her. But then they were alone.

"Let's walk," he said. He turned away from her, away from the pier, away from any authorities who may or may not be watching, away from the confessions she needed him to give her.

"No," she said.

"Suit yourself." He kept going. Staring at his back, Amber

felt desperate and angry. She couldn't follow this man again. She wouldn't trail him like a trusting puppy the way she had before. And she couldn't let him walk away, straight back into her nightmares where he was free to wander around.

"Do you know how long it will take to do the research on that?"

Detective Harlan Scott had cuffed Serena and put her in the back of his car, then with one manicured hand flipped through the papers she had brought as he drove toward booking. He was most intrigued by the suicide note she had supposedly written.

"You can ask an analyst about that, right?" she asked. "Some handwriting expert? I didn't write it. You can see what Roman planned."

"This isn't some Hollywood drama, Ms. Diaz." His pencil mustache slanted at her scornfully in the rearview mirror. "We don't just pull up the computer databases and in ten seconds find out that Roman purchased an expensive bottle of wine from France three weeks ago or five years ago. It takes time. Even if the wine was his, you might have stolen it."

"But I didn't," Serena said. "Look—I came willingly. A jail cell is the safest place I can be while Roman is out there. Hold me for as long as it takes for you to do a full investigation. I'm just asking you to start the investigation now, in a huge hurry. Roman's going to kill Brock Anderson."

"That would work out nicely for you."

"Please listen to me. I will submit to anything you tell me to do. I will cooperate fully with everything, everyone. I'm here. But my friend is out there trying to stop Roman from slipping through your fingers again. Please check it out. Call Brock. Go down to the beach. Send a team to Beverly Hills before Roman moves everything out."

Scott pulled onto the 110 and merged with the flow of traffic, headed toward downtown LA. "You don't even have an address."

"I can take you there. Please. Before you take me to the station. It's not far."

"I can't just storm a house based on someone's word. Especially someone like you. We need warrants."

"Just knock on the door," Serena spit out through clenched teeth. She tipped her head back against the seat rest and looked up at the ceiling. What would it take to get him to believe her? "You know, the problem you and the FBI have always had in catching Roman is that he never stays in one nook or cranny for long."

Detective Scott glanced at her in the mirror. He tapped those diamond-tipped fingers of his on the steering wheel.

"Roman is a much bigger fish than I am," she said. "And I'm telling you where he is, right now, right this second. I can tell you where you can get all the evidence against him that you need. But you have maybe less than a half hour."

He wiped a hand down the front of his face.

"Use my phone." It lay on the front seat of his car with her other belongings, with the stack of incriminating papers. "Call Brock. Roman will answer it. He wants me. Use me to get what you need."

Detective Scott picked up the phone and within seconds had pulled up the number. He activated the speakerphone. The ringer sounded once. Twice. Three times. Four.

Someone answered, sobbing, the hysteria chopped up by thunking sounds of wind coming across the line.

"You didn't come! You weren't there! Where are you? He was going to kill me!" Brock.

"Does he still have you?" Serena asked.

Brock seemed to find his breath. "No. He's got the other one. The woman who came instead of you."

"Where?"

"I don't know. I can't see."

"Where are you?"

"At the pier."

Detective Scott was already on his radio calling for assistance.

"Stay there," Serena instructed Brock. "Police are coming. Brock, I want you to call this number." She rattled it off. "The man who answers is my friend Will. He'll tell you what to do."

"Why should I trust you?"

Now that her student was out of harm's way, Serena felt annoyed by his whining behavior. *Grow up already*, she wanted to say. Instead, she opted for something slightly softer: "Because we just saved your life and you're not completely out of danger. But do what you want."

She leaned back in the seat with nothing left to do but entrust her future to the judgment of others. Her mind went to Amber, who was in the most dangerous position of all. She wondered how Kaleo was faring.

Detective Scott spoke up. "We can get to Beverly Hills just as fast as we can get to Santa Monica," he said, bypassing the turnoff that would take them downtown.

Serena leaned forward, freshly hopeful, suddenly supportive of manicured detectives. "We need to get there faster," she said.

Amber watched Roman walk away. Unable to follow him, unable to lure him back, unable to overpower him or trick him into a confession of his crimes, she felt like a failure. A failure who would spend the rest of her life depending on people to rescue her.

That's not true, a voice in her heart challenged. She wasn't sure whose voice it was—Christopher's maybe. William's. She might have even heard Serena's confident tones mixed in.

That's not true. You just saved my life.

The words were Serena's that time, for sure.

And Brock's, she heard Kaleo say.

You're a lifesaver. It was her brother speaking to her then, the man who had saved her life more than once, literally and symbolically. *If everyone only cared about one other person, we'd all be okay.*

Amber stood in the sands while Roman opened the distance between them, realizing that she was not a failure at all. She was a lifesaver, just as her brother had been. A rescuer. Brock was safe. Serena was still alive. And Amber was quite okay, so full of the care of others that she realized she had some to spare, for all the women yet to be rescued.

"Roman!" she shouted after him.

He stopped and turned around.

"Roman, you don't have any power over me anymore!"

The laugh that chased these words out of her was completely involuntary.

"You will never, ever have power over me again, and I will spend the rest of my life rescuing people from you. I'm going to ruin you!"

She bent down and scooped up two handfuls of sand in her fists. The overflow of it spilled out between her fingers in skinny little streams.

"I'm going to finish what my brother started, and do you know how I'm going to do it?" She had no idea, specifically, but the fire in her chest burned hot and she didn't question it. "I'm going to stay a step ahead of you. I'm going to find women who are just like me and fill them up with courage before you can touch them. I'm going to tell them the truth before you can tell them lies. And I'm going to dry up your supply, Roman. They'll be like sand through your fingers." She held up her fists and the wind caught the grains, carried them away. "You'll have nothing to abuse anymore. Nothing to eat but your own insides."

Roman waited for her to continue, which dampened her spirits just a little. When it became clear she didn't have anything more to say, he returned to her. He walked back with his hands in his pockets and his face to the ocean, and for a moment she worried that he might pull his gun out from wherever he'd tucked it away and shoot her through the heart without looking her in the eye.

Amber stood her ground, fists hanging at her sides, still clutching remnants of sand.

He invaded her space. The tips of his shoes bumped her bare toes. He leaned into her the way he had when he'd kissed her for the first time, while she was still a child. She closed her eyes to squash the memory jarred loose.

"Your brother," Roman began, releasing the heat and stink of his breath across her cheek, "died like a coward."

Amber's eyes snapped open.

"You think he humiliated me when he came after you and pulled you out? No, humiliation is what I did to him before he took his last breath. Humiliation is what happens to a sobbing man while little girls watch, and he knows he can't save any of them, or even himself."

"You murdered Christopher."

"It was worth the wait."

"You were the one who called him Monday morning."

"It was so simple and Christopher accomplished so much more than I thought he would."

"You *planned* to kill him?"

"I was only planning Phil Lancet's fall from grace." Roman shrugged. "But Christopher couldn't help playing the hero. The way I see it, he killed himself."

There was a part of Amber's mind clamoring to be heard, the part that was instructing her to cry, and to crumple in the sand, and to drown herself in the ocean. To simply give up fighting unconquerable evil. And there was another part, the part filled with the voices of her friends, reminding her that this, right here, was what she had come to do. It was happening at the exact moment she thought she had failed. And although it might kill her, this was what she needed to do.

Together she and her friends slammed the door on her weaker self.

"You're the god of all pimps," she mocked. "What a title."

He had his hand around her neck, his thumb pushing up under her jaw, holding the power to cut off her breath with the smallest effort. Her gasp dragged against the pressure.

"Show some respect."

He placed his other hand around her waist, and his touch on her skin opened up a dark place in her mind that not even the voices of her friends were loud enough to silence. The blackness would swallow her if Roman didn't kill her first. She tried to stay focused—there was the wire, tucked inside her bra. There was William, listening on the other end, maybe with the FBI. Maybe not. Even alone, there was William. She closed her eyes and locked onto William, who would hold her out of that black void or fall into it with her if he could.

"You took me away from my home," she choked out. "You raped me. You drugged me. You sold me to men too numerous to count."

"And I'll do it again if I decide to, just as I've done it to hundreds like you. Don't underestimate your insignificance," he warned.

"Take your own advice," she hissed, and she raised her arms to his face and threw what sand remained straight into his eyes. She pressed in with the heels of her hands, grinding it into his face. He released her immediately, roaring and striking out at her arms.

Run, the voices told her. *Amber, get out of there!*

She had the chance, the agility, the familiarity with the shifting sand.

"Get out! Go!" It sounded like William shouting. Screaming in her ear. Alive. Real.

But that black hole had already sucked her into its vacuum, and instead she went after Roman, as blind as he was to everything but rage.

FORTY-TWO

KIERA'S HEAD WAS A SOUPY FOG OF TEARS AND some kind of pain-killer that channeled all the hurt out of her body and deep into the corners of her mind. The room stank and filth on the floor cut into Kiera's knees as she leaned over a bucket. She had never wanted to die as sincerely as she did right now. All the drugs in the world couldn't save her from images of murder, which kept coming and coming and coming no matter how long she slept.

Becca crouched near the locked door where a voice had reached in to them less than two hours ago. The kind voice of a kind woman who couldn't have meant what she said when she told them to shut up.

"It was just someone messing with us," Becca declared, but she stayed there on her knees. "They do that."

Kiera knew Becca had hoped the lady's voice might belong to a friend and was embarrassed when it amounted to nothing. Kiera couldn't think of how to die. They had taken everything useful: the string from her sweatpants, the sheets from the bed, the chairs, the electric cords. She closed her eyes. The dank air of the house whistled as it passed in and out of her nose.

Voices joined it. Kiera jerked back, then pressed in to listen again. Footsteps on the stairs, then an argument.

A man, stressed and impatient: ". . . procedure. He'll want them."

A thump met the door and Kiera flinched.

Then a woman, farther away, with a low, sweet voice. "He left me in charge of the procedures. He wants to start over. No traces, no ties."

Becca scooted out of the arc the door would make if it burst open. Kiera felt the warmth of her body pressing next to her. The human touch was comforting and agonizing.

"The girls are valuable," the man said.

"More where they came from. They'll slow us down."

"He'll want his property."

"Then get it. Let the cops find you holding it in your very own hands." The woman's voice dropped as she moved off. "Phil's dead. Roman's burning his bridges. It's time to go."

The stressed voice moved away from the door, chasing the argument back upstairs.

"They're leaving," Becca said.

"Good."

"No, they're leaving *us*."

The heel of Becca's foot struck the door just below the handle. The boom filled the room and seemed magnified by the enclosed hall beyond. Kiera grabbed both sides of her head.

She groaned and Becca waited to see if the people would respond.

Becca kicked the door again. *Boom*. A cannon, or gunshot. Kiera retched.

"It's hollow, you think?"

What was hollow? The door?

"If I can kick a hole, we can reach through and unlock it from outside."

"Still need a key," Kiera said.

Becca kicked again, but with less determination. The silence that followed seemed deeper than it had before.

Then Becca let loose in a wail, kicking at the door and bouncing off while Kiera screamed at her to stop, both girls shrieking until the older one lost her balance and fell into the corner of the bed, heaving.

Kiera sat back on her bottom and leaned against the wall. It was cool and solid, smoother than the floor. She cradled her head, fragile as an eggshell.

"We're going to die," Becca said.

"I want to die," Kiera declared. She was cold. She ached. If she licked the floor, would the germs kill her? Her mother used to threaten such odd things when the chores weren't up to her standards. How did Becca keep fighting? Kiera hadn't even lasted three days.

Exhausted, she dozed, jumping from her new reality to a world of drug-induced nightmares. One prison to another.

Her mother was looking for her. *Kiera! Kiera!* Calling from behind the trees in a forest where Kiera was hopelessly lost.

Kiera!

When she woke, Becca was going at the door again.

Kiera let loose her frustration in a bloodcurdling shriek.

"Kiera!"

Becca was wrapping a blanket around her. The booming continued.

"Stop," Kiera pleaded.

"Kiera, they've come." The blanket secured her shoulders. Becca's strong arms held it there.

Boom! Boom!

Becca tucked Kiera's cold forehead under the warmth of her defiant chin.

Boom! She felt Becca's body form a shelter.

Crack!

Light speared the room and Kiera's eyes. People spoke too loudly. Too many voices. Men's voices. She turned into Becca's protection, waiting for rough hands to reach out and snatch her away.

Becca held on to her.

"Let me, please." A woman spoke this time. Kiera lifted her head. Her eyes still weren't ready for the glare coming in from a light out in the hall. But she could make out a figure squatting in front of her.

"I'm Serena," the shape said. "I'll help you."

"You can trust her," Becca said. "She used to be my teacher."

Roman got away.

Amber marked him with nail tracks and maybe a few bruises, but even blinded he peeled her off easily. An elbow to her rib cage, a head butt to her jaw—really, she knew she was lucky he left her alive. William called 911 the moment Roman turned back toward her taunts, but what followed unfolded too quickly for him to run across the parking lot, over the loose sand, and down to the shoreline in time.

On the beach, Will held on to Amber and refused to let her go. He sat next to her on the sand where she had lain down, never wanting to rise again, and examined her jaw, which was already swollen and oozing. She could taste the damage. He wiped the horrible mess off her chin with his fingers and then pulled her into his chest. The breeze whooshed up over his back, lifting his hair and pushing it forward into Amber's eyes.

"You were perfect," he said.

He kissed the messy part in her hair.

She couldn't think of anything but what she had failed to do. The pain from her jaw was spiking up into her temples.

"I got everything we need," he said. "Every word he spoke."

"I let him get away."

"No—we've got more than we've ever had before."

All but what really counted, Amber thought: *the man himself.*

"You should have chased him," she said.

William held on to her as if she might get up and chase Roman down the beach herself. He anchored her until her rigid muscles softened and her hands were no longer fists, until she closed her eyes and believed that there would be another day for John Roman, another confrontation. Because now she knew she had what it took to face him.

Under the Santa Monica Pier, Kaleo stood aside while Special Agent Dale Montague conducted a swift interview with Brock Anderson. It was a friendly Q&A, Montague insisted. He wanted to know about John Roman and what he had done to Brock.

"You're the victim here," Montague said. "The more you can tell me while it's fresh, the harder the hammer will fall on Roman."

Brock's face was hard. "I'm not a victim. You have no idea what I've done."

"To Roman? With Roman? Do you and Roman have a history?"

Brock shook his head. "No. It's all the rest. It's Jett, Uncle Phil. It's Ms. Diaz. It's all the lies."

And here Montague raised his hand and glanced at Kaleo. "That's not my jurisdiction, son, but we're not alone here right now, 'kay? So I'm going to recommend you hold that thought until your attorney gets here. Or at least your parents."

"It can't wait," Brock said. "He'll kill me . . . Ms. Diaz—none of it's her fault. I got my scholarship into trouble, Jett told me he knew how I could fix it." And he proceeded to spill his guts all over the California sands.

In Beverly Hills, after the girls were taken by ambulance to a hospital, Serena sat like a mouse in the corner of Roman's office while Harlan Scott and his fellow officers swept the house. It was a chaos of hurried departure, but immaculate of evidence. Computers and their hardware had been ripped off their cords. DVRs had been wiped clean. Printers were removed. Papers had been shredded and left in piles. Hanging files had been emptied and left hanging. Not even a Post-it note or a receipt for groceries had been left behind. Otherwise, the furnished home looked ready to accept another occupant.

Scott stood in the office, hands on hips, and Serena's desperation rose to her throat. He was ready to call them off.

"Did you talk to William Brenner?" she asked. "The FBI?"

"They say Roman got away." He lifted his eyes to her and frowned. "If he was ever there." His open mind had begun to narrow over the last hour.

"Have they found the wine cellar? You know, where they held me? Where the wine bottle was kept? Maybe he poisoned it there. Maybe there are traces of—"

"If it existed we'd have found it," Harlan said.

Serena stood. "Maybe I could show you," she said, knowing how difficult it would be to find her way to any room in the house.

"Stay seated, please," he said. "Nothing here lets you off the hook."

From somewhere deep within the house, a splintering crack of wood traveled throughout the maze of halls. Scott stepped out of the office and looked right, then left, and lifted his phone to his ear.

After a moment he said, "Right," then turned to Serena. "Lucky you." He motioned for her to follow.

By the time the pair arrived at the top of the wine cellar, three other officers who were having just as much difficulty navigating the strange house had joined them. Golden light from inside revealed rosy stains on the carpet outside the door. The hefty wood panel had been battered away from the lock, which remained engaged. At the top of the stairs, the two men who had entered had raised their weapons and pointed them downward, into the alcove where the long table might have welcomed them to a wine tasting on another day.

Serena stayed in the hall but had no trouble seeing their cause for concern. Seated at the head of the table, a woman in a red dress lifted an empty wineglass in a toast. Beside her, the table's surface was scattered with flash drives, CDs, digital cameras, a laptop, and even old-fashioned file boxes of paper files. Serena's hope surged.

Was it possible?

"Does a wineglass make me armed and dangerous?" Denise asked. "Yeah, maybe an empty one does. I can see your point. Thought I'd get a warmer reception, though, for all the trouble of this." She shrugged toward the documentation of her boss's career and cast a mildly intoxicated gaze at Detective Scott.

"Nice nails," she said. "But you should have them buffed, not painted."

The officers put their weapons away. Serena stepped into the cellar. Denise chattered on, the alcohol making her nervous and unguarded.

"Took you all longer to get here than it took me to collect it. If the others had really wanted to, they could have shot down the door and killed me while you took your sweet time. But loyalty is only so strong in these situations." She tipped up the wineglass for one more drop, but there was nothing more. "Not very interesting reading, but it's not my fault: a financial record of his conquests, a list of every john who ever lived, aliases, property deeds, fraudulent tax filings. You get the idea. Only thing I couldn't find was a catalog of the girls—you know, names, addresses, death records." She sighed. "Burial plots."

"Identify yourself, please," Scott said to her.

"Abandoned daughter, abused whore, worthless slut, objectified yes-girl."

Serena hoped that no man in the room was too callous to miss the pain in the woman's words. She spoke into their silence.

"Brilliant thinker. Brave soul. Heroine of the hour. Her name is Denise."

Denise turned her face downward into her open hand and began to weep.

Scott lifted a lid on the box and glanced at the contents.

"Let's get an inventory."

People in the cellar began moving again, breathing, speaking.

"Denise what?" he asked.

"Denise Wilcox," she said through sniffles.

"All right, Denise, what would you say is the most important piece of information here?"

She lifted her face defiantly. "Already told you. The most important piece isn't here. All those missing girls . . . I could have helped them. I could have, but I didn't." Her throat clamped down on her words again.

Serena put a hand on Denise's shoulder, awestruck by what Denise had risked to do this and wishing Scott would be more gracious.

"Okay," he said, more gently this time. "Then what's the second most important thing? Give me a place to start."

"I'll give you a place." Denise shook her head. "But it's not here either."

"What place is that?"

"I can tell you where John Roman went. Where I was supposed to go too."

"But you didn't," Serena said.

"No, I didn't. No. No, no, no. Sweet angels in heaven, it feels good to say no."

SPRING

FORTY-THREE

"I EXPECTED FIRE POPPIES," KALEO SAID, BUCKLING a tool belt over his Levi's as he looked around.

Serena looked out at the bowl-shaped landscape that opened up in front of the Station Fire house. It was green with spring and white blooms covered the toyon bushes. The oaks were leafing out and the chamise was thick this year, and there was even a scattering of wildflowers on the sunniest slope. But no poppies.

"Why?" she asked. "The fire poppies only bloom after a fire."

"Something about the way people talk about the place." He pulled on a pair of tough-skinned work gloves. "Like it has surprises in it."

She smiled and returned her attention to her sketchbook. It was one of her field journals, actually, but today she was sketching her view of the house. Not as it was, but as it would be. Her father would arrive soon with the surveyor, who would confirm the property lines for Fire Followers' first safe house. Amber and Christopher's shared dream, soon to be a reality.

"And have you found any surprises here?" she asked. Not everyone did, she'd learned.

"Just you, Ms. Diaz."

Her pencil stroked the surface of the yellow page. "You're sweet as ever."

"And still I can't talk you into a romantic dinner."

"You know I'm madly in love with Christopher."

"I know that in some circles that's considered, uh, weird. Maybe even unhealthy." He leaned over her. "Religious," he whispered ominously.

She laughed.

It had become an ongoing joke between them. Of course there was nothing about Christopher preventing Serena from spending more time with Kaleo, but it was the kindest way to deflect his attention, at least until she found the right way to explain. She held tight to the belief that Christopher had seen this place as she had, or at least had a similar experience here. As good a man as he was, there had to be something besides altruism that drove him to stand between her and death. Perhaps the more time she spent here, the more she would understand. The more she would see.

Like the sight of three young women she'd never met sitting on the new brick steps, drinking lemonade and making fun of each other while Serena led them in role-playing for job interviews. Each girl had her own profound scars, hidden in real life but worn proudly in this place. Serena put the uniquely beautiful women on her paper.

Few who came here saw beneath the surface view. Maybe someday Kaleo would. Until then, he wouldn't ever fully understand her story.

"Well, you never know, Kaleo," Serena said. "Stay open to surprises."

He harrumphed in a good-natured way and strode past her into the house. "Just keep in mind that I'm not as patient as Will."

"Empty threats," Serena said.

She wondered when these women, strangers who might become new friends, would arrive. In the meantime, there was so much to get ready. She still couldn't believe the house was theirs.

The LAPD's initial investigation into the murder of Phil Lancet turned up two pieces of evidence: the empty bottle of expensive wine bearing Serena Diaz's fingerprints and a duplicate copy of the suicide note. When Harlan Scott produced the one Serena had given to him, they were able to prove both had been produced by a computer program and printer Denise had salvaged from Roman's house.

John Roman was arrested at his private resort house in Taos, New Mexico, exactly where Denise had said he would be, on the day he listed it for sale.

More devastating to Roman's case was the evidence that wasn't found until a close examination of his files divulged—in addition to a receipt for the wine—a short list of law-enforcement officers on Roman's payroll, one of whom had been assigned to the Phil Lancet crime scene. This discovery prompted a thorough reinvestigation in cooperation with the FBI. This time, the dirty cop was at the center. At the officer's house, authorities found original video recordings and photos that Phil had taken without Serena's knowledge, then edited for Brock's purposes. Roman had instructed the officer to hide these, to ensure Serena's conviction. This find, in conjunction with Brock Anderson's testimony, yielded everything needed to vindicate her.

But Serena's favorite find among the evidence Denise had saved had nothing to do with her: the title to the Station Fire house.

An investigation into the property records revealed that the home had belonged to a man whose daughter had been caught up in Phil's web. The tenacious father, like Amber's brother, devoted years to finding her. And when he did, that piece of property and a vow of silence were the ransom he paid to get her back. The Station Fire tore through the area the following year.

Father and daughter lived in a remote part of Maine now and wanted nothing to do with the ruined place.

"But maybe it can be redeemed now," he told Detective Scott. "Do something better with it than I did."

The property was swiftly and privately auctioned.

Amber Larsen was the only bidder.

And the gutted place became Fire Followers', bought and about to be restored with a life insurance policy that Amber discovered among Christopher's personal effects after his funeral. She was the sole beneficiary.

But Serena felt luckiest of all, for she had received something even more valuable than money or property. She had been gifted a new calling.

Serena's father arrived before the surveyor with unexpected company: Denise and Becca, who thought they might also have a part to play in the new venture, and Serena's mother, because the presence of another woman in the car was helpful and right. Kiera had been returned to her heartbroken mother before Christmas and sent optimistic reports about their progress together.

Will and Amber were at the title company, completing the paperwork that would make their ownership official.

Serena stood and joined her family as they came around the front of the house.

"You've got your work cut out for you," Enid said, surveying the area for the first time. All the new subflooring and steps and frameworks Phil's men had installed had been ruined by the winter rains. They would have to start over, with nothing but the stone walls and intact foundation.

"It should be all fixed up and cozy for winter," Serena said. "Amber and I plan to move in come October. We'll have six beds. Not much, but—"

"Six more than the world had before," Esteban said. "That is a wonderful thing."

Enid patted her husband's arm and smiled at her daughter. "This feels like a good place," she said. "I can't put my finger on it. Just a good feeling here. You'll have something we don't have down in the city."

"It'll be a good partnership," Serena said.

"That it will," said her father.

"I'll need your help learning the ropes—the laws, the licensing."

"Anything you need, *mija*. As you've always had."

Denise was picking her way to the far side of the house. "I thought we could put a garden in over there," Serena called out, having already seen what one might look like. "Flowers, vegetables." Denise surveyed the area with her hands on her hips, looking like she'd been born for this very time and place. "We could teach cooking classes," Serena said, having tasted some of Denise's kitchen magic during the woman's long second stay at the Safe Place—her first as an adult. Denise had become something of a fixture there and was considering a more permanent role on staff.

Denise nodded, looking pleased by the idea.

This wasn't what Serena had envisioned when she had fancied herself a teacher, but it felt right. No, it felt perfect. Far more perfect than what she'd done in the classroom at Mission Acres High. Mr. Walter had asked her to return. She politely declined.

"You're a good teacher," Becca said after a long pause. Her first remark since arriving. She was looking at the upstairs windows, and Serena wondered what she saw. "I thought about you a lot while I was away. That unit you taught our health class about how good the body is at healing itself, with the right support."

Serena laid down her sketchbook on the stone wall that bordered the front of the house. She took Becca's hand.

"Come help me with something."

Carefully the women picked their way into the house through the open front door, then up the pine stairs swollen and warped by rains that had blown in through the gap. In the loft, Kaleo was measuring for new lumber.

Serena took a Fire Followers worry stone out of her pocket and gave it to Becca, who smiled when she saw it.

"Some stories are really hard to believe," Becca said. "But we want them to be true."

"Some of them are true. The first time I ever came here, I found one of these in the window over there." Serena pointed. "Balanced on the frame."

"How did it get there?" Becca asked.

"No idea. I had thought Kiera put it there—she was here that day. She saw so much that no one should see."

"But she'd never seen these stones until Christopher gave one to her," Becca said.

"It's a mystery. But stranger things have happened to me in the past year, and I'm kind of getting used to it. I thought we'd put it back, as a reminder."

Becca walked to the window and set the stone in the frame. "Maybe you can have a piece of stained glass made for this."

"I like that idea." Serena joined her at the rippled glass, looking at the view she'd first taken in months ago. Down at the bottom of the bowl, behind the white flowers of a blooming toyon, she thought she saw a bright yellow hat, a knit cap from the wrong season covering the head of someone who didn't have a care for fashion. The person who wore it moved at the pace of a nature walker enjoying the spring day, pausing to appreciate the details of a bud or maybe to take a picture. Serena smiled and noticed Kaleo had joined her at the window.

"Do you ever wish for the chance to ask him what on earth he was thinking?" Kaleo said. And she knew he was talking about the friend he missed so much. They all did, though the ache seemed to lessen the longer they were here.

"On days like today I believe I know what he was thinking," Serena said. "I just wish he could have seen what's going to come of it."

READING GROUP GUIDE

1. Erin's novels typically revolve around life's "thin places," metaphorical events that expose the intersection between the natural and supernatural worlds. *Stranger Things* is the first of her novels to present a thin place as a physical location. Not everyone who visits the Station Fire house has the same experience of it. Compare Serena's, Christopher's, Phil's, and Kaleo's impressions of the ruins. What might account for their different perceptions and receptivity to spiritual realities?

2. Have you ever been in a place where you felt like you could "see," physically or spiritually, a greater reality than your present circumstances? Describe that experience. Why do you think it happened to you?

3. This story doesn't belong to just one or two characters, but to a large cast of players. What might this say about the story's positive outcome? How is this different from stories in which an independent hero saves the day? Does *Stranger Things* have a hero? If so, who is it?

4. Why did Christopher put his life on the line for Serena while there was still the possibility in his mind that she was a criminal?

5. The accusations leveled against Serena precipitate a crisis of self. Her reputation, her dreams, and her future are at stake.

Christopher's death heightens her awareness of crises going on in the lives of hundreds of other women. How does becoming aware of someone else's suffering influence your perception of your own troubles?

6. How is Christopher's selflessness reflected in Serena's ultimate defense of Denise? Are there ways in which his mission became stronger after his death than it was before? Is selflessness a more powerful force in the world than selfishness? Explain.

7. With Christopher's and William's help, Amber is able to heal and rediscover her inner strength. But she never completely breaks free of needing their presence and assistance. Should she? Explain.

8. William and Kaleo often argue over the need for swift action and thoughtful strategizing. What are the strengths and weaknesses of each approach to rescue?

9. Phil's insatiable appetite for risk, power, titillation, and challenge stems from a deep inner place of dissatisfaction. What true hunger do you think he is attempting to satiate?

10. In this story, there are victims of evil, perpetrators of it, witnesses to it, passive bystanders, active rescuers, and those who blur the categories' lines. How would you describe Brock? Becca? Denise? Which character best represents your own life experience with darkness?

11. What prevents people from reaching into darkness to pull others out of it? Consider obstacles such as ignorance, lack of resources, busyness, backfired efforts, and feeling overwhelmed. What obstacles did even the dedicated Fire Followers face? Describe a time when you overcame these roadblocks and helped someone out of a terrible situation. Are you likely to do it again? Why or why not?

12. How does the human trafficking crisis affect you, if at all? Did reading this novel change your view of the problem?

ACKNOWLEDGMENTS

IT TAKES A TEAM TO WRITE A BOOK. I'VE WRITTEN this one with the help of a massive cast and heartfelt thanks to:

Pastor Kelly Williams, for asking the original question: If a stranger died for you, how would that change your life?

Agent Meredith Smith, for championing me

Publisher Daisy Hutton, for the treasured opportunity to write stories

Editor Ami McConnell, for saving me from my many weaknesses

Editor LB Norton, for being my loyal Story Partner and bravely entering the dark depths to help me

Marketing and Publicity Director Katie Bond, for always seeing the bright possibilities

Marketing and Publicity Specialist Laura Dickerson, for being a tireless force

Publicist Audra Jennings and all the Litfuse Chicks, for presenting me to the world one interview at a time

Art Director Kristen Vasgaard, for a spectacular cover design

The entire Thomas Nelson Fiction and HarperCollins Christian Publishing teams, for your invaluable expertise, support, and enthusiasm

Social Media Specialist Leah Apineru, for teaching me how to navigate the tangled ropes, and for doing it on my behalf when I just can't

Criminal Defense Attorney Stephen Klarich, for important insights into California law

My beloved family, for enduring my distracted presence during deadline time

And finally, to all of my readers, for your e-mails and Facebook posts, for your reviews and recommendations, for buying my books for yourselves and for others, for spreading the word, for your prayers and your encouragement

COMING FALL 2014

MOTHERLESS

GUILT MIGHT BE THE MOST DANGEROUS
MOTIVE OF ALL.

THOMAS NELSON
Since 1798

DON'T MISS THESE OTHER NOVELS BY
BEST-SELLING AUTHOR
ERIN HEALY

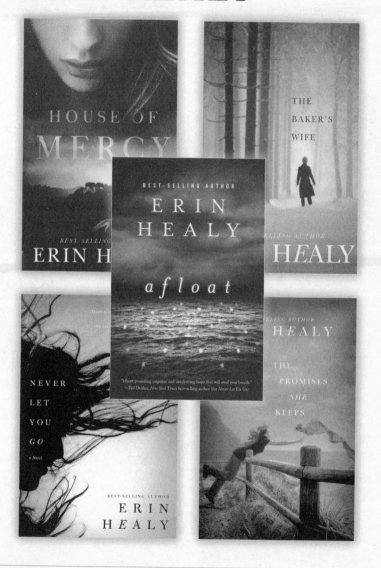

VISIT ERINHEALY.COM TO DISCOVER MORE.

AVAILABLE IN PRINT AND E-BOOK

"Dekker and Healy form a powerful team in crafting redemptive suspense."

—Lisa T. Bergren, author of *The Blessed*

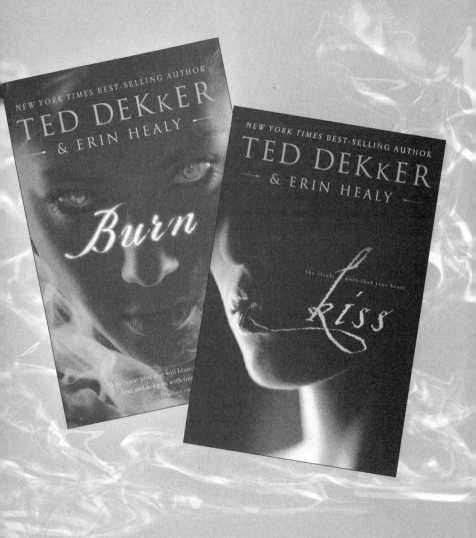

AVAILABLE IN PRINT AND E-BOOK

ABOUT THE AUTHOR

ERIN HEALY IS THE BEST-SELLING coauthor of *Burn* and *Kiss* (with Ted Dekker) and an award-winning editor for numerous best-selling authors. She has received wide acclaim for her novels *Never Let You Go*, *The Baker's Wife*, *House of Mercy*, and *Afloat*. She and her family live in Colorado.